Vladimir
Beekman

The Year of the Donkey

D1081100

Progress Publishers
Moscow

Translated from the Russian by *Liv Tudge*
Designed by *Andrei Salnikov*

Владимир Бээкман

Год Осла

На английском языке

03092098

Printed in the Union of Soviet Socialist Republics

Б $\frac{4702700200-421}{014\,(01)-87}$ 81-87

Author's Preface

Anyone reading this book will, most likely, have a difficult time pinning down the precise setting of the events it describes. How can one fix the longitude and latitude of Minore, an island which does not appear on any map? And yet I would make so bold as to state categorically that the Republic of Minore does exist in our civilized world. It just so happened that I was the first to 'see' it and to record some of the more noteworthy facets of life there.

So what exactly is this runty little island state of Minore? It is a completely modern bourgeois country, like so many in this world. It has political parties which are constantly at each other's throats and which campaign either on ossified dogma and prejudice or on mean-minded self-interest, but which share the same thirst for power. Minore has its grandiose film festivals, its bank robberies, its fervent followers of the dernier cri in fashion, and its crazy sports fans. The place has its idols and its terrorists. And the nation has wanted for nothing ever since it put its own land up for sale. Some unnamed international Consortium has purchased unlimited mining rights and unqualified authorization to export phosphate ore, which means that in the foreseeable future the island is going to disappear altogether from the face of the earth.

So what is this—a reflection of Nauru, a shadowy hint of Cyprus, or a remembrance of other countries, which are familiar to us if only from hearsay and which today pitch to and fro between reason and insanity, between indigence and abundance?

It suits me best to let my readers seek out their own answers to these questions: it is all a matter of watching closely what happens to my characters.

The Year of the Donkey is not my first satirical novel; the critics attached the same label to the novel *Night Pilots*, which I completed in 1975 and which was later translated into Swedish, Hungarian, Czech and Slovak. The novel's story line might be considered somewhat odd. Somewhere, on a miniscule Arctic island, is the forgotten crew of a long-range night bomber, stationed there by the fascists at the very end of the Second World War. And every week on the appointed day, entirely unaware that the war is over, they take off from the island and go on alert over Europe, waiting for the radio message that will order them to their next target. But the radio is silent. The command post from which the order would have come is long gone. So the phantom plane continues to slick down the skies, until one stormy night the long-awaited call sign starts to sound in the captain's earphones. And he, by the irony of fate, drops his last bomb on the town where he was born... The passivity of a conditioned, unreasoning mind, the fanaticism which transforms a man into a quasi-mechanical tool of destruction, of mindless compliance, the crass mentality of an existence without thought—behind all this one perceives a universalized portrait of both the Third Reich and the present-day revanchism which has arisen from its ruins.

The action of my most recent novel, *The Corridor* (1982), is rooted in documented fact. At the very outset of the Second World War, in the autumn of 1939, Hitler was pursuing his plan to germanize the occupied territories. He had the Baltic Germans, who had for centuries lived in Estonia and Latvia, uprooted and moved, without any prior warning and at lightning speed, to Polish territory. A veritable tragedy then unfolded for ten thousand utterly innocent people, whose story I tell in *The Corridor*, through letters written by Walter, a young Baltic German, to his beloved Eva, who has stayed behind in Tallinn. In one sense, this is a book about the bitter fate of the first displaced persons of the Second World War—those who trod a path that was later traversed by many other peoples.

I hope that this thumbnail portrait of the author will prove helpful in giving the reader some idea of the directions my creative interests have been following over the past decade. This is, after all, the first of my novels to venture into the English-speaking world, seeking friends.

Vladimir Beekman

My name is Artur Yanno.

All the while I have had this feeling that there was something for me to remember. It's just that I didn't know what it was. But now I know. That name! That is what it's all about. Otherwise this unstable world that is whirling nauseatingly around me and within my very self will never stop, and finally it will turn me inside out, will transform me into a twitching glob lost in the tides of the universe, like a clot of protein in the prehistoric sea.

My name really is Artur Yanno! I am a journalist. Or maybe I once was a journalist? To tell the truth, I am not completely convinced of my own existence after all that has happened, after that fearsome blow out there on the sun-speared square, like a boxer's punchbag smacking into my temple—the blow that flung me into the void, filling my head with an endless buzz and swallowing up everything, even my name.

I have been trying to remember it from that moment, I think. How does it... how does it go?... Ar... Ar... This is terrifying. Have I lost my name again? Where has it got to this time? I can't be without a name, not even for a moment! Quick, we'll start it all over. I am a journalist. Jour-na-list. Never mind what that is. My name is... My name is...

A white mist closes in...

Ar-tur Yan-no!

A hot wave of relief washes over me. Now once again I have a foothold, something to take hold of, to sink my teeth into as I whine piteously when the leaden oblivion surges in again, stronger than before, and tries to tear me away. If that happens, I will be swept off into the unknown, and that will be the end. While the unknown stays out there, so will the end. A savage fear, faceless and speechless, picks me up, carries me towards it. I really cannot bear this.

Artur Yanno... A slight jolt comes to me through the deck. The ungainly steel hull of the *Maltese Cross*, painted white end to end, has bumped into the mooring. From the speakers on deck and in the saloons comes the kind of cheerful music that inspires quiet terror, rouses yearnings for the departed days of merry-go-rounds with wooden ponies and swan-white pleasure craft. In the far distance, near the harbor pavilion, locals who have come to meet the steamer are crowding against a silver-painted iron fence and are avidly watching the last, almost indiscernible movements of the *Maltese Cross*, as she prepares to dock.

Their strange fervidly glittering eyes are fixed on the steamer. The more impatient among them are pushing their heads through the fence; just a little further and their ears will sprinkle down onto the dusty asphalt on the other side of the railings.

The arrival of the steamer here is a routine thing. Day after day, the *Maltese Cross* plies her scheduled route, one of the few still in existence—five hours from Serana to Antafagusta, and five hours back. Yet they are staring at the ship as though it were some sort of prodigy. Will they really be gawking like this tomorrow, and the day after tomorrow too? Or is there something unusual going on today?

The *Maltese Cross* had proved to be the only way of getting to Minore. Neither in Antafagusta nor anywhere else on the island is there an aerodrome where commercial planes can land. That's incomprehensible, especially now, when people with business to do, knowing what their time is really worth, travel only by plane, and those with no business to do pander to their enthusiasm for marine excursions by cruising on floating hotels that are not bound by any hard and fast itineraries.

I was delighted to hear that a plane would get me only as far as Serana, and that from there I would have to go by steamer, like it or not. Thus far in my life, I have always been too busy to travel for the fun of it—I charge about all the time, on planes or trains, and expresses at that. By the time you reach thirty in our profession you have to start keeping your ears pricked and be fast on your feet if you don't want some younger spark to pull ahead. Sailing on a steamer is one of those few things that have not lost the charm that they had for me as a child, probably because I have never done enough sailing to get bored with it. A boat seems to cut you off from the everyday life back there on the shore; everything around you is outside of time, as it were, sort of unreal and slowed to a stately pace. It is impossible to lose touch with yourself, to forget about sleeping or to skip dinner. That is the sort of thing that happens to me at times, and I myself am not exactly thrilled about it.

And still, the business about the lost aerodrome is really pretty strange, even silly. Someone should have dug around a bit. There might have been good background for a fairly reasonable series of articles, but as far as I can remember, no one ever followed it up. During the war, when Minore was a British protectorate, the island had an air base for long-distance bombers. That is a recorded fact of military history. And now that my agency has at last and finally made up its mind to accredit me for two years as special correspondent in Antafagusta—it is simply sickening, the way they fiddled about—now I find out that there is no air link with the Republic of Minore because there's no airport on the island. No one was able to give a sensible explanation of what had happened to it. Avik Nersesyan, who is the one we have covering hot foreign items with a local-interest angle, recalled that it was somehow connected with some economic chicanery way back when, but the details turned out to be irretrievably buried under layer upon layer of fresher tittle-tattle.

But all the same it is still a bit much to think that anyone, even in this day and age, could have contrived to export an airport, lock, stock and barrel.

That was the total extent of my knowledge when I set off, and my arrival found me no wiser. The crowd of people with the fervid glitter in their eyes on the other side of the railings could possibly be an object lesson on the islanders' thirst for contact with the outside world, but otherwise it explains nothing at all. Oh well, blow it. I'll work it out in good time. Just let me get my feet on dry land. I'll find my sources of information in the better sized watering holes in Antafagusta: there's no serious drinker on earth who will turn down a free round. Then it's tit for tat. A journalist thrives on news; thuswise, should you wish to make friends with a journalist and drink at his expense, stock up on scuttlebutt. And mind that you make it at least half a day fresher than anyone else's.

I, Artur Yanno, on my first visit to Antafagusta, have a head full of information gleaned from reference books. I stand on the deck, with my raincoat—my faithful light-brown raincoat, purchased last autumn but one in Prague—in my hands. I listen to the unbearably optimistic music that comes thundering and hooting from all the speakers, and I think: what's the chance of anything ever happening in this runty little state that might propel me, if I play my cards right, onto the front pages?

The main engine shuts down, the ventilators fall silent, and the trembling in the deck, which runs all the way up to my knee joints, suddenly stops with a powerful jolt. I gaze through the crack between the ship's hull and the mooring wall and I have the distinct feeling that everything around me—the steamer and the island itself—is rocking gently on the glittering, oil-filmed waters of the dock. That blow creates an instant bodily recall of that other blow, the one on the sun-speared town square; and a taut, ethereal breaker tosses me into a sealed bag of blank oblivion. In order to scramble out of it I must again make the agonizing effort to recollect my own name, straining until it hurts, in haste and in fear, because this time I might be too slow, and I am afraid that by the time I haul my name from the depths of my memory there will be no point to anything any more. Can it be that any moment now I am going to drown in the unknowing that is the end of everything?

Ar-tur Yan-no.

Those two meaningless words apparently possess a magic power. They are like an anchor biting into the sea-bed. The slide to who knows where immediately stops, the weightlessness goes away, and all of a sudden I care again which end is up and which is down.

Beneath my feet is firm ground. It is a floor, whose rocking I do not feel, although there is a perhaps barely perceptible swaying. I am standing in my room on the sixth floor of the Archipelago Hotel. The hotel's name is pretentious, to say the least: in addition to the main island, the Republic of Minore encompasses all of three unin-habited scraps of land, more like sandbanks than islands. They are simply the crests of hills rising up from the littoral shelf. Small nations tend to be deadly earnest about suchlike things, so it's better not to make a big deal about it. I stand there, gazing through a window that takes up one entire side of the room. Down below, on the narrow coastal terrace, the buildings of Antafagusta cluster closely together. The white governmental edifices from the colonial period stand in groups; beyond them are pocket-sized squares shaded by luxuriant clumps of trees; the lone private residences of the nobility and the merchants are part of the view; and there, for all the world as though they had been thrust forcibly between those blithely scattered houses, modern rectangles loom, their multitudinous panes glinting. Here too they have started using brownish tinted glass which provides protec-tion from the sun's rays and from the curious glances of passers-by, while not spoiling the view from inside.

Half-hidden behind the buildings, the *Maltese Cross* gleams white in the port, its back-tilted funnel with the black and red stripes no longer emitting even the faintest puff of smoke. Over there right now the stewards are cleaning up the saloons in the expectation of more passengers, and the barmen are pouring out the dregs so that they can top up the bottles that have already been opened. The mid-quality brandy, the one that sells best, can take up to ten percent adulteration with any old rubbish before suspicion begins to dawn on your aver-age non-sophisticate. And they are unfailingly good at it.

So I stand there by the window, vividly imagining the busy barmen and the stewards wielding their vacuum cleaners, when suddenly the telephone rings, delicately insistent. It is obviously a mistake, or at best one of those young ladies whose business consists in phoning round all the hotel rooms day after day to offer their services. No one in this town as yet knows the first thing about me, and the fact that a certain Artur Yanno is up on the sixth floor of the Archipelago Ho-tel, surveying the town from his point of vantage, is something known to me and me alone.

Not so.

'Mr. Yanno?' a well-modulated baritone rumbles in my ear. 'I am glad to welcome you to Minore, Mr. Yanno.'

I am completely convinced that what is hampering the spread of the videotelephone right now has nothing to do with technical com-plexity. It is just psychologically unacceptable, that's all. Who needs it? It is a repulsive thought—your sweet face, asinine with surprise or contorted with rage, appearing to some inquisitive stranger calling in from goodness knows where, without an instant's delay, the minute you pick up the receiver on an incoming call.

English, a rather lilting enunciation that is stamped with the in-fluence of Minoran—a language which, according to the rather de-batable opinion of some pundits, could have emerged when Phoenician,

Arabic, and a few other Semitic languages started working upon a putative primordial language, whose nature remains as yet unestablished. Were the ancient Minorans related to the long-lost Etruscans? Or to the Basques?

'Mr. Yanno,' the practiced baritone rumbles in my ear. 'My name is Ares Damian. I approach you in the name of the International-Democratic League of Minore, whose president I have the honour of being. We were exceedingly glad to hear the news of your arrival in Antafagusta. We are splendidly well-apprised of the fact that your esteemed country has always accorded due attention to the principles of international democracy, and therefore your arrival in the capacity of special correspondent is for us a truly significant, not to say momentous, event. Permit me on this occasion to invite you to a modest unofficial supper in the restaurant at your hotel—say, at half past seven. We would be honored.'

The silky baritone is starting to make my head spin a little, as though I were standing above a wide, swift-flowing river and staring raptly into the water: at such times I have a strong urge to throw caution to the winds and cast myself head-first into the current. I could not come up with a single reason to refuse. And why should I? Admittedly, Avik Nersesyan had impressed on me not to be in too much of a hurry to make acquaintances, because everything would be double dutch to me at first, and if I didn't watch it I would be tied hand and foot, like a fly trussed by a spider. Before I could say 'knife', I would be in harness to some political organization and would not be able to get out of it at any price. Well, that's all nonsense. I'm no ambassador—neither extraordinary nor plenipotentiary—obliged to weigh every step I take, everything I say, for fear of being gossiped about all over the place. A journalist exists solely to meet people—Satan himself, if necessary, and hit the bottle with him—his place or mine—if there's the slightest hope of digging out something new about purgatory or the underworld.

Damian holds his peace, giving me the chance to think it over, then adds, 'We plan this supper for a very select few—entirely unofficial.' Next, as confidingly as you please: 'Your help would stand us in very good stead, Mr. Yanno, for you are a journalist of international renown.'

I like good restaurants. It would be reasonable to assume that the Archipelago's restaurant is one of the best in town, it being such a respectable hotel. I am not a pig about it, but a good meal and a civilized drink or two are, like as not, the only ways in which I occasionally indulge my sinful flesh. Lord knows, the old body deserves no less—I mean, how often do I squeeze from it all it can give? A journalist is like the proverbial wolf, which only eats what its legs provide. In this day and age, when events unfold with stupefying rapidity and a filed report is obsolete in a matter of hours, all this dashing about becomes almost unbearable. If you don't weaken just a bit now and then, you will collapse like a broken-winded horse—and they shoot broken-winded horses, right? A talent for relaxing, really relaxing, should be considered worth its weight in gold.

My professional curiosity was piqued too. They need my help, do they? That promptly brought back the memory of my last African assignment. I arrived in Katsunga on the third day after the latest insurgency had been put down. The mercenaries had already been arrested and shoved into solitary, and efforts were being made to rattle them into telling who had backed them. The prisoners kept mum, more out of shock than on principle. The authorities were very keen to find out which opposition group or foreign power had been behind the insurgency. For the moment, all anybody knew was what had happened. At midnight, a motor-launch carrying an armed detachment had put in to shore. At the same time, an unidentified aeroplane had landed another group at the airport. Unluckily for the insurgents, on that very same night the commander in chief of the republican armed forces had been staging one of his habitual snap inspections. Everyone knew about it, of course, so not one single soldier in the whole army was sleeping that night. The enemy, putting in from the sea and dropping from the sky, provided just the target they wanted, given the circumstances. As a result of the hellish shoot-out that ensued, the only survivors were a few lucky fellows—white as well as black—who had had the sense to hide in ditches and sewer pipes and stay put, and then, when they crawled out at dawn, to do so waving white flags over their heads. By that time the shooting had stopped, and the prisoners were taken off to jail alive.

I was told that prize catch was the white commander of the seaborne landing detachment, who had yet to utter a single word and whose diary no one could read. More out of curiosity than anything else, I asked them to show it to me. When I got my hands on the black notebook, I almost let out a yell—words I had known since my childhood were dancing before my eyes.

They took me there. On the dirt floor of a cell in the central prison was crouched a human figure attired in underpants. The local gendarmes had confiscated all the rest of his clothes, reasoning that he didn't need them. The man was staring fixedly at one point, no doubt painfully trying to puzzle out exactly what had gone awry. He seemed not to notice us when we entered. I stood behind the prisoner's back, kicked him in the side and roared, 'You pinheaded twit! Who was the loony that sent you out here, to the middle of nowhere?'

The sounds of his native tongue had a miraculous effect. The prisoner roused himself, turned toward me, and at once started talking almost too fast for me to translate.

Later, on my departure from Katsunga, I was driven to the airport in the President's limousine, and the Secretary of State told me that I was the first foreigner ever to be recommended for the Revolutionary Cross. Who knows, maybe they'll send it some day, registered parcel post, if they don't have another coup before then. For me, though, the excellent commentaries I filed from Katsunga were what really mattered. And supposing something of that ilk pops up here too?

In the next five minutes I root out a fresh shirt from my suitcase and run my hand over my chin. At times there is something to be said for being a natural tow-head and growing stubble that is an indeterminately light color. A guy with a darker complexion would not get away without shaving again, but I'll pass, and that saves me almost quarter of an hour.

The image of the hotel room suddenly distorts, goes all ripply, wrinkles just like a photograph in a flame or the picture on a television that has suddenly gone wrong. In my ears, louder and louder, sound unfamiliar words, which, in my short time on Minore, I have grown quite used to hearing. But who is repeating those words, if not I myself? For a time I see nothing, and those words sound louder and louder. Then suddenly I discover that I am the one who is saying them, and at that point their meaning flares up on my mind.

It all began on that unlucky, thrice-accursed day, towards evening, when a panting Kolo came running up the hillside to my door and bawled, 'Stemo! Stemo! Chuck in your damn goats, chuck your nets—we're rich now, you and me! All them stones that stick up out of the ground and break our ploughs—it's pure ore! You know what that's worth! They'll soon be forking out that much to us we'll be millionaires!'

I thought he had gone off his rocker, and all because of our grinding poverty and the hunger that never went away. The other villagers had always thought that Kolo was weird, and now he looked to have gone completely batty. I had known him since childhood. His family had moved in from the plateau when Kolo was still quite small. A little while later, a persistent rumor crept round the village to the effect that Nikanor, Kolo's father, had beaten the life out of some traveller one night there on the plateau, had taken his money, and had used those few pennies, they said, to buy a scrap of land in our village, because his conscience gave him no peace where he was. No one could prove it, yet the rumor ran from house to house. I took no notice at all. Although Nikanor, a gloomy peasant with a brigand's curly beard, was shunned by many, I reassured myself with the thought that if he actually had beaten the life out of the traveller, Kolo would have been too little at the time to have had any part in it, so we stayed friends.

There on the plateau they ate only potatoes, since nothing else grew there, and tiny potatoes at that, about the size of a pigeon's egg and always green on one side. Kolo told me that was because there the rock was covered by a layer of earth so thin that it did not protect the taters from the sun. Because of those potatoes, breast-feeding women found their milk drying up after a couple of months, and after

11

that the little ones were given potato pap in a rag to suck. It was simply a wonder that the men had what it took to make children at all. But the children of the plateau, from the day they were born, were just not normal. They were sort of slow-witted, and spent an unbelievably long time musing over whatever it may be, and when they had finally thought it through, they would invariably start the job wrong end up. It just couldn't be helped.

Kolo didn't change a bit, not even when he grew up. When it came to clearing his field of the rocks that came creeping back out of the ground every year, he unfailingly began at the top of the slope. The rocks, of course, rolled down, and, by the time he was done, the entire field was studded with them and the whole job looked like it needed doing over again. Several times I tried to suggest that there was a better way of doing it, but apparently his head was already so arranged that no lesson could stay put in it for long.

Our field was about as big as a dining table and all downhill, right on the edge of the plateau. Down below, the sea shone blue. Sometimes we would go down with nets to catch something extra to put on the table. Our plateau was not a plateau at all—it was only some thirty meters above sea level—but we called it that anyway, because it sounded good. From its notched edge there was a sheer drop to the sea, and that's where the brownish grainy rock which makes up our entire island can best be seen; it had been trodden by many generations of our ancestors who lived in direst poverty and never suspected that they were really walking on a mother-lode of gold.

Kolo certainly wasn't the one who discovered it, needless to say. Once upon a time, a very long time ago, one of the island's rare visitors in those days—a Dutch tourist and obviously a peculiar sort of person—took with him a hefty chunk of that brownish primordial rock and carried it home in his suitcase, evidently for lack of anything else to take. It seems that he kept the rock on his desk at first, showing it to his visitors, and then, when the novelty wore off, he took it into the hallway and sometimes used it to prop the front door open.

No one knows how long after this, a friend of his stopped by—a geologist he was, or maybe a mineralogist. The rock just happened to be holding the door, and the visitor stubbed his toe on it in the dimly lit hallway. Well, and it wasn't the first time that someone has hobbled his way to a discovery. So the visitor crouched down to see what kind of boulder this was on the floor, saw the unusual mineral, and, stirred by professional interest, cadged the stone for himself. And a week later he came bounding back, all in a lather, asking: where did you dig up that fabulously rich phosphate ore? With the world becoming overpopulated before our eyes, every loaf of bread, every bag of fertilizer worth its weight in gold, and the spectre of hunger looming over us and our children, it is unthinkable to leave a deposit like this in the ground.

That was back in the time of the British, long before the war.

On the plateau, which wasn't all that big—perhaps a little over twenty square miles—there suddenly appeared strangers, in such numbers as no one had ever seen before. Most of them were sharp little chaps in plaid jackets with cheque books in their pockets. They started buying up plots of land from the locals, on the authority of various heretofore unheard-of companies, half of whose names started with 'British' and the other half with 'International'. The price they were offering was perfectly decent: our arid plateau had been worth almost nothing to that point, and for the kind of money they were offering you could even buy yourself a little house in Antafagusta, if you bargained properly. But those who fell all over themselves to sell off their holdings at that time later had good cause to groan and gnash their teeth. The money they had got looked like peanuts a few years later, when the phosphate boom reached its peak.

In those days, our family did not sell one iota of land. Not that anyone was insisting much that we should; they were all trying to get plots nearer to the center of the tableland, to keep the real estate all in one piece. The story was that they were planning to build a mine there, with an entire settlement next to it, where all the islanders would find work aplenty. A lot of us considered that to be downright impossible. But back then they got no further than sinking some trial workings before the war began. They managed to dispatch a total of perhaps ten or so steamers loaded with phosphates. It was a good thing, in a way, because otherwise where would they have built their aerodrome during the war?

When the war was over, the Consortium appeared, buying up plots of land from the rightful owners and opening its first quarry alongside the military air base. We often went there to gawk; it could not possibly have occurred to us then that this accursed pit would soon swallow up all our holdings. I had just buried my mother and father, who, as frequently happens with people who have lived a long life together, died within a week of each other, and we carried them off to the village cemetery within the same space of time, and raised gravestones over them. It was all mine then, and our little dry-stone hut in the shade of a large Italian pine, the scraps of open field, and the stony sheep-pasture were so dear to my heart that I would not have given them up for all the gold in the world. When employees of the Consortium came to talk me into it, I laughed right in their faces.

Besides, I did not want for money. The war had just passed that way, leaving us a little nest-egg. At the very end of the war, a huge American bomber that was coming in to land crashed to the ground with such force that all its wheels were wrenched away, and they sped off, one after another, overtaking the plane. The landing strip pointed right at our house. A little while later, when the plane was lying on the strip with its belly torn open, being consumed by crackling flames, four hulking great rubber hoops came thundering down, smashed the walls and roof, demolished the house and, bouncing over

13

the rocky outcrops, carried on down to the sea, until they finally vanished from sight, sending up tall pillars of water.

The devastation was something awful. Our house and sheep-pen were a mass of scattered stones, as if they had taken a direct hit in an aerial bombardment. At the time, luckily, we were in the upper field, from where we helplessly gazed down upon the image of destruction. All our goats and sheep were also at pasture on the slopes, so that only the black ewe that had given birth the day before and her two lambs perished. Fear and sorrow beset us then, and no mistake. They sent soldiers and a lorry from the aerodrome to help, and by autumn we had built a new house. But the Americans did a generous thing when peace was declared: they reimbursed us for the losses we had suffered because of the war. For the black ewe and the barn we received a sum more appropriate to a purebred Arab race-horse from a King's stables.

My father changed those dollars little by little, only when really driven to it, so that I ended up inheriting a goodly sum. Besides, I had bread, and I caught fish with my father's nets, and the idea that I could buy myself all those thingumabobs that are now cluttering up my flat, my cellar and my garage did not even enter my head. I quite simply did not have the brains to imagine that so many different things could even exist in this world, and that people could fancy that they are all essential to life.

But, as I said before, it all began on that thrice-accursed day when, one airless evening, a panting Kolo ran to our door and bellowed, as though he had been set barefoot on hot coals, 'Stemo! Stemo! Chuck in your damn goats, chuck your nets—we're rich now, you and me! All them stones that stick up out of the ground and break our ploughs— it's pure ore! You know what that's worth! They'll soon be forking out so much to us, we'll be millionaires!'

True enough, we might perhaps become millionaires if it goes on like this. Only there are some other things tied in with it that don't suit me half so well. And is it just me? I don't know a single person here who really feels good about anything, although we have all long forgotten the bad times.

Perhaps that is the price of wealth?...

Ar-tur Yan-no...

What is this ridiculous nightmare I've just been having? Some huge black wheels bearing down like an express train upon a little slate house, knocking down the walls, flinging slabs of stone across the hillside, as if someone had blown it up, and racing on, bouncing over brown outcrops of rock, over the withered grass down the slope, toward the blue sea below, smacking into it and flinging up fountains of water. Where could I have seen anything like that? In the cinema, perhaps?

The vision suddenly starts to blur, disappears, and, without the

14

slightest strain, I realize that my name is Artur Yanno, that I am a journalist, accredited for my first stint in Antafagusta as a special correspondent. 'Since none of our people have been there before, they will judge us from the things that you pick up on or turn down,' the deputy director of our agency said as he saw me off, 'so mind that you give no one any reason to disapprove of anything you do.'

They will judge? And who exactly will they judge?

The square is flooded with sunlight, as if it were not a level surface but a concave mirror which draws all the sun's rays in and does not let a single one escape. Over the burning hot iron of the car roofs, the air is so agitated that it looks like water seething from invisible springs. The entire square is packed with cars. Damn it all, sooner or later they are just going to suffocate on their scrap of earth amid these iron boxes. The cars allow no one to pass, and you go flinging yourself from side to side, as though you're doing some absurd Andalusian dance, and I—wouldn't you know it?—am in a hurry. I don't have the time right now to play the fool on this asphalt frying pan! Twelve o'clock has struck already, and our meeting was set for noon.

There is a moment when the back of an unknown man, clad in a tight summer jacket with black and white stripes, comes into my field of vision. The stranger up ahead of me is doing his own Andalusian dance, and from time to time he seems to stop short as he manoeuvres round a car, but that could perhaps be simply an optical illusion, because he's still out there giving as good as he gets. This unknown man's back conveys the feeling that he is impatient and highly strung, and for some reason I find that unpleasant, but there's no helping that, and besides, what business is it of mine? It's stupid to feel anything you don't have to feel.

We fling ourselves about like ants in an iron labyrinth, filmed in slow motion, and all at once I sense, with absolute clarity and in every pore of my skin, that something is about to happen, something awful that will put a stop to this senseless capering.

All of a sudden the striped back vanishes. A car door slams. Something bright blue flickers, and an instant later something inexplicable occurs. A sharp jolt, a tornado, an earthquake—and I know no more. Everything around me, and inside me too, begins to sway, unceasingly and endlessly, like the warm water by the shoreline that is packed with tiny weeds.

From that moment I have been dominated by a crushing fear. Just suppose now that I cannot remember something that is absolutely essential, in whose absence everything else will lose all its meaning? At first I do not know what that absolutely essential thing is or where to look for it, but then it gradually comes clear to me: it is my own name. I have to remember my name at all costs, because otherwise I will not be able to stop the swaying that is trying to turn me inside out, for I will have become nothing more than a twitching clot of protein on a wave rolling in to the shore—a glob with no face and no name.

Finally I have the upper hand! I have dropped my anchor. I feel infinitely exhausted. Now, at last, I will be able to rest. I no longer have the power to recollect, recollect, recollect.

I hurry and stumble down the hotel corridor, which is completely and utterly brown. The walls are brown; the floor is covered with a brown carpet, along which I am scampering in unseemly haste; even the soft light falling either from invisible windows or from concealed lamps has a brownish tint, as if the rays have passed through yellowed leaves.

Those idiotic cuff-links, they're what's making me late. What the devil can I have done with them? How absolutely stupid can anyone be? Having worked myself into a lather in a fruitless search, I ended up having to thread a needle with trembling fingers, so as to secure my cuffs with invisible stitches. All the same, I'm going to feel revolting now, and I'll be pulling up my shirt sleeves on the sly and attracting everyone's attention. It's a curse, it must be, because obviously to the very end of my days I will never learn how to get all the little essentials into my suitcase in any proper order! And if it were the first time this had happened...

I fail to notice a sliding door that blends with the wall panelling and with which I have drawn level. It opens up abruptly. I instinctively move aside, so as not to block the path of whoever is coming through the door. Into the corridor splashes a voice, transformed by an amplifier into a faceless, synthetic sound. It assaults my ears, but the words do not penetrate into my mind. The door shuts immediately but the person who has emerged into the corridor does not walk past me, although I have made it possible for him to do so. Instead, he cannons right into me. I feel a stranger's hands grasping my jacket lapels.

'You're a journalist, right? You are a journalist, aren't you?'

I nod automatically, not having had time to make anything of this. The hands take an even stronger hold of my lapels. A tall woman, her hair fashionably cropped, is staring insanely at me through a pair of huge octagonal spectacles, which bulge out like fish-eyes, and starts nudging me little by little toward the door, like something she has bagged. A madwoman, I conclude without wasting a moment in thought. The psychiatrists aren't kidding when they declare that virtually one in three, or even every other person, in the world today is suffering from some sort of psychiatric aberration. Perhaps it was like this before, but then, evidently, most of them had a kind of quiet insanity that involved a lot of silent glowering in corners. These days, lifestyles have changed so much that any half-wit thinks that he has the right to force his will and his viewpoint upon other people. It's really too bad. I just can't come to blows with a woman, and she makes the most of that and keeps shoving me forward. I feel like a fly in a spider's grip, and the rapacious glint in those bulging spectacle lenses makes the comparison even more compelling. A little white plastic panel strikes my eye. On it is written, in blue lettering, 'IEA', and below that, in slightly smaller letters, 'a UNESCO-associated project'.

'Wherever have you been? Why didn't you show up for the opening? You must come at once to the plenary meeting!' the unidentified female upbraids me in a loud whisper. 'Today we're holding our jubilee meeting, as if you didn't know that perfectly well! Fifteen years of Association work, and the two hundred and eightieth peripatetic session. This is a scientific event! It absolutely must get coverage in the international press!'

Her eyes are burning, as if from a sudden flare of lust. I am starting to feel odd: mad people inspire an unaccountable fear in me. I flap helplessly, but this woman is unbelievably strong, and leaves me not the ghost of a chance. I am suddenly overpowered: my will caves in without further ado, and I no longer determine the course of events. My resistance is broken. As a result, I find myself in a conference hall, where my seductress pushes me forcefully into one of the numerous armchairs there that are shaped rather like a bent penny. They stand in concentric semicircles around the chairman's table, where highlights sparkle on a microphone and a bottle of mineral water. Behind the table are two chairs, one for the chairman himself and one for the speaker.

'Oh good lord!' the bespectacled Amazon sighs behind my right shoulder, with sudden, unfeigned womanliness. 'What a monstrosity you are! I've been looking for you everywhere!'

With these words, she takes her hands off my shoulders and disappears towards the back, where softly upholstered walls radiate into the dusk.

My first impulse as a free man is an urge to jump right up and take off. This is some kind of ridiculous mistake, and I have to get away, pronto. No one is expecting me here—after all, they don't have a clue who I am. But there is something about this room that draws me. Only the chairman's table stands out in the all-encompassing semi-darkness. The place reserved for the chairman is occupied by a gentleman in a steely-colored suit that is manifestly not off the peg. His graying wavy hair descends to his collar. No doubt he is an academic, a foreign member of countless scientific societies. Impressive gentlemen like this are constantly eyed and photographed at every international gathering, be it of butterfly collectors or experts in forensic post-mortems, and are invariably elected to preside over every conceivable sort of scientific society. The speaker, though—and this you can tell without hearing him speak—is one of those young professors who these days go around the universities in droves with short-order doctoral dissertations under their arms, doing a little research here and a little reading there, busily improving themselves and unceasingly arranging symposia. It would be nothing short of an injustice to expect them to finish anything; they have absolutely no time to delve much into their subject. Before, when there were not so many universities and colleges, and fewer of these fellows too, when teachers and researchers were always in the public eye, this kind of professor, tagged as he is by a conspicuous air of charlatanry, could never have contrived to carry things off so successfully. This is a product of higher education run rampant. He is dressed, as a matter of course, in a scruffy pair of denims and a jeans jacket. Young as he is, his egg-shaped head is completely bald, if you don't count the sparse locks of hair of an indeterminate shade which hang from behind his ears onto his collar. Viewed from the side, that head looks awfully defenseless and vulnerable, for all the world like an egg that has been shelled. The professor's voice is high-pitched and boyish; it still hasn't broken, though he must have been through that phase at some time in his life. Young urchins like him are so rabidly involved in doing their thing in every sort of group and society and then some—and have been, ever since they were in school—that they have simply been too busy for that awkward age. And so they grow into superannuated urchins. It is suddenly clear to me that the professor reminds me of someone, though who that someone might be I cannot say for the moment.

'Returning to this session's scheduled topic—the influence of the earthworm upon cultivated terrain, as inferred from the relevant petrographic and sociobiological factors, and the instrumentalities impacting thereupon,' the professor intones into the microphone, as he glances attentively around the room, 'I would wish to remind you of the classical pronouncement penned by the great Charles Darwin in 1881, which is, of course, well known to us all but which nevertheless is something that bears repeating, at all times and in all circumstances. As you recall, Darwin made the following statement: "Worms have played a more important part in the history of the world than most persons would at first suppose. In almost all humid countries they are extraordinarily numerous, and for their size possess great muscular power. In many parts of England a weight of more than ten tons of dry earth annually passes through their bodies and is brought to the surface on each acre of land..." I would urge you, my respected colleagues, to reflect on this for a moment.'

A suspenseful silence reigns over the room. I begin to feel that I am picking up some miniscule vibrations—down there, deep in the earth beneath the Archipelago's foundations, earthworms are munching their way through the soil.

'Subsequent research has merely confirmed the accuracy of Darwin's propositions. By their tunnelling activities, earthworms continually mix and aerate the soil. While taking in decomposed vegetal debris, they also swallow soil in large quantities, which acquires new and valuable properties while passing through their digestive tracts,

19

there being enriched with calcium, magnesium, ammonium, and also phosphoric acid, and is subsequently expelled in the form of what are known as worm castings. Worm castings are pellets with an alkaline pH, which thus serve to lower soil acidity. They also contain measurably larger quantities of useful microorganisms. What other creature so benefits Mother Earth with heroism so quotidian, yet so unsung?'

The hall rings with applause. Not wanting to stick out like a sore thumb, I also clap a few times. Then, when I turn my eyes back to the professor, I suddenly realize what he looks like. An earthworm, to be sure! It's nothing but a giant earthworm. Even the way he swings his elongated head right and left to scan the room through his spectacles has something of the earthworm about it.

'Since earthworms are capable of producing daily amounts of faecal matter which approximately equal their own body weight, their effects upon the soil may be quantitatively calculated. There are between five hundred thousand and two million earthworms, on average, per hectare. In favourable circumstances, that number can rise to between five and seven million, or even higher. This adds up to between two and three tons of live earthworms per hectare. An equal weight of soil passes through their digestive tracts every day, being transformed into castings. As a result of the loosening effect which the earthworm has, soil volume increases by fifteen, or indeed up to thirty, per cent. Calculations have shown that the surface layer of soil, to a depth of a half a meter, or even a whole meter, passes in toto through the guts of the worms which inhabit that soil, once every one or two hundred years.

'Esteemed colleagues! If earthworms did not ceaselessly renew the soil worked by man, the fertility of the arable layer of our lands in all the more populous areas would long ago have been definitively exhausted, and we would now be living in a lifeless desert, while the greater part of humanity would have died of hunger, never having lived to see this day.'

What is being applauded now—the industriousness of the earthworm or human debility? The professor adjusts his spectacles in their gold frames, and his face takes on an anxious expression.

'What we have been talking about to this point are universally recognized items which, most regrettably, many of us not infrequently fail to bear in mind. Now, though, I would like to touch upon a new and exceedingly ominous turn of events, which I have recently been researching. The point at issue is that, in his endless striving to increase the biological output per square unit of land, man has begun to introduce increasing amounts of chemicals into the soil. While a portion of these are pure poisons—herbicides and pesticides—the most regular and the largest applications are of mineral fertilizers. It would be frivolous to suppose that all these substances do not exert a certain influence upon existing biological communities. No interference with the established balance of nature can pass off without some repercussions. The earthworm lacks the senses of smell and taste, as we understand them. Along with soil and organic debris, it swallows both poisons and fertilizers, and, as a result, is often killed by ingesting excessive concentrations of chemical substances. The willing worker says his final farewell, and the fields are left to mourn him.

'Thus, dear colleagues, if we do not succeed in achieving, immediately and on an international scale, enforceable limitations on the production and use of mineral fertilizers, in no time at all we shall have to deal with lifeless farmlands made up of noxious clay with the texture of soap, entirely impregnated with corrosive chemicals, where even the most hardy weeds, not to mention cultivated plants, will wither. And, really, what is there to be said about arid lands, where the earthworms, as they habitually do during dry spells, will burrow down to a depth of two meters, will construct protective capsules out of mucous which they themselves secrete, and will settle down to wait for better times? Meanwhile, on the surface of the earth, dust storms will be carrying off the parched soil which by then will have turned into powder.

'All this will become deplorable reality if we permit the earthworm to survive only as an illustration in natural history books. This is something which we cannot allow—generations yet to come would never forgive us!'

The professor has evidently finished. He scarcely has time to raise a handkerchief to his forehead to wipe the sweat away before an incomprehensible ruckus starts up in the back section of the hall, in an area submerged in semidarkness. I make the sudden discovery that the chairs here swivel. How very convenient! I turn to face in the opposite direction. By the back wall, which is engulfed in gloom, about fifteen or so people are scuttling about, frenziedly waving their arms and unrolling banners. One of the green bolts of fabric reads: 'Minore for the Minorans!' 'Earthworms—yes! Phosphates—no!' another slogan exclaims. One sign bears a heraldic insignia—a little barefoot lad riding a goat and holding a fishing net. Above that portrait is a semicircular inscription which reads 'ASSn OF OWN-LAND-ERS', while below it is emblazoned a bright red emblem composed of the letters 'GFP'. After a lengthy to-do, a third banner is unrolled. It is the biggest of the lot and evidently carries the basic rallying cry, which is 'How much longer will our wealth go rolling down the gullets of eternally hungry superpowers?'

'Ladies and gentlemen, please!' the chairman implores, leaning toward the microphone. 'Under no circumstances will we become embroiled in politics and interfere in the internal affairs of a country where we are guests!'

The noise grows. Scarcely has the chairman completed his appeal when from the rear, emerging from the people skittering hither and thither with banners, steps a young man, an exceedingly wild-looking young man who is wearing on his shoulders something resembling an animal pelt. His long dark hair, untouched by scissors in living memory, hangs straight on both sides of his thin face, and a fanatic fire burns in his close-set eyes. Not paying the slightest attention to the chairman, he snatches the microphone from the table, brings it to his mouth for all the world like an apple, and yells, his white teeth gleaming, and seeming to take a bite out of it with every word,

'Guests? And did anyone invite you? You're here on the say-so of those who run this place. We are fighting for our land, and we recognize only those guests who support our just struggle. If your earthworms blind you to Minore, then good riddance to bad rubbish!'

Some of the people sitting in armchairs leap to their feet. The woman in octagonal spectacles runs up to the table from behind, and yells hysterically, 'Shame on you! This is a gathering of scientists, of great minds...'

Her words are drowned in a fearsome din, which sounds as though the hotel and all it contains have fallen into a cavern dug by earthworms. The gloomy-looking young man has flung the microphone to the floor.

Chunky hotel porters in glossy leather caps come running into the room. There are a lot of them here, and they are porters only in name—perhaps that is what they're called on the payroll manifest. But in reality their job is to stop things from getting out of hand and to keep tabs on people. A hand-to-hand skirmish breaks out. I finally shake off my torpor and, turning my back on the combatants, make my way out into the brown corridor. I am dogged by the fear that the woman in octagonal spectacles will come and grab me by the lapels again.

I have almost the same feeling—that of an animal caught in a trap—sitting here at the restaurant table, across from Ares Damian. The man's sheer bulk and massive round head are overwhelming. His black eyes gaze unblinking from beneath riotously bushy eyebrows, with hypnotic effect. Damian dyes his curly Romany hair so carefully that one would search in vain for a single grey thread, although, given his age, there should be quantities of them.

'Well, yes, of course, those are our darling Own-landers kicking up a fuss again!' he exclaims in pear-shaped tones and gives a knowing nod. 'The cretins! They are our main ideological adversaries and the pallbearers of all and any progress. They don't have a jot of support among the people, because the people thirst to forge ahead to a higher standard of living. And that's why they make their appeals to foreigners. I can assure you that there is never a single international event in Antafagusta, and we have them frequently, where they don't show up with their slogans. I blame our prime minister for his indecisiveness. They should have been given a gentle little throttling long ago. They rant on about human rights, but give them their way and they'd muzzle all those who think differently or toss them into jail. Solanine-

22

soaked degenerates!'

As a start, who could ask for more? Great, let's begin our acquaintance with Minore right here. What do the Own-landers want? Where do they come from? And what does solanine have to do with it?

Damian would have been very happy to brush it all off and get on to something else, but he needs me. Putting a tight rein on his stormy temperament, he concedes that it's this or nothing.

'Our dear old plateau, where major projects are now under way and virtually no one lives any more, was inhabited by some real paupers before the phosphate era. They grew potatoes, and nothing but potatoes, because nothing else would grow there, and the ones they grew weren't much bigger than peas and were always green on one side. There was a mere sliver of tillable soil, not deep enough to protect the tubers from the sun. Because of those potatoes, breast-feeding women found their milk drying up after a couple of months, and after that the infants were fed with mashed potatoes. So the children's bodies were subjected to steady doses of solanine, which, as you probably know, is a poison that forms when the layer immediately below the skin of a potato tuber is exposed to sunlight. Normal concentrations of solanine present no danger to adults, but its effects on the infant body are far stronger. Stunted development was always endemic on the plateau. Generation after generation of lethargic people with exceedingly limited intellectual capacities were raised there. Evidently by way of compensation, they developed a simply prodigious degree of stubbornness. We have a saying that a plateau dweller will smash his way through a cliff face. In addition to this, they are awfully apt to stick together and will push forward one of their own at the drop of a hat. In their eyes, any native of the plateau is by definition the best of the bunch. The plateau dwellers who moved into the town have formed an organization called the Association of Own-landers which has an exceedingly witty motto: "We want our own land for ourselves!" Their one goal—a return to the goat, the fish and the potato—is represented by an emblem made up of the letters "GFP". They want an end to the phosphate mining and an embargo on foreign entry, so as to preserve the invaluable ethnic purity of Minore. Their noisy contention is that otherwise we will soon be a national minority on this island and will be forced to integrate with the aliens hired by the Consortium. A worse calamity they cannot imagine—they'd rather have the great flood any day.

'They take every chance they can get to make a stir, to attract attention. I should apologize for the fact that my deputy, Dr. Ingoberto Reus, who was waiting here with me to meet you, was called away at the last minute to the scene of the fracas. We had intended that he, as the officer responsible for dealing with the problem concerned, would acquaint you with the plan in whose implementation we are seeking to enlist your magnanimous assistance.'

Damian gestured broadly toward the empty chair next to him,

23

where I could see a white napkin, dropped there in haste.

'You mean people got hurt?'

'No, no—Ingoberto is a doctor of law, a barrister. The best in Antafagusta, by the way, just in case you should ever need advice or help in any legal matter. Some of the Own-landers' leaders have been taken in and have demanded that he be present at the interrogation. Otherwise they refuse to respond to questioning.'

'Just a moment. As I understood it, Dr. Reus is your deputy in the International-Democratic League.'

'That is absolutely correct.'

'But the Own-landers are your ideological adversaries, right? Then why would they ask for him and no one else?'

Damian throws himself back in his chair so brusquely that the front feet lift off the floor and bang back down.

'Yes, but you know,' he declares, quite mollified, 'political sympathies are one thing and professional duty is quite another. Besides, the most idiotic law enforcement officials in our talentless government cannot be presented with the opportunity of acting outside the unremitting control of the democratic consensus.'

At this point the picture before my eyes starts to blur. Indistinct snatches of words come sneaking into my ears, making it difficult to listen to Damian, who is by now getting to the point. I can no longer distinguish individual words and phrases; I can just grasp the general drift of the conversation through the mysterious static. It is as though one transmission is drowning out another, with a receiver that is not selective enough to filter out the noise. Damian wants me to help them set up a memorial in Antafagusta to someone called the Herald, who is the forefather of International-Democracy on Minore and whose first name I simply cannot make out. It is something on the lines of Tomasson, but I am pretty sure I have got that wrong. I am overcome by the unfamiliar words that echo in my head, poking into my cranium from within, until I actually start repeating them.

'They'll soon be forking out that much to us, we'll be millionaires!' Kolo kept exclaiming, as though those were the only words he knew.

But on that day there had been nothing to give an inkling of changes to come. Only the man at the chemist's subscribed to a newspaper. It's really funny to think what savages we were back then—not a transistor, not a television to be had, and who among us could even have guessed that anything of the like had been invented and existed in this wide world? Kolo had been down to the chemist's to get some cough medicine for Niki, his sickly little brother, and just happened to hear the man behind the counter telling someone about an article in the paper which said that foreign scientists were of the opinion that all of Minore was made up of fabulously rich phosphate deposits, and that if every Minoran were given an equal share of its cash

24

value, then every last one of us would be millionaires.

To this I replied, 'Kolo, you're nothing but a numskull, and you don't get the point of anything. Even if someone decides that this stone is worth something, nobody will give us a brass farthing for it, you'll see. If that weren't so, the place would have been swarming with wide boys way back, but there's neither sight nor sound of them, you can see that for yourself, and that means you won't set eyes on any million either.' Kolo just stood gawping at me, his lip sticking out, and I put on my one good shirt and went down to the sea, where Murana was waiting for me among the rocks, afire with impatience. I left Kolo alone with his troubles. That whole conversation about the money that was going to come cascading down on us wasn't worth a rap to me in comparison with one—just one—of Murana's kisses.

Murana was a very beautiful girl in those days. She is beautiful still, but in a different way. She has grown lean and nervy; her face has darkened and narrowed, and sometimes I catch a spattering of despair in her eyes. I think that the accidents have done more than anything to change her—first the one, then, a few years later, the other. But perhaps the years have also taken their toll. In any case, in those days Murana was a round-faced slip of a girl with enormous eyes and luxuriant black hair. She never sat still for a moment, and, after a long day working in the hot fields, thought nothing of dancing the night away with me in the village tavern, until the back of her print dress turned dark with sweat.

It had been decided when our parents were still alive and I was sixteen and she was fourteen that Murana and I would marry. Only we had to wait until the time was ripe. Murana's mother had died young, of tuberculosis, and Murana lived with her fisherman father down below, right by the shore, in a tiny little shack. They didn't have enough land to plant even a measure of beans, but every year Murana raised a dozen or so ears of maize by the door-sill and between them she would set a handful of garlic cloves. Murana would go to the village to help in the fields, and was paid back with a little grain when autumn came. Everything else they got by bartering the saltwater fish that her father caught. The early postwar years were good from that point of view because the fish grew fat and multiplied while people were busy fighting. It is also true that some folk turned their noses up, saying that it was all due to the drownings, but during the entire war no more than two munitions transports went down near the island, and anyway most of their crews made it to shore in lifeboats, so that kind of talk was not worth listening to.

Later, when large foreign fishing vessels took to entering our coastal waters, the stocks of fish were very rapidly depleted. They cleaned the sea right out, as thoughtless as anything. Sometimes Murana's father came home from the sea, like all the other fishermen, without a single tiddler, and gradually, things got to be the way they

25

have remained to this day, there being far more sundry trash, plastic bottles and oil slicks to be met with at sea than fish. It often depends on the direction of the wind, but sometimes our sea looks like a rubbish tip close to shore, and mountains of motley junk pile up when the tide turns. All that stuff is thrown overboard from the ships. And what gets piped out into deep water doesn't bear thinking about.

The despoiling of the sea was the real reason for the grief that was visited upon their home. Had need not come knocking at the door, Murana's father would not have had to ignore the storm warning. But coming home from the sea for a week empty-handed is reason enough for a fisherman to take risks, so he went out that morning, although the rim of the sky to the northwest boded no good. And he did not return that day. His boat was found bottom up a few days later near a distant islet. As had been the custom on Minore time out of mind, Murana's father could not swim. We never swim out of our depth. But when I think about it, I can well see that in a bad storm even the best swimmer would be overmatched.

When Murana was left all alone in the world, we decided that there was no sense in waiting any more and that the two of us would manage more easily together. So we got married. There was no big celebration, just a quiet dinner with Kolo, and Leila and Maria, Murana's friends. A wedding like that would horrify your average Minoran these days. The good life has changed our habits unbelievably. A few years back, when Kolo's mother and father were getting ready to marry off Niki, their youngest, the bride's parents categorically insisted that no fewer than two hundred people must be invited to the wedding. This was their only daughter, and nothing less would do. Anybody would have thought that they were putting up their only daughter for auction!

We lived for about a year in my little house. Murana got into the way of taking care of the sheep and hoeing our slanted scrap of land. And then change came into our lives. The government signed an enormous phosphate-mining deal with the Consortium, and all the land in our village came under the concession. We were told that we would have to move off our holdings—not without compensation, of course, but that did not make it any easier for us. A fearsome thing it was to leave those familiar places, and none of us could even imagine how we could live any differently than our fathers and grandfathers had lived before us. But the pen-pushers rabbited on and on, until none of us had the strength to refuse them any more. Only old Ossian held out to the end: he would not sell his scrap of land and he was not about to move anywhere. Since his shack stood on the outskirts of the village, right by the lip of the slope, they finally left him in peace. I'll bet they had figured that the old lad would go to his reward before his little house got in the way of a quarry. And so Ossian was the only one from our whole village who kept his own roof over his head.

They gave us flats in new buildings in Antafagusta, and they started paying us twice a month for every ton of phosphate taken from our parcels of land. It was the first time in all our lives that we had had so much money, and we did not have to do a thing to earn it. Anyone who wanted to, of course, could go and make extra by working for the Consortium. There were vacancies aplenty in the office, as well as on the machines. There was even a call out for construction hands, posted on every corner. But most of those who went to work were townies or those ragtags who did not even have a scrap of their own land to bring in money from the phosphate mining. Soon the Consortium wangled official permission to ship in foreign workers, because otherwise the work in the quarries and on the building sites could well have ground to a halt. We were getting our money anyway, and we wanted to live life to the full at last. We had some darn difficult times behind us and it would have been just stupid to go and knock ourselves working for a living. We didn't care if the Consortium wanted a big port, where machines could be used to load the phosphates directly into the ships' holds, or if it needed roads to transport the ore from the quarries to the port. We never gave a thought to where our money was coming from. Every month, as if by magic, it was simply deposited into the bank and we very quickly got used to it.

That was when I bought my Honda—an iridescent gray beauty she was, with a huge square petrol tank and any number of gizmos and multicoloured headlights, a glittering vision of thick, chrome springs and exhaust pipes with funnel-shaped bells. When I gunned the engine, those funnels let out a powerful bass roar, which made my head spin a little. I had my hands on the next best thing to man-made thunder. And when my motorcycle tore off and sped down the road, it took my breath away.

In those days, mopeds were the big thing all over Minore. Every last one of Antafagusta's steeply canted alleyways reechoed with the thin whine of the motorettes on those puny French Peugeots and West German Sachs, and their little brakes squealed endlessly all over the place. Mopeds were the cheapest form of transportation and required no personal effort to run, and, since money was still a novelty to us, we spent it grudgingly. I despised the mopeds, called them motomules, and saved up for an extra six months until I could buy myself a real motorbike with some power to it. Except for the bikes that the policemen rode, it was the first big Honda on Minore.

Minore suddenly became unbelievably small. The only highway we had back then was one which ran around the island. It is still there but they have broadened it and doused it with asphalt. Later they did lay a few other roads, which crisscrossed the island, but the Consortium's excavators quickly crunched them up into little bits, like pliers chopping copper wire, and we were left with our one and only ring-road. In those days it was still narrow and surfaced with crushed rock. When I put my foot right down, a high wall of dark yellow dust rose up behind me and the rocky outcrops where the plateau plunged down to the sea sped past only an arm's length away.

At first I took Murana with me on these motorcycle rides. She clung to me, hot against my back, and sometimes, on the sharpest turns, gave a quiet little moan of pleasure tinged with fear. Then, when our Roxana was born, I unwillingly took to riding alone. I got into the habit of going once or twice around the island every morning, and the same in the evening. In between times, I ate dinner, played with the baby, took care of my Honda, chatted a little with Murana, or sat for an hour or so in a bar with Kolo. Kolo had come up with a more tranquil pastime. Every week he would buy a new pair of shoes and parade around in them for seven straight days, I think it was be-cause, as a child on the plateau and right to the point where he grew to manhood, he never had any shoes at all. As far back as I can remember, Kolo went barefoot winter and summer, his cracked heels glinting at his trouser ends. So now, sitting at the bar, he would put his foot up against the bottom of the upright or onto the foot-rest of his stool, and, right in the middle of a conversation, would suddenly start contemplating his shoes.

I smirked to myself over this childishness. My hobby seemed a lot more manly to me. I persuaded myself that, by riding about the is-land in this way, I was keeping an eye on the life around me and its changes. On my trips I took note of everything that was going on along the road. I knew where the quarries were being widened, and where the spoil-heaps were growing.

Could I ever have guessed how it would end?

That instant in time swims up again before my eyes, as soon as I start thinking about it. It is as though I will never free myself from the moment when the fearsome suspicion flitted into my head that I had really gone and done it now.

I was coming out of the long curve before the last stretch which ran along the shoreline to the outskirts of Antafagusta. There are two tourist hotels on that part of the road now, but back then there was nothing, just some oleander shrubs, and rocks that had tumbled down the precipice. The setting sun was striking slantwise into my eyes, making me squint. Entering the straight, I opened the Honda right up, to let her rip across the distance remaining between me and the town. Before my eyes even now there is a razor-sharp picture of the thin, bright-yellow speedometer needle, like a little ray of light, trembling around 120.

I noticed a vehicle approaching in the distance. It was a familiar red Yamaha, a hulking great powerful thing with a 1000 cc engine, whose owner lived somewhere down by the harbour. When we met, we would exchange a greeting, as was the custom then among the few of us who had large motorcycles. This time, as usual, we saluted each other with a wave of the hand, and immediately I was over my head in the soft, dense, smokescreen of dust that the Yamaha had kicked up. For a minute, the whole world outside the curved visor of my crash helmet was yellow and impenetrable. I held my breath, so as to keep the stuff out of my lungs.

When I started making things out again, suddenly there they were on the roadway: four shadowy figures in a cloud of dust. I gathered from the loose-fitting clothes and the guitar that they were hippies. Every autumn in those days, when the weather started cooling off, hippies would come in from the mainland, intending to winter on Minore without a roof over their heads. We were none too keen on them, that was for sure. Their slovenliness and their behaviour, which looked brazen to us, offended our sense of decency. But, since they kept themselves to themselves and got in no one's way, we put up with them. Or, rather, we had resigned ourselves to the inevitability of their company, because it was impossible to drive them away with anything we said, and even the police could not steel themselves to get rough with those defenseless denizens of nowhere in particular.

To this day I cannot understand where they sprang from. Perhaps they had been on the road before, and had just moved aside a little when the Yamaha approached, or perhaps they had climbed up onto the highway from the side nearest the sea, meaning to get into town before evening. I am tormented by the afterthought that I ... maybe I failed to notice that the man on the Yamaha was trying to tell me something. True, that thought is now completely beside the point. There was by then no more than twenty meters between me and those figures. I was going at full tilt, and I sensed instantly that it would be foolish and dangerous to brake. I just took my foot off the accelerator and jammed my finger on the horn. There was still a hope that they would scatter in all directions when they heard that ear-splitting sound, and I, albeit at some risk, would shoot right through the middle. I did not believe that anything bad could happen. Does anyone?

The motorcycle bearing down on them, its horn blaring, threw the hippies into a panic. Like one man, they flung themselves to one side, towards the sea. 'Terrific,' was the thought that flitted through my head. 'I'll be able to get by if I go over to the other side and skirt close to the verge.' The commotion among those longhairs, their muddleheadedness and clumsiness brought on a superior smirk. I, for my part, was directing the headlong rush of the motorbike and of my own body in space with fingertip precision.

But the hippie who was furthest from the far side of the road—I never knew whether it was male or female—suddenly got all tangled up in his tunic and fell as if poleaxed, straight across the roadway. The rest were busy making a dash for it. I wrenched the Honda sharply to one side, and actually saw the front wheel flying by the bare feet of the hippie, who was lying spreadeagled in the road. Then the bike slammed into the sandy verge and flipped over onto its side, and the fearsome blow knocked me senseless.

By the time I came around, I was in hospital, swaddled head to foot in bandages and plaster of Paris, so I could move neither hands nor feet. Frightful paroxysms of pain flared up all over me, and most dreadful of all was the pain in my left leg, which, I thought, obviously got the worst of it because I had gone left side first into the rocks.

It was a couple of days later when they told me that I no longer had a left leg and that I should be delighted to be alive at all.

If I could have got out of bed at that moment, I would in all likelihood have made away with myself. I did not doubt for an instant that a person with one leg is not a person and has no good reason to live.

I drag my eyelids apart, and light trickles into my eyes. Blurrily at first, and then more and more clearly, the figure of a doctor, dressed in a white gown and bending over me, looms up before my eyes.

'Artur Yanno,' the doctor says encouragingly.

Do I know him, then?

I try to nod my head, although I don't recognise him. Besides, I am tortured by what I don't know. Through benumbed lips, I try to speak.

'Doctor, am I really... Artur Yanno?... Or, perhaps... Stemo?... Why do I feel that I am ... sometimes one and sometimes the other?'

My strength gives out. The doctor leans closer, speaking softly and soothingly, but I don't understand a thing. Gradually the sharpness fades, the doctor's face blurs into a shapeless blob, and my eyelids close.

I am swathed in a twilight that resembles a dense, grayish-yellow cloud of dust.

This is the life! I am reclining in state, ensconced in a soft chair at the Figaro hairdressing salon, with warm, damp towels on my face, a lavender-scented cloud swirling above me, and the space around me, which is divided up into a multitude of cubicles, filled with unobtrusive music that flows from all sides at once out of quadrophonic speakers. Everything here is the last word in technology.

For a long time I saw no good reason to break my longstanding habit of shaving myself, and instead spend an hour or more every day lounging about in a chair at the hairdresser's. I mean, the Figaro is not some no-account barber's shop, where they are finished with you in fifteen minutes. Here everything is done thoroughly and unhurriedly. It is a sort of ritual, which brooks not the slightest haste, like a coronation ceremony. Never in my life have I seen a hairdressing salon with such a variety of superlative equipment. Nobody here bats an eye at the veritable panoply of foreign machines to massage the scalp, curl the mustache, and comb the sideburns. Sometimes it seems to me that, on account of its large mirror-like windows and mock late-Baroque interior decor, the Figaro salon, which is located on Herald Square, Antafagusta's main concourse, even overshadows the National Theatre, where the government funds restoration projects to the tune of several million a year. The only difference is that the National Theatre is basically a tourist attraction, while the Figaro salon is personally patronized by everybody who is anybody on Minore.

It was not the Figaro's splendid decor, mind you, which finally turned me into one of its regular customers. I'm not that vain. The Figaro simply happens to be the venue for meetings of the most influential and well-informed political club on Minore. For several months I had been secretly astounded by the way my fellow newsmen from other agencies seemed to have the inside track on everything. They were forever filing reports with their home offices on events which were covered in the local papers two or three days later, and often in a patchy or hazy manner at that. Meanwhile, I was told off several times for missing some important local story. I had already tried to get in with the people who compiled news releases for the state information service, but that was a real waste of time. Finally, Carlos Martinez—a newsman from the Prensa Latina agency who had been watching my constant bungling—took pity on me. One day, at a Foreign Ministry press conference where we were having explained to us yet again the Minoran government's favourable opinion of the nuclear-free zone issue (which was news to absolutely nobody), he tactfully drew me aside and said, 'Listen, why don't you go to the Figaro salon for your shaves?'

'Because I reckon I can take care of that better at home,' I replied.

'You're wrong there,' Carlos observed, fingering his classic Castilian beard with a distracted air. 'Some economies can turn out to be very costly.'

This conversation got me worried enough to find out what exactly was going on. So one morning I crossed the threshold of the Figaro salon for the first time. On the glass door, under the company name, the phrase 'Everything for Healthy Hair' was traced out in small, thick, gold letters.

Shortly after my arrival on the island, I had, admittedly, heard with half an ear that Prime Minister Eldon's brother ran a hairdresser's shop in Antafagusta, but at the time I attributed no particular significance to that bit of information. I dismissed it as an absurdity that was par for the course in this runty little state. It never once occurred to me that Dan Eldon's salon might not be your ordinary everyday establishment, but a social institution, a distribution point for rumours that suited the government, and a place where moods were shaped and sometimes political deals, plain and simple, were struck. One could always hear something worth listening to there, or perhaps launch a useful rumour and be fully confident that it would reach its intended destination.

I, in my innocence, had assumed that they were all motivated by pure vanity. My own lack of shrewdness exasperated me, and I tried unsuccessfully to comfort myself with the unconvincing excuse that no one had so much as intimated to me that all was not what it seemed. Who would point a boar in the direction of the truffles?

The proprietor greeted me with open arms. I felt like the prodigal son.

'At last!' he exclaimed histrionically. 'And there was I, thinking that I would have to set up a special cubicle for you, for otherwise you would not grace my humble establishment with your presence!'

I did not hear much the first time. All new things need a breaking-in period. For starters, the proprietor introduced me to two senators, who grilled me on my opinions of the economic policy which Minore was pursuing and who did their best, without even waiting for an answer, to drum into me that this policy was nothing less than totally unexceptionable.

But the groundwork was laid. From then on, I have had a standing appointment on weekdays from nine to ten thirty, and on Fridays, when I have my hair washed, I arrive half an hour earlier. That is when I usually come upon the Antafagusta's chief of police, who regales me with the past week's chronicle of criminality.

So here I am, still smiling at his tale. The chief of police left a good half hour ago and my old pal Ares Damian, who usually takes his place, is late, for some unknown reason.

The chief of police had been telling me how well and truly disconcerted he had been the previous morning when two of his sergeants

32

came back to the police station accompanied by a naked man of athletic build attired in nothing but a pair of brightly coloured socks. The man was wrapped in a white sheet that had MORGUE emblazoned on one corner, in large, violet letters, and he was shaking his head incessantly and making inarticulate noises.

A sluicing with cold water in the shower room appeared to clear the stranger's wits a little. The sergeants had found him at the crack of dawn in Antafagusta's central park, where a pair of feet in brightly coloured socks had been seen sticking out of the bushes. At first glance, the body seemed to have breathed its last, so the sergeants, overcoming the disgust inspired by this naked cadaver, called out the van from the morgue. But when they took hold of the body under the sheet, so as to lift it onto the stretcher, it turned out to be completely warm, to be wiggling its toes and making unintelligible noises. Thereupon the policemen decided that it was time to check in at the station.

The story came out piecemeal. He was the senior coach with a Serana baseball team, and had arrived on the *Maltese Cross* the day before, to spend his holidays in Antafagusta. A crowd of young Minoran merrymakers had latched on to him, and invited him to a restaurant. That was the last thing he remembered. After a lot of head-scratching, he finally announced that the liveliest one of the lot, who kept ordering mint liqueur and trying to sing, was called Mr. Ecks. He could not even remember that much about the rest—only that they were all very fine chaps.

'So fine that they left you without underpants,' one of the sergeants said sarcastically.

'Yes, well they did have a picture design on them,' the unfortunate trainer muttered apologetically.

What absolute nonsense, I thought. The dire straits they were in during the war and immediately afterwards, when any bit of cloth was a treasure, have long been erased from the Minoran memory. But when I recall the underpants with the picture design that were stripped from that trainer, I see once again the faces of the Minorans behind the iron railings, come to greet everyone who was disembarking from the *Maltese Cross* and the odd glitter they had in their eyes. What was that? A tic that afflicts those who are always craving for more? The uncontrollable urge to lay hands on all the silly gewgaws that cannot be had for minares?

Though they do not, after all, want for a single necessity of life, the government is very tight-fisted about the import of consumer goods. All the foreign exchange they get in payment for the phosphates or whatever is transferred to accounts in solid foreign banks, so that Minorans yet unborn will be taken care of when the phosphate era ends. And its end is already on the cards. To build those accounts up as quickly as possible, the government has established a particularly advantageous exchange rate for foreign tourists, so that

33

they will stuff their pockets with minares when they arrive. And the tourists come to look at the National Theatre, to drink mint liqueur, to let the Minorans get a good look at them. And the unbridled orgy of possession for its own sake—one glance at their clothing, at their hand luggage is quite enough—evidently has its charms for the locals.

A theme for an article, an economic analysis of the way things are, begins to come together, bit by bit, in my head. I must remember that. When I have more time I will need to work out which economic laws I can use to tie it all together.

Damian's still not here. Damian's late today. My thoughts are interrupted by a new client. I can hear his childishly resonant voice, distinct to the very last syllable, although he is not speaking loudly.

'Maestro!' the newcomer is saying to Dan Eldon, in imploring tones. 'Maestro, couldn't you try and do something to get my hair to grow, even a little? Even just a tiny bit! There is no way I can get up in front of my students this term with my hair so short—that won't do at all. They're liable to boo me off. It's about as bad as showing up in the lecture hall these days wearing a jacket and tie!'

The salon owner replies in a tranquilizing murmur. But of course he can help his client out of this adversity. There is no misfortune in this whole world for which he does not have a fitting remedy. Only a month or so ago he received from America a brand-new, high-frequency ultrasound machine which, if the brochure is to be believed, could grow a beard on a birch log. The man with the childish voice is led into the corner, to a piece of equipment with an exceedingly extraterrestrial look about it, and they start fastening him into the pilot's seat, so as to jam on his head a hulking great round helmet made of metal and plastic. The client, scared and suspicious, starts off by giving it some very funny looks.

Well, if it isn't that professor—the earthworm specialist from the IEA meeting! I suddenly cheer up.

'Hello there, Professor!' I call, giving him a wave.

'Professor Walter Umbermann.'

He tries to rise from the chair and give a slight bow, but the seat belts promptly sit him back down again.

'Artur Yanno, journalist. I heard you speak at the IEA meeting.'

The professor's oval face wrinkles up in a smile, and for a moment he forgets how scared he is. Dan's two assistants take advantage of this, and pull the helmet down over his head. The plastic obscures Professor Umbermann's face from view; all you can see now is his mouth.

He is warily silent as Dan and his helpers, glancing at the instruction book now and again, wire the thing up and flip some switches. Finally the gadget settles down to work with a steady hum. This apparently does not bother the Professor overmuch, and he continues the conversation.

'How splendid that you are interested in a problem, which, without

34

exaggeration, is one of the most vital issues in the world today!' he exclaims in his high-pitched voice. 'By no means do all journalists realize how significant it is. You know, some of them even have the effrontery to style us "wormologists", and "maggotites" too. I have just qualified for a UNESCO grant, with support from the International Earthworm Association, and I shall be doing research here on Minore. I have an idea. There should be some mutant earthworms here—mutants, you understand, in the sense of being adapted to specific local conditions. Given that the Minoran soil is rich in phosphates, they ought to have developed a higher tolerance to phosphate fertilizers, not so? Those worms, if I can find them, will constitute an invaluable genetic pool for future crossbreeding, don't you agree?'

'Have you found anything yet?'

'They assure me that there are no earthworms on the island at all!' the Professor exclaims plaintively. 'I don't believe it! That simply cannot be. Obviously, they have never looked for them properly. But with this grant, I will find them, even if I have to dig day and night!'

'And then what?'

'I will develop a fertilizer-resistant species. That is my idea. To be completely successful, I'll still need worms with a low sensitivity to nitrates, from the nitrate-rich soil of Chile—and then I'll just have to crossbreed them.'

'You think it'll work?'

'Science knows no obstacles—at least, not in our day. I still don't know exactly how to go about it, but it is, in my opinion, entirely feasible. Just think what it would mean! If we could populate our farmlands with a new species of earthworm which is resistant to mineral fertilizers, we would not need to stop using those fertilizers. And then we could derive benefits from the fertilizers and from the worms, at one and the same time. According to my calculations, that would make it possible to increase agricultural yields by at least three hundred percent. Hunger would be forced into retreat!'

Dan Eldon came up to the Professor, asked how he was feeling, and threw a switch. There was a smell of ozone.

'I don't actually know what this thing does to the hair-bulbs—something good, it is to be hoped,' Umbermann said suddenly, 'but the mind becomes uncommonly buoyant under here. I will have to drop in more often. Can you imagine—everything I have just been talking about is no more than the first stage of my grand design for the earthworms. Why have I never realised that before? It has just dawned on me, all of a sudden, that one can and must proceed further!'

'Toward a wonder-worm of some sort?'

'You'll stop making fun as soon as I tell you what this is all about. I do not know if you have ever heard that certain earthworm families contain species which are some ten times larger than our common worms. *Rhinodrilus fafner*, a native of South America, for example,

35

3*

can grow up to two meters in length and up to an inch in diameter. Or take *Megascolides australis*, the very largest earthworm, which is found in Australia. Some specimens are anything up to two and a half meters long. It's a veritable snake! Just imagine for a moment how it would be if we succeeded in hybridizing those giant worms with our common *Lumbricus terrestris*, which is a mere thirty centimeters long, or with the highly fecund gray *Allolobophora*, which has a population density of five hundred per square meter! Large worms mean high productivity. We won't even need to bother breaking up the soil, so there you have an end to ploughing and an end to erosion! And wouldn't they increase the fertility of the soil, though! It would all pass through their guts, and the longer it went on, the faster it would go. A single unbroken chain of fertility, literally a bioindustry!'

'An engaging prospect, doubtless,' I was obliged to agree.

'True, my adversaries are saying that as yet no biologist has succeeded in producing a viable hybrid earthworm that is capable of reproducing itself, but then there is a first time for everything!'

The Professor began to squirm in his chair, an earthworm to the life, rapidly and purposefully moving down its tunnel.

'And think of the enormous castings,' he sighed soulfully.

'An irreproachable idea,' I seconded. 'It's just crazy enough to really shake things up.'

Umbermann suddenly cried out. I could have sworn that he was glancing about anxiously under his helmet, afraid that someone might be eavesdropping. His reedy voice instantly grew weepy.

'Then I beg of you, don't write and don't utter the slightest word to anyone about my idea until I have got to grips with the mutant crossbreeding. I am afraid that those wretched chemists will get wind of this and that'll put the tin lid on it. They'll flood the ground with their latest junk and bye-bye earthworms! All my life they have been victimizing me. I just can't get rid of them. We even studied together, in the same class. They say that everything is chemistry, from beginning to end, and that there's no need for any earthworms or suchlike slimy things. That, according to them, is the primitive epoch in the natural order, science for cavemen. All you have to do is introduce the necessary reagents into the soil in the correct proportion and it will be broken up to order, and fertile enough to make you think ten million earthworms had been working every hectare. I am so afraid that they will find out and spoil everything. They can sniff me out like hounds after a hare.'

Just then the tardy Ares Damian came through the door, homed straight in on the chair that was waiting for him, flopping into it with such force that the metal bits on the seat squeaked dolefully. Damian's corpulent frame hid Professor Umbermann from me, but in any case the Professor was so drained by his lengthy tirade that he seemed in no condition to continue. A sniffle or two carried over the buzzing of the high-frequency generator, then the Professor lapsed into silence.

'Damn it!' Damian mumbled, his eyes glittering. 'We'll either have to hurry it up or forget the whole shebang.'

He was keeping a wary eye on the proprietor's movements, and stopped talking as soon as Eldon started toward him. So the conversation was not to be broadcast. For starters, Damian had a civil little chat with the proprietor, who instructed his assistant to prepare the client's hair for dyeing and then went off to his other patrons, leaving Damian free to continue.

'The position has changed in no time flat. We're in a rotten fix with this memorial. Everything could fall apart. We've got to do something to forestall them.'

At that moment the assistant returned with some towels and began to drape Damian with them. I could see that it would have given him great pleasure to fling them all over the place with a snarl of rage, but the good sense of an experienced politician forced him to keep a grip on himself. Assistants are the proprietor's eyes and ears, and that's all there is to it.

Damian's ill-temper did not sit well with me, because I had actually been trying to find a way out of the dilemma. Reasoning that support for the memorial that the International-Democrats wanted to put up would be seen as a useful and progressive gesture, I had suggested as much to my superiors immediately after my first talk with Damian. The answer came back with unexpected swiftness: get on with the pieces you're commissioned to do and stop sticking your nose into things that don't concern you. That bawling out left me in a stupid predicament. I had already as good as promised the support to Damian, and he would unfailingly have me down as a fraud if I took to the hills. Now, Damian is an influential personage; his opinion carries some weight around here. And I'll still have to work the Antafagusta beat, whatever happens.

It is not easy at all to get on with superiors who treat their subordinates like pawns, as I had already found out to my great discomfiture. Three years previously I had been sent to represent the agency at an international congress of journalists. I set off in a great mood. After all, my sort rarely gets the chance to represent anyone or anything; most of our time is spent chasing after representatives. Everything went swimmingly at first, but at the closing session some southerner suddenly hopped up and breezily suggested that we should take up a collection for a memorial to the Unnamed Reporter, the Unknown Soldier of our brotherhood. How many of them had died in accidents or in skirmishes, pressing hard on the heels of a big scoop?

I hemmed and hawed, and ran to phone my agency, having been given no instructions on anything along those lines. But when I got home I found myself in trouble for tarnishing the agency's prestige, because my signature had showed up somewhere at the tail end of the subscription list.

Now I had done the opposite, and that was wrong too.

And so I decided to continue what I had started, but on the quiet this time, keeping my superiors in the dark. A journalist is not a diplomat; he has a thousand and one ways of getting things done. And as for the outcome, time alone will tell. But now, if you please, Damian is rooting around like a mad buffalo and wants me to risk my neck too.

Dan came up and started the job. He worked unhurriedly and with manifest pleasure, like a true artist. Not one single hair on Damian's head was allowed to escape his sure touch.

As his hands did their work, Dan had time to let us in on some less significant problems. A sunken Spanish galleon with a cargo of treasure had been discovered off the east coast of Minore. Some guys had gone down with oxygen tanks, to try their luck by combing the bottom for gold ducats. When the Coast Guard cutter started closing in, the look-out opened fire with a machine gun, started up the motor, and charged out to sea, dragging behind him the two skin-divers in their black rubber suits, dolphinesque at the end of nylon cables. Being hauled across the surface by a speedboat, if it hadn't killed them, would surely have rattled their insides six ways from Sunday. And next, seventeen miles from Cape Santa Clara, at the north end of Minore, an old hulk named the *Octavia*, which was owned by Niarchos, the Greek shipping tycoon, and was sailing under a flag of convenience, had struck a reef and sunk the previous autumn. After the boat went down, its owner announced that it had been carrying iron scrap. But then fish and other sea creatures started going belly up, and an analysis revealed an excessive amount of cyanic compounds in the sea water. The only answer was that the old fox, in addition to hitting on his insurance company, had got a healthy rake-off for picking up toxic waste from some chemical plant and sinking it out at sea. The government had determined to appeal to the International Court at the Hague, to force Niarchos to raise his refuse from the seabed and take it somewhere else.

When I stood up to leave, Damian whispered to me surreptitiously, 'Be at home after dinner. I'll send a car for you.'

Once again I felt how awkward and inane my situation was, and mentally cursed my superiors for their unshakeable conviction that a position of authority bestows wisdom and that from the ninth floor of our head office they could see perfectly what was to be taken seriously in some little corner of the wide world and what was plainly not worth the candle.

So for a short while I am again closeted with Damian's spherical little chauffeur, who apparently does double duty as a bodyguard, in the lift of a large, undistinguished block of flats. The lift judders its way slowly upward. When I first stepped into the lift-car, my nostrils had been assailed by an acrid odour of urine that made me catch my breath. I had glanced involuntarily at the floor, and had seen

38

that all four corners, to a height of seventy-five centimeters, had pulled away and were swollen with damp. The chauffeur wrinkled his face.

'They pee in here. Always when they're alone and sometimes a whole gang of them.'

'Who?'

'Beats me. The tenants, I suppose. It's a big problem in all government housing—places where they give out flats for next to nothing. I mean, no tenant pays more than four and a half minares a month—that's fixed by law. And some of them, y'know, owe two years' back rent. They pee as an expression of gratitude, I guess.'

'What about the concierge?'

'What about her? She'll get paid whether she does anything or not.'

'Then she should be sacked!'

'Much she'd care. There are fewer and fewer people who still have enough go in them to do anything. I myself stay in my job more out of respect for my boss than because I need the work. All of us here live off the earnings from the phosphates.'

We continued upward, amid the pungent ammonia fumes. Damian had a clandestine flat in a residential block that was in no way different from others of its kind. He liked to think that in this way he merged with the hoi polloi, and that the public at large would remain unaware that he was receiving mistresses, political wheeler-dealers and secret messengers there. In actual fact, his neighbours had long had him figured out, and now all of Antafagusta knew who the ex-premier's guests were. The town was far too small for anyone, be he a vagrant or a celebrity, to keep anything secret for long. I rather think the old man did not have the slightest inkling that the other tenants had dubbed their entire residential complex 'Damian's house', no less. And, to top it all off, the tyke who lived next door had drilled a hole through the plaster-board in the wall of Damian's bedroom and had screwed a peep-hole in there, so that all the inquisitive adolescent males in the area now knew what exactly Damian was doing with his latest conquest, and how often. The enterprising youngster sometimes even let his very best friends in to watch the more steamy scenes, for a fee. Damian liked small women, well put together. He wouldn't even look at tall girls, evidently because he didn't want them making him feel inferior. Anyway, he often exchanged one paramour for another who looked very much the same. He used to go by their hair colour, until he discovered to his disgust that they were dyeing their hair so as to make several repeat visits to his bed. After this discovery, which really stunned him, he abruptly limited his choice to females from the plateau, who were not sophisticated enough to deceive him like that.

An informant of mine in the security services once admitted to me after his seventh glass of mint liqueur that the ex-premier's flat had microphones floor to ceiling. There were even two in the lavatory, although he wasn't really sure whether that was to cover a breakdown or to get stereophonic sound. And in the cellar of a neighbouring house there was a task force which listened in and made recordings. So I had decided simply to hear Damian out and not let myself get drawn into anything.

Damian sent the chauffeur outside to keep watch and poured three straight shots of mint liqueur. I touched my glass, for appearance's sake, and waited to see what would happen next.

Those who would have you believe that Minoran mint liqueur is simply creme de menthe don't know the first thing about it. They simply have no imagination. True, its taste is highly reminiscent of Chlorodont, the archetypical toothpaste, but in fact it is made of a particular variety of mountain mint which grows only on the Minoran plateau and nowhere else in the entire world. The significance of this drink to the national economy is so great that, in its negotiations with the Consortium, the government deemed it necessary to extend for another twenty years its ownership over that part of the plateau where the stands of mint are thickest. Now the annual mint harvest is dried and stored, against the day when the quarries swallow up the mint fields. Mint liqueur production is a government monopoly, and violators are punished with the same severity as counterfeiters. The drink itself is purveyed to the few royal courts which still exist, though I simply fail to understand how those effete creatures can stand this diabolical drink. Mint liqueur is definitely no less than sixty degrees proof—put a match to it and it bursts into a blue flame, and when you drink it, it just knocks the wind out of you. Cutting it with tonic or soda is considered an outrage on Minore. True, ancient custom permits women and invalids to drink the liqueur mixed with asses' milk, but very little of that has been imported from America of late.

Damian was the first ever to treat me to a mint liqueur. When I rolled my eyes and started gasping like a fish out of water after tipping down my first glass, he roared with laughter and was obviously tickled pink.

'Hah, a man's drink! Do you know what it's made from? Just guess! In the old days the entire market square here in Antafagusta was paved with oak beams. They stood a good two centuries of wear. And all that time, people from the plateau would be bringing their donkeys down to the market. Up on the plateau, the donkeys fed on mint, and in the market they dropped and dribbled this and that. Little by little, those beams were soaked through with it. And when we tore up the wooden pavement, we got the brilliant idea of brewing it into mint liqueur.' He thought that was hilarious.

In actual fact, the mint liqueur is simply matured in oak barrels, which is where it gets its tannin flavor and extraordinary strength. But when you drink it, it's not too difficult to believe that Damian's recipe is close enough to the truth. In any event, all the tourists go crazy for it—that baseball coach from Serana, the one who lost his

40

underpants with the picture design, had got plastered on nothing other than good old mint liqueur.

After the third glass, Damian clicked his tongue and, without the slightest preamble, flung out, 'The shitheads!'

I bided my time. Now it was coming, for sure. Damian gave me a searching look.

'They have come up with the idea of transferring the Herald's remains back to Santa Clara! Ron Eldon, that miserable abortion who calls himself a premier, has suddenly decided that it is befitting for the Herald to lie at rest where he was born and where he made his re-markable stand. Shifting the burial site was, supposedly, a major ideo-logical blunder. As if he—the Herald!—does not belong to all Minore.'

I composed my face into an interested expression.

'What trouble I went to back then, during my tenure as prime min-ister, to have the coffin containing the Herald's remains moved from the crypt in Santa Clara to Antafagusta! I had words about it with the Archbishop himself. For three solid months I did nothing but watch over the signature-gathering in the villages. I sent all my bodyguards, every last one, around the island to list their relatives and friends, to get names from the gravestones in the cemeteries. The officers—well, they even went looking for names in books, when they were really stumped. And for all that, I did get the number of votes required by the constitution! But the actual ceremony when the remains were transferred—I wish you could have seen it! We rented a gun carriage from Serana. Two veterans who as little boys had heard the Herald speak were out recounting to all and sundry how the noble Tommazo thought the world of Antafagusta, the heart of his beloved Minore. And, do you know, people wept...'

Damian was so moved that he brushed away a tear. A true states-man is always a bit of an actor and ever so slightly hammy at that.

'And now Ron Eldon—that old rogue, that swindler—is about to obliterate it all at one stroke, and purportedly out of patriotism. But I can see perfectly well what's going on—he's playing up to those thrice-be-damned Own-landers, he's fishing for votes among people who want everything on Minore to stay as it has been from time im-memorial. Once the phosphate income stops, both he and his entire budget will be high and dry, so he has decided to go and cozy up to those half-baked blockheads.'

Damian upended another glass of mint liqueur and sighed noisily, 'We'll have to get the memorial up before Ron Eldon can carry out this fiendish plan of his. We'll have to be nimble and crafty too. But he won't be able to swipe the Herald's bones out from under the me-morial, not once it's up!'

Damian's words reminded me of a recent encounter I had had in an abandoned village, which I had come upon as I was driving up to the phosphate quarries. There, where the road turned onto the pla-teau, by a tiny stone house that stood near the cliff, I saw an old

41

man swathed all in white, sitting on a bench. Something made me stop the car and get out. My attention was captured by that old gentleman who was still as any statue. His white hair, hanging down over a forehead that could have been cast in bronze, was stirred by the morning breeze. I wanted to sit at his side, in silence, and perhaps get him to talk to me if I could.

The old man gave no sign of having noticed me. I sat down close by, on a boulder that was etched by wind and rain. We were both silent. Sitting here, alone with the bare rocks, the deserted sea, and the forlorn expanse of the sky, I felt I was in a prehistoric world. The wind whistled in the sedge, and from time to time a sound carried from the distant quarries which could have been dinosaurs rumbling their discontent while the earth trembled under their weight.

About fifteen minutes went by before I decided that it was time to begin the conversation.

'It's breezy up here, all right.'

The old man did not even glance in my direction. A minute or two later, though, he murmured placidly, as though talking to himself, 'That's good. I don't like to breathe air that has already been in and out of me. Or of anyone else.'

I took a quick look at his hut, where the wind was promenading unhindered through the cracks, and thought that he was no more threated by stale air in there than he was out here.

The conversation died. I thought I'd to try a little offhand sociology next.

'In Antafagusta someone has got the idea of raising a memorial over the Herald's tomb. I can't decide whether it's a worthwhile notion or not.'

The old man's wizened face puckered up even more, and it wasn't until I heard his voice that I realised he was laughing.

'Wouldn't old Tommazo just laugh if he could but hear. A memorial to him, now, old reprobate that he was! I almost bust a gut back then when they dug him up in Santa Clara. They tumbled the bones into a new box all lined with gold and then they carted him on a gun carriage all over the island. No, brother Tommazo, I said then, you'll see that this won't be the end of it. Bid your rest farewell. Once they've descended on you, you can be sure that in their insolence they'll dream up something else. And so they have. Of course they can put up a memorial, why not? But, believe you me, it would have done Tommazo a sight more good when he was alive. It would have made it easier for him to shake off his creditors, y'know!'

'You really knew him?'

'Him—who else would I mean? The Pope of Rome, happen?'

Old Ossian told me no more on that occasion, but that was enough to convince me that this thing with the Herald and his posthumous fame was not so simple as one might have concluded from Damian's hectoring tirades. People's reputations never exactly accord with reality.

But, after all, it's like that everywhere. So what's the big surprise?

I think I should have kept myself right out of it. If I had never seen it, that image of destruction would not have persecuted me relentlessly through the months and the years, through all my sleepless nights, which are becoming increasingly frequent and occur so often now that I am beginning to fear my own bed, to dread that it might entice me into a trap, into the perpetual captivity of the hours before dawn that jangle with hopelessness. More and more often, no matter how tired I am, I want to escape from my bed in the evening, not to succumb to its call, to run as far away as I can, at breakneck speed, to keep my eyes peeled so that all these tormenting fears, those terrors of mine that are rooted in human existence, will not catch me unawares in the hours before morning when the mysterious mechanism that controls sleeplessness goes to work.

In any case, it would apparently have been better all round had I not chanced to witness that event. Suppositions of that sort, alas, always come as an afterthought. These are things that can never be predicted.

Once in a blue moon we decided to revisit our old haunts. I had become so accustomed to my artificial leg that I walked with only a slight limp. We made our way upward, to what had once been our field, which looked down upon my father's long-abandoned house and the shore. A pile of brown slate shards marked the ruins of the hut where Murana's fisherman father had lived. Not a single stalk of maize had been raised there for so long, but the few sprouts of wild garlic were doing fine.

My little home was still there. For some reason it pleased fate to have me witness the devastation of my father's house.

While Murana and I were surveying the tableland, where a dusty haze lay like a blanket and the excavators nodded, sinking their steel teeth into the earth and tipping the contents of their huge buckets into the beds of blue lorries that were hidden in clouds of yellow dust, one of the excavators crawled up to our house. And sealed its fate. Its huge wheels, shod in black tires, made their way across the uneven ground, like the legs of an insect. The machine had a bucket that was rocking, glinting at the end of a long boom, and its onslaught—which in one way was sort of impersonal, entirely mechanical, but in another somehow had a dreadful sense of purpose—was a repulsive thing to see.

The iron beetle was getting closer to our house, was stalking it. The machine paused for a moment, then gave a broad swing of its bucket connected with a solid blow.

That blow was like an explosion. And once again, for the second time, I watched from above as slate tiles leapt into the air, as they coasted slowly in various directions and then, with an even more bizarre languor, spinning and cartwheeling, fell back to earth.

Murana screamed and grabbed at my shoulder.

In that instant, I distinctly saw the excavator stamping its thick legs in satisfaction. I could have sworn that I saw little fountains of yellow dust spurting up from under its wheels. The machine was celebrating its victory over a defenceless little shack. Looking back now, it is difficult for me to tell what I actually saw from what I imagined.

That dreadful moment had almost as strong an effect on me as that distant day, during the war, when far away on the plateau, the Flying Fortress slammed down on the landing strip, its damaged engines howling, and then, a long time later, four huge black wheels came rolling down soundlessly toward our hut, like in a nightmare, pitilessly flattening everything in their path, even the sheep-pen that held the black ewe and the lambs she had just borne. Wide awake, I saw those wheels again, as I had often seen them in my nightmares. The only difference was that this time they stopped for a moment near our house and began stamping up and down, as if pleased with the black deed they had done. It was unbearable to watch.

Suddenly, an intolerable, searing pain struck my left leg below the knee, at the juncture with my technologically flawless prosthesis. I groaned.

Murana told me later that she had had her work cut out getting me down the slope.

4

The International Film Festival turned everything upside down in Antafagusta for a week, until everyone got used to it. For the first seven days, though, no one spent any time on politics, not even in the Figaro salon. Everyone was fussing around the countless film stars and going to receptions thrown by the various delegations. As a rule, the more modest a country's placing in the programme, the more sumptuous the receptions it gave. After all, it had to do something to justify its presence at the festival.

The municipality of Antafagusta had dreamed up this film festival some fifteen years previously, when the big drive to attract foreign tourists and foreign exchange to Minore was just beginning. By a happy coincidence, this was exactly what the big producers and independent small fry in the film business needed. They were looking for new ways to publicize their films, as cinemas were going broke one after another in the developed countries because television had taken over from the art of film-making. The exotic reputation of Minore, an almost unknown quantity, would double the attraction of feature films which had premiered in Antafagusta. The old centers of cinema art were not what they used to be; their renown was tainted with fibs and jiggery-pokery. So from the very outset the superstars of the film world were glad of an invitation to the Antafagusta Film Festival. All the illustrious past masters—Antonioni and Bergman, Bardem and Buñuel—had already attended, either as judges or as nominees for best director. The gold and silver donkeys that were awarded in Antafagusta were greatly sought after. You could say that they guaranteed a film's success.

The film festival gradually brought all the rest of it to the island— covens of sensation seekers, noisy pop-concerts, outrageous fashion shows, family fall-outs among the film stars, and surges of sundry rumours. The *Maltese Cross* was booked to the hilt for two weeks straight, and they had to add a second steamer—the Susanna—to the route.

No one foresaw that anything much out of the ordinary would happen this year. Then, three months before the festival opened, at the very beginning of the bathing season, when the sand-sifting machines were still at work on the hotel beaches and unmarried ladies worn out by vague anxieties were arriving to test the water, Christian Chardin—one of the most popular Parisian arbiters of fashion—rolled up in Antafagusta with a bevy of models. He had become a veritable idol the previous autumn. With one wave of his hand he could oblige thousands of wealthy women to toss out their entire wardrobes and start from scratch. Textile manufacturers thought he walked on water.

He had a fixed booking for a certain number of pages in several popular fashion magazines, so that he could show off his top designs in every issue. His arrival was much like the entrance of an Olympic athlete: the road from the port to the hotel was lined with the serried ranks of the fair sex all chanting, 'Char-din, dar-ling!'

The day after his arrival, the idol gave a news conference and a private fashion show. Fashion and the social scene did not normally interest our agency, but I went all the same, as much out of curiosity as anything, especially since I had almost had my invitation stolen. Some person or persons unknown had unsuccessfully tried to crack the hotel safe.

The nabob of fashion was there in person to greet us in the lounge of the Princess of Antafagusta Hotel, which was hung about with dark lilac silk. Christian Chardin was lolling in a large armchair, his legs dangling heedlessly over the arm. He was wearing dark blue trousers of fine wool made up to look like sail-cloth, trimmed with a fringe, and was shod in crudely-made violet suede boots with broad toes and garish bright yellow insets. In addition to that, he had on a dark red shirt, completely unbuttoned, with long front laps that were knotted over his stomach. Chardin, his face a study in boredom, was fingering a gold medallion that had got all tangled in the hairpiece on his chest, and was switching from side to side a head that was adorned with a curly Afro cut.

Having been informed that everyone had arrived, he did not change his position or stop toying with his medallion, but announced, in the weary voice of a man who has seen a thing or two in his time, 'Gentlemen, today you may count yourselves beastly lucky! It's not every day that journalists are given the opportunity to attend the birth of a completely new departure in fashion. Or could it be that I am mistaken? This is an event of international significance in the history of culture, take my word on that. It will create as much of a stir as did the advent of mini-skirts once upon a time, and I deem myself fully justified in hoping that you will present it to the world as such. Chardin's new beach fashions will go down in history, and in a moment you will be able to see this for yourselves.'

The arbiter of fashion swung his legs up effortlessly, and, with a loud stamp of his crudely-made boots, rose from the armchair. His legs slightly apart, his head butting forward, he turned to face his audience, and held that manly pose for a couple of minutes, to give the photographers a chance. It was obvious that Chardin had a hopeless addiction to fame.

Having made sure that everyone who wanted a photo had got one, Chardin continued,

'As you know, some time ago, world beach fashion produced the topless style, which sparked some heated controversies. A mere three years ago, the police were rousting from the beaches any ladies who had left their bikini tops at home. Yet now the entire French and Italian Rivieras have adopted this natural, unconstrained style, and it has already spread to the Adriatic coast and points beyond. However, progress never stops. Fashion cannot stand still—that would be nothing less than suicide. And so, on this occasion and with an expenditure of intense creative effort, I have developed a new style for which I foresee a great future. This style has the boldness of modernity, it has great vigour, and—I wish to stress this particularly—it makes a woman young again!'

He made a theatrical pause, heightening the curiosity of his audience, and surveyed the assembled journalists with a watchful, hardfocussed gaze. A chance flash-bulb went off and a shadow of displeasure passed over the maestro's face. He was not wearing his wellrehearsed photo-opportunity look.

'Which part of the female anatomy is the loveliest? That is no rhetorical question. For a creator of fashion, it has a strictly practical import. If we answer it correctly, completely new horizons, broader than ever before, will open up to us. We shall no longer have to spend our time in experimentation, and will be able to concentrate upon what is most important. In search for an answer to this question, I stood for seven hundred ... excuse me!' He stopped the note-takers with a peremptory wave of his hand. 'Seventy is quite enough. It sounds more believable... So, then, I stood for seventy hours in the Louvre behind the Venus de Milo. No, no, you did not mishear. *Behind* the Venus, not in front, where crowds of museum-goers whose sense of true beauty still slumbers jostle together. All they know is that the Venus de Milo is a famous statue. They are ill-equipped to take pleasure in her aesthetic perfection. And it became clear to me that the loveliest part of the female anatomy is—the buttocks. Such consummate symmetry, such tenderness and sensual eloquence! And what have we been doing? For entire millennia, driven by misplaced Puritanical bashfulness, we have been covering them up, bending every effort to hide them! Gentlemen, from henceforth this lamentable state of affairs shall be no more. I have created a completely new and original style of attire which in the international idiom of our profession will be called "bottomless".

Chardin gave a military-looking hand signal. An unseen orchestra struck up, and on the dark red carpeting that ran along the back wall of the lounge, marking out the stage area, six models appeared in single file, tottering on high heels, and each stark naked except for a miniscule triangular scrap of cloth covering her private parts. Their faces were all the same: they had identical hairstyles and identical little breasts which jiggled identically to the beat. The only way of distinguishing them was by the colour of their G-strings. But when the young ladies, performing deft little kick-steps, turned their backs to the audience, certain other differences became apparent. Some had transparent nylon netting across their bottoms. The G-strings of the others were held in place by nothing but laces or flesh-coloured strips of elastic. Swaying their hips and buttocks in a practiced manner, the models marched along the carpet in an impeccably precise rhythm. The pale bodies against the background of dark lilac silk were irresistibly reminiscent of the dancing white horses at the Hofburg in Vienna.

'You see, gentlemen, that there is an infinite multiplicity of possible variations. Any lady wearing this style will be able to maintain her self-hood. The individual will not be forced to conform!' the nabob of fashion exclaimed fervidly. 'And now permit me to show you two designs, the chefs-d'oeuvre of our collection—Eve After the Fall and Sexy Jeans!'

Chardin clapped his hands loudly above his head. In a twinkling, the six models disappeared through the door. They literally seemed to melt away before the eyes, like a morning mist, and a moment later two new models entered the lounge, striding out triumphantly. The first was a blonde, powdered to a dazzling whiteness, wearing a green velvet G-string cut in the shape of a fig leaf and held in place by lengths of flesh-coloured elastic. The second, a swarthy brunette, had on a pair of knickers made of dark blue denim in front, and stitched along the sides; the back, though, consisted of loose-weave black netting.

'Eve scarcely requires any commentary, evidently. The design bears the impress of Old Testament sensuality,' Chardin declared. 'In reference to the Sexy Jeans design, however, I would like to point out that the adroit and subtle combination of a rough, masculine material worn by farmers with the absolute femininity of fish-net, a perennial trademark of prostitutes the world over, creates a sensual effect which—as you must admit—would make anyone sit up and take notice. And so, gentlemen, I am counting on your good offices in assisting our new departure to take the fashion world by storm in the coming season. And now permit me to offer you cocktails!'

The models jounced their breasts one more time, as if they were both suddenly chilled, twitched their haunches, made an about-face, and strode toward the door. Immediately the first six girls entered through another door, each carrying a tray set with glasses, and began to circulate among the guests. They were soon surrounded by a dense crowd of journalists. A general hubbub arose and flash-bulbs popped.

Chardin, with a glass of mineral water in his hand, watched the mob from a distance, a wistful smile playing on his lips.

The next day's papers were full of photographs and stories covering the fashion show at the Princess of Antafagusta. The town bristled with anticipation: something very new was coming. Queues instantly formed where gauze scarves were sold.

And all the same, the shock turned out to be a transitory one. The first of Chardin's acolytes, admittedly, were given a ride from the beach to the police station in police department vehicles. However, the station desk clerks protested and threatened to strike. All those unclothed backsides in the workplace embarrassed them and made it difficult for them to keep their minds on their jobs. The Own-landers, who stood in defence of the more modest ways of yesteryear, and the Society of Unmarried Ladies of Minore—or the Company of Old Maids, as people styled them—mounted a demonstration or two on Britannic Boulevard, which ran along the beach from the port to Cape Cataracta. In the course of these demonstrations, the more hot-headed lady activists contrived to get some naked bottoms tarred and feathered, at which point the police were constrained to inter-vene and put a stop to this form of protest as being too hazardous to the health. Junior-school children snickered and pointed from the promenade for a week. And within a month, women in bottomless beachwear were strolling quite calmly along the shore. The more doughty souls had got up the nerve to cross the road and walk to the nearest bar, and no one even turned to look at them any more. The world gets used to all manner of things very quickly these days. I would think that the rapidity with which the sensation died down was an unpleasant surprise to Chardin himself.

By the time the film festival opened, naked buttocks were already commonplace. To kill time before the opening ceremonies, I was strolling back and forth along Britannic Boulevard, one thousand two hundred and fifty meters each way, and on this entire stretch I en-countered only a solitary pair of visiting Finns, who, with a thorough-ly northern matter-of-factness, were making good use of huge Japanese telephoto lens to capture a set of particularly pert hemispheres. The passers-by were giving them wondering looks, and making good-natured jokes about it, which did not, however, deter the Finns at all.

Suddenly some pushing and shoving started near the Festival Hall. Two demonstrations were about to clash. The Own-landers were coming from the direction of the port, carrying a huge placard which proclaimed 'GFP and Minority'. By 'Minority', they were not refer-ring to some lesser number, but rather to their dedication to Minore, and it was just their ineptitude in foreign languages, which they had elevated to the level of a principle, that was doing the dirty on them. The leftists, who had gathered on Cape Cataracta and hoisted their slogan—'All to the Contrary'—there, were coming from the other side. They were stepping out smartly, and demonstratively leading with their left sides. Neither of these parades wanted to give way to the other, although there couldn't have been more than sixty demonstra-tors in all. The six hundred surrounding them had just come to watch. One of the leftists—a young man with long, uncombed locks—start-ed clearing a way for his boss, an old codger with a flaccid face the colour of mortar and thin whitish hair that fell in waves to his collar. In so doing, the young man knocked into an Own-lander carrying a placard. He lost his grip on his burden, and it smacked down on the heads of the leftists in the front ranks. And immediately a fight flared up, as if they had all just been waiting for a signal.

49

'Bloated oppressors!' the leftist cohort cried.

'Judases, peddlers of the Fatherland!' the Own-landers screeched in reply.

Fists and sticks were brandished on high, the first punches began to rain down, someone was hit and gave a piercing howl. I pushed closer. I had an investigative piece to write about the political conflict on Minore. My superiors had put in a specific requisition for a critical piece, and the less you have to make up, the better it sounds.

But before the fight had had time to warm up, some police vehicles appeared, their sirens wailing. They cut right into the crowd and slowly edged forward, gradually pushing the groups of combatants apart. The crowd grew agitated and started to spread out.

There now, I thought, properly peeved, someone just couldn't wait to phone for the police. I don't know why, but there's always somebody who can't take the heat. They couldn't have hung on until the scrap had got going! What kind of details can I get from this?

But, oddly enough, the police did not pay the slightest attention to the brawlers. The vehicles, their roof-lights flashing, drove right up to the side entrance of the Festival Hall, and blocked it off. The last of the Own-landers, who was trapped between a police van and the wall, slipped under the vehicle with lizard-like agility, and took off, never once looking back. About a dozen policemen in steel helmets poured out of the vehicles, some carrying mine detectors on long poles and others with submachine guns strapped to their shoulders. They all disappeared through the door at a run.

The dumbstruck Own-landers and leftists stopped fighting and mingled with the onlookers. The leftist leader, the old codger with the sparse gray curls, still wanted to get his followers going, and was whispering something to the young lads around him but getting no response. The most they could manage was to shift an Own-lander a little out of the way, so as to clear a space and get a better view.

The few policemen who had stayed by the vehicles were forcing the crowd back with their submachine guns. More sirens began to wail in the distance.

My attention was drawn to the police captain. I had met him a couple of times at sessions of the legislative assembly, where he was sergeant at arms. Hoping that he would remember me, I pushed towards him, but he never let on.

'Get back!' he barked, rolling his eyes and waving his pistol high in the air intimidatingly. 'Get back, and I mean now!'

With one hand I thrust my correspondent's credentials under his nose, while with the other I dropped into his unbuttoned holster a packet of cheap imported cigarettes, which were sold in the Press Club for foreign currency to anyone presenting a foreign passport. The captain looked askance at his holster and piped down.

'What's up?' I asked.

'A bomb!' he whispered. 'We had a telephone call. It's set to go off

50

in ten minutes. They're looking for it.'

'Who's claiming responsibility?'

'Some terrorists—the Lilac Brigade or the Green Hand, devil only knows the difference. They've bred like homeless curs. Must be good weather for it, or something. Now move along there, please. They'll be coming out any minute, either with the bomb or without it...'

I stepped back a little, though that was not easy to do. The gawkers kept arriving along Britannic Boulevard, and every one of them was impatient to get a good look at what these policemen, armed to the teeth, were up to around the Festival Hall.

A quick thought occurred to me: the experience gained by the generation of Europeans who lived through the war—which makes a person look for a place to hide at the very sight of armed men—means less than nothing here. Men carrying weapons, especially large numbers of them, always used to foretoken danger. Here, though, they only roused interest.

A young boy—thirteen or so, by the look of him—was standing next to me. Unable to tear his enraptured gaze away, he was all eyes for the policemen.

'You'd do better to clear off,' I advised him. 'Aren't you scared they're going to start shooting?'

The boy gave me a look that was unfeignedly enthusiastic. 'Let them start. Wouldn't that be something—pow-pow-pow!'

'Idiot, you could get hit!'

'Heh!' was all he said. And straight away, forgiving me for being a sclerotic old coward, he went back to staring at the policemen. It was obvious that the danger of stopping a stray bullet had not even sunk in. For him, this was all a fascinating spectacle, something to break the daily routine, if only for a while. He was blissfully unaware of any danger.

The police reinforcements—two more vans carrying steel-helmeted guardians of law and order—were arriving. Without a word of explanation, they started shoving the crowd aside, freeing up a path to the promenade. The people, without the foggiest idea of what was going on, were just reviled by these custodians of the law. One of the leftists from the ring-leader's entourage climbed onto the roof of a Citroën and broke into a roistering speech against all and any fuzz and in defence of all and any human rights. When the car's owner tried to drag the orator off the buckling roof, the leftist brought his heel down smartly on the owner's fingers and continued his speech as though nothing had happened, although, what with the general racket and the wailing of sirens, it was hardly likely he could even hear himself.

A pair of policemen bounded out of the hall and flung the doors open wide as though some high-ranking personage were coming through. In the doorway appeared a third policeman, his face whiter than chalk under the rim of his helmet, and in his outstretched hands was some kind of package, some mysterious object. He walked slowly,

51

like a somnambulist, feeling his way with his toes and lifting his feet high over any uneven spots. And without a word being said, it was clear that he was mortally afraid of stumbling, that in his hands he was carrying the type of burden that is not to be dropped, come what may. And only after he was some ten paces away from the hall did the others appear in the doorway.

Meanwhile, the police reinforcements had managed to open a narrow corridor through the crowd, a gray strip of asphalt that cut across Britannic Boulevard and led to a stairway which descended to the beach. Down there, policemen were rushing madly to disperse the beach-goers—whether their backsides were covered or not.

A police officer in a jacket festooned with gold braid gave a peremptory yell, whereupon several policemen lifted their submachine guns and fired a couple of rounds into the air over the crowd.

'Lie down!' they bawled deafeningly.

Everyone instantly dropped to the ground. The orator came down off the Citroën roof with a clatter, leaving scratches and a dent there to remember him by. The man with the bomb continued on his way, at the same measured pace. When his right foot froze for a moment by my face, I dragged my hand out from under the person next to me, and glanced at my watch. If the captain had got his facts right, then there were two minutes left to go. Or had he said 'approximately'? And what if the caller had made a mistake? Or if the clock in the bomb was running fast?

The policeman with the bomb slowly proceeded. I raised myself up a little and looked around. The entranceway to the Festival Hall was carpeted with people lying face down, like a thick layer of fallen leaves. A few bodies away from me, on the promenade side, a trend-setter with an unbroken tan lay prone on the ground—goodness only knows where she had popped up from. From the back it was difficult to make out whether she was wearing Eve After the Fall or something else. As I watched though, a hulking great hand with gnarled fingers appeared out of nowhere and, in a decisive movement, grabbed hold of a naked buttock as though it were a rubber punch-ball. I waited for the inevitable reaction, but the terrified woman buried her head in her arms and evidently was at a loss to understand what was happening to her.

Everything congealed into silence. It was obvious that something was about to happen.

Then, down on the beach, there was a loud explosion. After a few seconds, sand and bits of shingle began to spatter down upon the people lying on the boulevard. I stood up.

The festival opened an hour and a half late. The whole building was searched, step by step, so as to turn up any possible surprises. The guests were let in after a careful scrutiny, one at a time, through a chain of policemen who stood with their arms linked. Anyone who seemed suspicious for any reason was taken aside and searched to see if he had a concealed weapon. The even more dubious ones, despite their protests, were unceremoniously ejected.

A young lady, tall and very easy on the eye, dropped an earring as she made her way through the solid wall of policemen. I managed to snatch it up literally from under the crowd's feet, and its delighted owner favoured me with an enchanting smile. I realised immediately what I had done to deserve so much gratitude. The earring, which I had held in my hand for a few moments, was silver-plated but stamped with a gold hallmark on the underside. I have excellent vision and for years have been schooling myself to pick up barely discernible details. There is a law against the private possession of gold on Minore. It can only be sold through a state purchasing point, and otherwise is promptly confiscated. So I became privy to the unknown lady's secret.

Of course I sat beside her. She asked me who I was and what I did and then, heaving a deep sigh, confessed that she envied journalists because they travel all over the world and see so many interesting things. I was flattered and bragged a little about the trips I had taken and my knowledge of the world. By the time we left the showing, we were already old friends.

Britannic Boulevard had suddenly gone crazy this evening. Cars and people, shrouded in the stuffy evening air, were rubbing their flanks up against each other in a perverted sort of way. Shrill groups of street musicians were playing on corners, and the idlers who were sitting at tables, swigging beer and mint liqueur, were lazily throwing them nickel coins worth a good half-minare.

Out of the darkness that led down to the beach spilled a noisy bunch of people in wild and wonderful carnival costumes, in fluttering tunics, with caps on their heads. Among these leaping, twisting beings danced a woman in a black form-fitting knit outfit, her face covered in red and green spots and her hair twisted into several stiff, jutting horns. My companion—her name was Delia—shuddered and clung to me. I laughed.

A thick smell of petrol was rising from the cars. In fits and starts, they were rustling their way down Britannic Boulevard. The fronds of the palm trees that stood between the opposing streams of traffic drooped down, wilted by the exhaust fumes. Right in the middle of the intersection where a winding side-street came out onto the Boulevard, a thin man holding a torch was cavorting. Suddenly a large smoky flame flared up above his head. The man with the torch carried on hopping about, and the flame above him died down.

We were interested, and moved closer. As well as a burning torch, the thin man also had a large blue plastic flask. He stood up now, lifted the flask to his lips and tipped his head back, filled his mouth with liquid, then brought the torch to his face and sprayed the liquid out. An elongated reddish-yellow flame danced over the glittering car roofs. The passengers looking through the big windows of cars that were slowly inching along, shrank back fearfully in their seats. The flame died, and black smoke rose high into the palm trees. The man seemed irrepressibly overjoyed. He bounded from side to side, waving his torch, and then again brought the flask to his lips. Another tongue of flame cast unquiet highlights upon the car windscreens and the dark shop windows.

Delia shuddered and dragged me on. It was as though this flame-thrower might direct his next geyser straight at the cars, and then these petrol-fed creatures would burst into flame together, and in two shakes all of Britannic Boulevard would turn into a solid river of fire.

'Quickly!' Delia cried.

I complied. The trembling unease of this woman was exciting. An adventure in the making? Well, is that anything to be scared of? My agency isn't about to forbid me that. A sense of limitless personal freedom made my head spin. The evening town instantly shifted into the realm of the unlikely. I brightened up no end.

As we turned off Britannic Boulevard into a badly-lit alley, an airborne flame again blazed out behind us, under the palms.

Up ahead, dim lights were beating solitary paths up the mountain.

If only I had known what my adventure would lead to!

My body has grown light—so light that I no longer have a body. I float above myself, dissolved in the swaying currents of air. I cannot understand how it can be that man, his free spirit, must be fettered to the pitiful and unfeeling, sluggish and sickly lump of flesh that is called the body. The spirit was created to fly, to burst at will through time and space. It cannot be confined in a ponderous casing that is like a stone sack, shackles, a ball and chain. This is how the spirit suffocates.

How happy I am to be free of all that. I am light and fleet, but no more than I want to be. I am complete master of myself, and therefore of the whole world. Of more than the whole world—of the entire universe!

But then the intoxicating lightness is skewered with a foretaste of danger, sharp as a needle's point. Has the white satan got his claws into me again? Even after once pulling through, will I have to pay all over again for those few moments with long and agonizing days of detoxification, when all the fears and burdens of existence, things I thought were long gone, will surge over me all together, like water breaking through a dam?

This is horribly familiar. I am fearfully afraid of my own past. But the past is never far away.

In an utterly despairing moment like this, I raised my hand against Murana. I was completely out of control. Not just my amputated leg but my entire body, my pitiful, trembling body, was suffused with intolerable pain, and curly-haired manikins with stumps for legs were prancing round me. They laughed in my face, ridiculing me, and yelled that I was a legless cripple, incapable even of mounting my own wife, so that she had to get her satisfaction from other men. Jealousy was driving me mad. Shaky and distraught as I was, I had recently been keeping an eye on Murana when she talked to any other man. I would be in no condition to touch her for several days, not after a hit. And so I finally concluded that she must be seeing someone else. The manikins with stumps for legs, who always appeared when I was in a very bad way, knew how to get to me. But of course, who could it be but the greengrocer's assistant! That day I saw—saw with my own eyes—him and Murana rolling naked on the floor in our living room, her slim hands running passionately over his solid, bulging body. That sight made me howl like an animal, snatch up a hatchet that we used for chopping meat, and go after Murana, to extract revenge for my torment.

She ran into the kitchen, her eyes brimming with indescribable fear, and she scarcely had time to turn the key in the lock. I whacked the hatchet into the door panel so hard that the wood cracked, and the upper edge of the blade went right through. But that fearsome blow brought me out of it. The curly-haired manikins who ran me ragged disappeared all at once and then I sank to the ground behind the door and began to sob. I knew perfectly well what I had almost done.

When Murana finally ventured out of the kitchen, she told me through pale, trembling lips that her patience had run dry, that she was afraid to stay with me, for her own sake and the child's. Either I would immediately go in for treatment and become a human being again or she would leave me forever. Wretchedly, humbly, I swore to her that I would go to the clinic and I would soon be the same as before, if only she would stay. I kept my word, and spent six months in a drug centre, where by dint of fearsome torments I shook free from my self-destructive mania.

Have I given in to it again? I go rigid with horror. There is no life for me any more without Murana, no life at all, especially not after what happened next.

And it all began so innocently. A marijuana cigarette or two—who considers that a sin these days? They made me feel better, but without painkillers. I really don't know what happened during the operation—they pinched some nerve-endings, perhaps, but ever since I came out of the anaesthetic, my amputated leg has not stopped aching for a single moment. Changes in the weather, an awkward movement on my artifical leg, sometimes a slight upset would be enough to turn that intermittent, drawing ache into a drilling pain which became increasingly difficult to bear. In the depths of my soul I just could not come to terms with the fact that I was no longer the same: I ought not to have brooded so over the loss of a leg. That is why I am hypersensitive to pain. I should have knuckled under to it, but I rebelled, and would not accept my fate.

I kept scrounging painkillers. At first, they gave me all I wanted, evidently assuming that in this way they would succeed in schooling me to my new condition. But then the doctor told me to buck up and not to dwell so on the pain, because he did not want to turn me into a drug addict. I lost my temper with him and began to seek out other doctors who would write me the prescriptions I needed, for a small consideration. And then one time Kolo shared with me a joint that he had wheedled out of some tourists who traded in merchandise of that sort. It was extraordinarily pleasant. Suddenly I needed no doctors, and for a few hours I simply forgot about my aching leg. I got into the habit of going down to the port, where I would spot, among the crowd of tourists, those who were carrying marijuana. With time, I developed an infallible eye for newcomers who had the merchandise I needed. True, the police caught me twice. They used to plant agents in the port, to nab money changers and drug dealers. Thanks to my disability, though, I got off with a fine both times. My comrades in misfortune, who still had all their extremities, were slapped behind bars for a year or two, on the same charge. But new ones came to take their place, and the port was never empty.

At the same time, though, my experience was doing me a bad turn. The marijuana sellers only needed one look at my trembling hands before they would start dragging their feet, like—'To be quite honest, we don't have any joints for sale, just these few sticks here in our pockets, and those are for us.' It was clear that I desperately needed to make a connection, and they were playacting, so as to jack the price up disgracefully. It was simple enough to figure out what they were up to. I gritted my teeth in impotent fury, but all the same I paid whatever they asked. I just had to have the dope.

But it was a cushy time, for all that. Things got worse when I graduated to hashish and heroin. And I can remember exactly how that happened.

On that day, the *Maltese Cross* had brought in an unusually large number of tourists. To attract foreign currency, our government had just introduced a particularly advantageous exchange rate for tourists, and foreign travellers with nothing better to do but take trips were pouring from the steamer. I was pleased by this; I could expect a rich haul. And then, as I darted among the passengers leaving the customs hall, to my surprise I heard someone call out,

'Stemo! Stemo Kulamar! Is that you?'

It was Samuel Arbis, Samu, a boy I had once gone to school with, had even shared a desk with. During the war, we had actually been joint proprietors of a real pistol. An armoury officer at the American air base who had become overly enamoured of Minoran mint liqueur had been selling weapons to all comers. In time, he glutted the market so thoroughly as to do himself a serious disservice, because the prices fell to such a level that in the summer of forty-three you could buy a weapon from what you saved from your school lunch money. So Samu and I lost weight for two months, and then bought ourselves a huge Colt. Lord only knows what we needed it for—little boys don't usually trouble their heads much about that sort of thing as a rule—but from then on we turned up at school proudly packing a gun. On even dates it was in my school bag, while Samu flaunted the holster on his belt, and on odd dates it was the other way about.

As soon as the war was over, the entire Arbis family emigrated. It was a very complicated and doleful time, in one way, for us Minorans. The threat of invasion by the Axis powers was a thing of the past. We no longer needed anyone to defend us, and the people's mood made a sudden swing against the English and the Americans. Perhaps one of the reasons was their disgusting prosperity, which we had observed throughout the war from very close up. Everyone, after all, knows what it takes to rattle envy's chain. The first elections brought   a completely unexpected victory for the Own-landers—nothing like that ever happened again—and the new government started up a veritable Saturnalia directed against everything from overseas. They persecuted everyone, down to the cleaning women at the British administration building and the American air base, and even more so after the English left, giving us our independence. You'd think we got it just so we could start acting like complete clowns.

Looking back, it seems to me—and, no doubt, to many others—simply unbelievable. But it really did happen that way. After the English left, we were horrifyingly poor. We had nothing to our names except our goats, our potato fields, and our fishing boats. We had no means of supporting ourselves. All those who had earned their bread by working for the colonial administration or on the American base were suddenly out of a job. The Own-lander government itself was so hard up that it sacked the entire service staff at the former governor's mansion, and the ministers themselves, along with their secretaries, had to take their turns cleaning the stairways and halls with rags and mops. The Prime Minister himself drew up the duty roster every month. That was when we began to persecute the unemployed officials in a particularly spiteful manner, as if they were to blame for our poverty. It was officially announced that they had betrayed the national interest.

The old air base barracks were converted into an educational labor camp, called an ELC for short, and they started sending people there who had compromised themselves through collaboration, as the newspapers put it.

The people in the ELC were set to work from morning to night. Work was supposedly going to do more than anything to reshape them into loyal citizens. For a start they were given choppers to cut up the old automobile and aeroplane tires which the Americans had left lying around in heaps when they decamped. The scraps of rubber were collected together in a big mound and various schemes were set afoot to make use of them. Some were poured into gunny sacks, to serve as fenders in the port of Antafagusta. And when all the dock walls there were fixed up with fenders to last them for at least the next two hundred years, they launched an experiment in using the rubber scraps as a filler for surfacing pavements. It was soon discovered, however, that this needed too much bitumen, which anyway had to be mixed with sand or else it would not solidify at all in our warm climate, and simply glued the rubber scraps to the soles of people's shoes, so that no power on earth could get them off. People shuffled around town in what looked like those revolting black felt slippers that are handed out to visitors in some museums. Finally, the ELC authorities gave it up as a bad job and left the fruits of their labour under the open sky, seeing that neither rain nor wind could do the scraps any harm. Later, when the Consortium moved into the territory once occupied by the base, looking for phosphates, the rubber mountain was in the way, so they simply set fire to it. The hummock smoldered and smudged for five solid weeks, and the reeking smoke lay thick over the entire island all that time. It was as though Minore was having a low-grade volcanic eruption.

After the rubber project, the reeducation subjects were made to carve souvenir ashtrays from phosphate rock, in four set sizes. True, the ashtrays came out a dirty brown colour, and were rough and porous. They could never be cleaned properly and they broke easily. Sometimes they just cracked on their own, without anyone touching them. Eighty thousand beautifully designed labels, stamped 'Made in Minore' in gold, were ordered from the Madrid Mint, to go onto the finished products. It was decided that they would be sold as souvenirs in all the bakers' shops, bars, chemists' and newsagents' kiosks in Antafagusta. When the Own-lander government fell three years later, secret reports compiled by the Ministry of the Economy, which were published by the new incumbents, made it clear that in all that time only two ashtrays had been sold. One had been purchased for the Own-landers' party headquarters, but it was never established for certain who had bought the second or for what purpose.

Ares Damian, the Prime Minister of the new International-Democrat government and himself an experienced marketeer, sold the remaining ashtrays, priced as phosphate ore, to a Japanese fertilizer firm. In profound secrecy, they were loaded onto a bulk cargo ship which sailed under a Panamanian flag, and dispatched to Nagasaki. When the deed was made public a while later, the Own-lander opposition raised a fearful howl, accused Damian of crass anti-Minoranism, of betraying Minore's vital interests, and of flouting the nation's dignity. The government paid no attention to this, and used the Japanese remittance to build a drainage system which carried the urban effluent out to sea beyond Cape Cataracta and made it possible to open the town beaches again. From the very beginning, Damian had dreamt fondly of developing international tourism on Minore.

Well, but the Arbis family missed all this. They were off as soon as the Own-landers started their witch-hunt. Yustus, the head of the family, had spent the entire war at the air base, working as a maintenance technician on the main gates. Since the Americans could not take the trouble to get out of their vehicles, the main gate-locking mechanism was made to open automatically when a particular light and sound signal was given. But the soldiers and officers returning from Antafagusta in their jeeps were for the most part one over the eight on mint liqueur and did not usually manage to get the brakes on before their radiator grills were jammed into the gate. So Yustus had to repair the automatic gates two or three times a day, and more often on Saturdays. And he always had his welding equipment—an acetylene container with tubing attached—at the ready. The work he did was valued and well paid, and the Own-landers could never have forgiven him for that. Yustus Arbis gathered up his family, paid a goodly number of dollars to a fisherman, and put ashore under the cover of night somewhere near Serana. At that time, a lot of people were escaping in like style, some because they really had to, others simply out of fear that was mostly unwarranted. Many, however, lacked the mettle to tempt fate and wait to see if anyone would come knocking at the door with an official summons.

Samuel and I sat in a cafe, nursing double mint liqueurs, and he related what had happened to him later. He and his father had started out by washing up in restaurants, first in Serana and then, having saved up enough money for the move, in Toronto and New York. They gradually got on their feet. Samuel looked like a man who had done well for himself: gold-rimmed spectacles, a diploma from the Massachusetts Institute of Technology, a patent for a 'mole'—an ingeniously designed air-driven underground cable-laying machine, his own small firm, and business contacts all over the world.

'Nothing of the sort would have happened to you if you had stayed on Minore,' I said to him with a sigh. 'What power would have driven you from your home and forced you to get your brain in gear? You know, I have worked out that in the majority of cases it depends on the individual whether he ends up a professor or a drayman delivering beer. A professor or a trader is the end result of those times when circumstances weigh heavy, when there is a gnawing fear that it's going to take a real effort just to survive. But remove that fear, and ninety times out of a hundred a man will come unstuck, will content himself with whatever life throws his way, and it won't even occur to him to pull himself together, however difficult that may be, if only to prevent the spark that was embedded in him at birth from going out with a quiet little hiss.'

'That could be,' Samuel agreed. 'Only I'm no great shakes. Do you remember Leo Neckarborn?'

You bet I did. At the foot of the cliff, by the sea, about three quarters of a mile from the hut where Murana's father lived, there used to be a village called Bonegripe. It has long been abandoned, and now lies demolished by people and by the sea. I don't know where

59

it got that name from: it's not every village that gets called Bonegripe. Perhaps the dampness of the sea air had once made people's bones ache worse than usual, and the name had come from that. Or perhaps it was the loneliness and solitude that preyed upon them. The lads in that village were scrappy, wiry, and stubborn. They probably realised that they would come to a grinding halt in their old age, and so were eager to get up to as much mischief as they could while they were still young. While I was at school, the leader and best scrapper of all the Bonegripe kids was Leo Neckarborn. The story was that he owed his terrific surname to an ancestor who, once upon a time, had skipped from a passing Austro-Hungarian battleship and had made it to the island in a dinghy.

Leo had ginger hair. His big-nosed face always bore the traces of past tussles, and his knees were forever scabbed too. He was two years older than us, so towards the end of the war he was called up and assigned to the auxiliary troops that guarded the aerodrome, and he would strut about, looking ever so proud, in an old khaki uniform with shorts, which had not been standard American military issue for ages. By then he would no longer condescend to fight with us; he had his dignity to preserve. He got away during the evacuation of the base in an extremely risky fashion, by crawling unseen into the bomb hatch of a Flying Fortress that was about to take off. And there he stayed until the plane landed somewhere in England, when they pulled him out, half-dead from cold and oxygen deprivation. But it was his only possible escape route. Auxiliary troops were not included in the evacuation, and he had no money at all to pay for a boat. His father had died at the very beginning of the war, when a German U-boat had surfaced off Santa Clara and had sunk seven Minoran fishing boats with a burst of machine gun fire, and there were two younger boys in Leo's family too.

Leo had only managed to spend a total of four years in school, and it wasn't until he was in the auxiliary that he learned enough English to swear and say other rude things, but not a word more.

'Then just picture this. Leo Neckarborn is now a well-known solicitor. He has two assistants and an office in the centre of London with water-seasoned oak panelling. I have to be in London at least once a year on business, and I always drop in to see him. He gets a bottle of genuine mint liqueur out of the safe, and we reminisce about our childhood. He's a specialist on wills and inheritances. That's where most of the money is, apparently. But you can just imagine—he has to know off by heart all the British law codes published over the past seven centuries. Some of their laws haven't been changed in all that time. And the speeches he trots out in court!'

And that example, like many others, confirmed all over again that life itself had forced the Minoran emigrés to shift for themselves. A man absolutely must stand up for himself, or else he goes right off and then someone has to take charge of him. Neither that day nor the next was I able to rid myself of an increasingly powerful sense of my own inferiority.

After that encounter with Samuel I could no longer keep things in hand. I searched for drugs with a stronger and stronger kick. I began to disgust myself. Everyone else was out in the world, and I alone, had no education and no calling, a cripple living on the state dole, on those three minares which the government takes on account from every ton of phosphates mined on my land, the balance of sixty-seven minares being deposited in accounts which will secure the future, ours and our children's, when the phosphates run out on Minore twenty or so years hence, according to the calculations of experts in these matters.

I quickly started going downhill. I could not shake the sensation of drawing inexorably nearer to a gaping black pit which would put a natural end to my senseless existence.

The money flowed through my hands like sand. It got so there wasn't even enough to last out until the next payment came. On the toughest days I started borrowing from the few friends I still had, but, while it got more and more difficult to pay off my debts, the amount left for my heroin dwindled faster.

That was when they hooked into me. Shrewd young fellows they were, carbon copies of each other, in identical tightly buttoned jackets and with Christlike beards. They would sit me down, they would sympathize with me—a proletarian roundly forsaken. They would pass me a joint and lend me money. And they asked for nothing in return. Only much later did I chance to hear that they called themselves ultra-leftists.

To tell the truth, that was completely irrelevant to me. In those days, if the devil himself had offered me a joint and money I would not have turned him down.

The money flowed away with incomprehensible speed.

Murana was having difficulty keeping bread on the table. She started working at the greengrocer's, sorting and stacking the produce. It promised some income—not much, but some.

I was awash with impotent rage. Before my eyes there arose images of the strong and stocky assistant tumbling Murana on a green pile of fresh cabbages, on a grey mound of potato sacks...

That was when despair itself thrust the hatchet into my hands.

A doctor in a small white cap seemed to float out of a thick mist and at the same time his voice came to me from somewhere far away. I decided that he must be talking, because his lips were moving; the image on the retina of my eyes and the sound in my auditory canals were not yet connected. I had to work quite hard to bring them together, and only then did the picture become whole.

The doctor was conversing with someone outside my range of vision. I was too weak to turn my head.

'...very strange thing, this degree of identification. The merging of two streams of consciousness, and occurring with no regularity whatsoever, in spasms... the literature contains descriptions of individual instances... we'll be taking encephalograms and doing an overlay...'

With an incredible effort, I drag my benumbed lips apart to ask, 'Doctor ... what's the matter with me?'

The doctor breaks off his conversation with the other person, and looks attentively into my face, assessing how capable I am of understanding him.

'Nothing much, Yanno. A bad concussion and shock. You'll just have to stay in bed a while, and then everything will be fine again.'

Nothing much, nothing much, shock, bad concussion and shock, but what could have concussed me like this? Did I get sunstroke there on Herald Square amid the seething currents of air, or did someone knock me down? And what was it that caved in on me with a crash from which my ears are still ringing like anything? A bounding back in a striped jacket and a fearsome crash on the burning-hot square...

Everything shifted again. The doctor in the white cap was spirited away and my thoughts stuck together all at once, like fruit drops at the bottom of a jar. My memories merged into a single opaque block, and I was no longer sure whether I heard the crash there on the square or whether it came from the beach. Perhaps, I was still lying with several hundred of my companions in misfortune on Britannic Boulevard, my nose thrust into the dirt and policemen armed with submachine guns standing watch over us. The shakiness of my memory demoralized me. Not for one second did I feel convinced that I had the thread of memory in my hand now and I could move forward without fear of stumbling into another dead-end.

Suddenly it was as if heavy wads of cotton wool had fallen away, unplugging my ears. I could hear tranquil, ageless music in the garden of the British Embassy. I guessed straight off that they must be holding a reception to mark the one hundred and tenth anniversary of the Minoran-British defence pact. On that day, one hundred and ten years previously, the six-inch guns of the Cruiser *Intrepid* had been booming out there in the anchorage, while today's cannonade was coming from the champagne bottles in the embassy garden. Two generations had passed through this vale of tears in the interim; that was the only difference. Swirly white iron chairs were grouped here and there in the grounds, which were laid out like a miniature English park and were the Ambassador's pride and joy, while waiters in stiff Victorian livery—swarthy, sturdy lads from the Archipelago Motel restaurant who moonlighted as police informers and were always sent to serve at embassy receptions, even though the organizers usually only asked for a washer-up and a barman—handed round the mind-boggling mixed drinks in which the Ambassador excelled. He never missed a chance of getting behind a bar and mixing lethal cocktails from all the bottles he could lay his hands on. He was firmly convinced that only savages drink their hard liquor straight. Almost the entire diplomatic corps was at the reception: the summer tedium in placid Antafagusta spared no one.

Some time ago I had hit on a sneaky way to get through to one of the ambassadors. It seemed that I had managed to find out what made him tick. I had to stop stalling. Damian was tightening the screws and my superiors, by all appearances, had not the slightest intention of changing their minds. From them I could expect neither support nor assistance.

That morning, I had bumped into a gloomy Damian in the Figaro salon doorway, only to hear him whisper reproachfully, 'Eldon is intending to begin the campaign to move the Herald back to Santa Clara next week. The propaganda department has already told the papers to start work on their editorials. Listen here, something has got to be done! We cannot, in the situation we're in and without any support, announce to the world at large that we are going to put up a memorial!'

I knew that Damian had taken up a collection among the members of his own party, but the result had been exceedingly unimpressive. The three hundred and seventy-four active International-Democrats had contributed a total of precisely three hundred and seventy-four minares. That kind of money would buy, at best, the plaster bust of the Herald that stood on Damian's desk, but certainly not a monument. Now all hopes were pinned on help from outside. Damian was profoundly convinced that this help must be enlisted by none other than yours truly. His own efforts had invariably come to nothing: scarcely were the first words out of his mouth before he was reading his opposite number the riot act for not caring enough, which for some reason was not too pleasing to people who were supposed to be forking out.

I soon found the ambassador I was looking for standing in the shade of a large magnolia with leaves as shiny as tin-plate. He and the Botswanan Consul were sampling a bright-yellow egg cocktail and discussing the problems of African development.

Ambassador Leverkühn, an undersized, rotund man endowed with an inexhaustible supply of geniality, was dressed in a white dinner jacket that made him look like a puffball which had recently sprung from the ground. I was used to seeing him in a different get-up. Having almost nothing to do in Antafagusta, Leverkühn had devoted himself entirely to ornamental horticulture, since the Minoran climate favoured that sort of thing. Every time I drove past the residence, I would see Ambassador Leverkühn working in his garden. Evil tongues insisted that the director of Antafagusta's Botanical Gardens, who was not exactly indifferent to the good things in life, secretly supplied Leverkühn with very rare plants and was paid in foreign currency. Envy makes for inventive minds, but it is a fact that not long after a late supper in Leverkühn's greenhouse, to which he had invited a select party on the occasion of the flowering of his 'Beauty of the Night' cactus, the *Minore Evening News* had run a wistful little piece written by some social activist, a champion of the conservationist cause, which said that the Botanical Gardens' only 'Beauty of the Night' had succumbed to cactus beetles and had been withdrawn from the display.

I would think that the director of the Botanical Gardens quieted the pangs of his conscience by looking into the not too distant future. The time would inevitably come when the phosphate quarries would swallow up the town too, and then would it really matter whether the rare plants perished in the Botanical Gardens or in the embassy greenhouse? So let them do someone good while they lasted. Besides, it was clear as day that the Botanical Gardens would be sacrificed to the voracious excavators before the residential areas, which meant that plants taken to the embassy would have a year or two longer to live.

I spent a long time staring at the Ambassador, arrayed all in white and calmly chatting with his bluish-black colleague, before I finally recognised him. He dressed quite differently when he was gardening. Leverkühn was a native of an area in the Alps where the Swiss, Austrian, Italian and West German frontiers met, and, in addition to an inexhaustible joie de vivre, had acquired in the land of his birth an unquenchable passion for Tyrolean and Bavarian costumes. Given any opportunity, he would put on an Alpine bowman's hat decorated with a colorful feather, and the green shorts of a mountain man, with broad braces joined by a bib that had edelweiss flowers embroidered on it. He wore mountain boots and white knitted knee-length stockings, and his round knees shone with a pink innocence that was utterly unmindful of the pros and cons of diplomatic etiquette.

It was said that this sartorial foible had cost Leverkühn, who was considered a subtle and capable diplomat, an ambassadorial post in one of the old European capitals, where his bare knees would have given rise to any amount of nasty scandalmongering in local conservative circles.

'Ah!' Leverkühn exclaimed, catching sight of me. 'Come here! Where two gentlemen are discussing politics, there is always room for a third—a swindler.'

'A swindler!'

'To be sure! Only scoundrels work in the big agencies, and don't try to pretend that you are the exception to the rule. Would an honest man ever become a pressman of his own free will—or were you sentenced to it? Well then, let's hear what big story you are planning to let loose after today's reception.'

'I haven't decided yet. Perhaps something like this—according to reports from well-informed sources, certain European states have begun to work on a new and more resultative policy for Southern Africa. Are you pleased?'

The Botswanan burst out laughing: his large, azure-tinted white teeth gleamed. The Consul's face shone in the sunset's reflected glow, and it was, no doubt, these glinting highlights which made it difficult to catch the expression on his face. All his jollity notwithstanding, his face was like a mask; I don't know why. The Consul was laughing without a care in the world, but his laughter was not a comfortable sound. It was impossible to tell whether it betokened genuine gaiety or scorn. Leverkühn waggled a finger.

'Now there's a hint I can see right through. And what kind of news would that be? Name me any country that is not contemplating a new policy initiative in Southern Africa—everyone has contrived to come to grief there to date.'

The Botswanan gave an even more enigmatic laugh.

'But tell me, as a journalist who knows everything in the world and, on personal conviction, quite a bit more besides, what does the white man represent in Africa today—a snippet from a self-assured class of overlords or simply a schoolboy who has forgotten what he's been taught?'

The Botswanan stopped laughing and, as though preempting any question that might be coming his way, gave a dignified bow and left, his face fixed in the same impenetrable expression. Leverkühn, with a touch of envy, watched him go.

'Something tells me that you and I are rather more luckless school-boys than we realise ourselves. With our stock understandings, we're ill-equipped to plumb the innate wisdom of that continent, of that race. And in our helplessness we lay all the blame on mysticism...'

The Ambassador bent down, drummed with his puffy little palms on the white chair seat and did a few ritual skips around it.

I decided that the time was right.

'Mr. Leverkühn, to the best of my knowledge, many of the principles of International-Democracy may be traced back to the works of German philosophers.'

He was instantly on his guard.

'What are you driving at? One has to keep a weather eye open all

65

the time with you! What now—do you want to saddle me with responsibility for all the unsuccessful experiments in the world that have rested on those principles?'

'Most certainly not. It simply occurred to me that, this being so, you are in a position to make an extremely impressive gesture here on Minore, which would, incidentally, redound to your credit.'

I briefly told him that the International-Democrats were intending to raise a memorial to Tommazo Oon, and directed the Ambassador's attention to the desirability of a modicum of financial support. Leverkühn's eyes went owlishly round. He was thinking. His crafty mind had begun to whirl with thoughts about what the suggested step would do for him and whether or not something underhand was going on.

'And the government?' he asked suddenly. 'I mean, Eldon is very touchy about any outside interference. This is true to type for all bigwigs in small countries. On that score we've had experience aplenty of our own. They trump up some laughable pretext, declare you persona non grata, and—see you later.'

'No such thing,' I tried to convince him with all the assurance I could muster. 'Though it's true that Eldon is a Christian Liberal, Tommazo Oon was long ago elevated to the position of enlightener of the nation. Party squabbles have no role to play here. National pride, and all that. You've seen for yourself the respect they all have for their Herald.'

'All right, then. But tell me—what's in it for you?' His professional circumspection was awake now.

'Well, it's simply that if Damian himself, let's say, turned up in your office, banged his fist on the desk and barked, "Respect for the Herald is your bounden duty, so let's see the colour of your money!" you would show him the door, and he has no illusions about that. And I am a journalist beholden to no one and do only what I consider necessary.'

'But all the same, you do have a personal interest in this?' Leverkühn continued to probe. 'Come clean, now—you'll get nowhere trying to foist me off with a pig in a poke.'

'Firstly, I myself am, in a certain degree, an internationalist, and a democrat in like measure. Isn't that enough for you? Then try to imagine that I, despite belonging to the despised fourth estate, am also a living, breathing human being. Perhaps I too would like at least once in my life to put my hand to something which will not be thrown out with tomorrow's rubbish, like the paper that usually carries my byline.'

'Excellent—I really am trying to imagine that. But are you sure that the Minorans will take such a gesture at face value?'

'Without a shadow of a doubt. And not only the Minorans—this story will set world public opinion back on its heels, you'll see. I'd lay anything that the British Ambassador will break his golf club in

66

a fit of pique because he, the world's greatest authority on all things Minoran, didn't think of it first.'

Leverkühn gave a malicious smile. He and the British Ambassador were rivals to the death. While one had the upper hand through the rich and varied selection of drinks in his bar, the other carried the day on the strength of his garden and greenhouse. On the diplomatic plane, they were forever thrusting spokes into each other's wheels, with amiable smiles.

'Very well, ' Leverkühn assented. 'We must put ourselves out for our brothers in the developing world. They don't discuss aid for developing countries in our Parliament for the fun of it, do they? Let them shell out once in a while. What amount do you consider appropriate?'

He's bitten, I thought with satisfaction, he has most definitely bitten. It was very hard for me to keep my composure, but I didn't want to arouse his suspicions.

'Well, I would think about five thousand...'

'Ten!' the Ambassador exclaimed, bouncing a little like a tennis ball. 'If a job's worth doing, it's not proper to be stingy about it. I am not exactly the representative of Monaco or some such place! My finance minister could not care less whether it's five or ten. It's ten and that's that!'

Having made this decision, Leverkühn once again clinked the glass containing his favorite egg cocktail with mine, and hurried off to roust out other diplomats and take soundings. Something bigger was obviously in the offing.

I felt a sense of awkwardness—a measly little feeling, perhaps, but enough to tweak me. However, my experience as a reporter told me that it was nothing to get fussed about. There's no sun without shade. Not long ago, the *Minoran Reports* had published an essay about Tommazo Oon which portrayed him as a great enlightener. It was not my fault that only the week before I had happened to find out from old Ossian what his crusade had really been all about.

As usual, we had been sitting in the wind by his hut, our gaze wandering far below, to the seashore. A little distance away, by the ruins of Bonegripe, the sea was bright blue, but right on the shoreline the water was so transparent that from this vantage point it was possible to make out the huge boulders on the bottom and the fish swimming between them. White cliffs, littered with rock fragments, descended to the sea, taking on a rusty hue at the water's edge. This was the bedrock which lay below the phosphate deposits. Nearer to the centre of the island, that bedrock formed a giant bowl whose bottom was below sea-level, so that after all the phosphates had been mined, there would be nothing left but a jagged atoll, a border of rock rising slightly above the surface of the water. But that was almost impossible to conceive just then, there in the company of Ossian, who

5*

sat like constancy incarnate in front of his hut, where many generations had lived out their lives.

'I remember right well when Tommazo opened a school, a trade school... The whole island talked of nothing else, it being the only school of its sort in these parts,' Ossian told me. He had already grown accustomed to my grilling him on the Herald and was perhaps a little flattered by it. 'You know, in the old days there was an almshouse in Santa Clara. All the old folks with no one to provide for them were brought there. The community supported them, with the help of the church. Collecting boxes were set in the churches for that very purpose. Pinched and straitened it was, but they had full bellies and a roof over their heads. After that there defence pact, the English had built themselves a big two-story building for their barracks, and then, when they saw that the shore folk could think of nothing but how to feed themselves and them on the plateau were altogether too slothful to rebel, they took the soldiers from there, so as to spend less. And the building stood empty until it was turned into an almshouse. The place had seen neither paint nor putty all its born days. When the wind came in from the sea, all the windows rattled and the old folk trembled with cold. But on the other hand, that's no bad thing that they were so well aired, or else the place would have stunk like a rabbit hutch, as almshouses are like to do.

'One autumn a Turkish sailing vessel, manned by smugglers, came up on the rocks off Santa Clara. Down at the cape there is a most perfidious current, and when the sea is high you don't notice that you are being carried full onto the rocks. It happened in a storm. Some of the sailors drowned in no time, and the rest made for shore in a boat. Now, old folk are inquisitive as goats. Every one whose legs still carried him hied himself off to the shore to see the Turks. A wave took and capsized their boat, and the more sprightly old men, who had been fishermen before, hauled the sailors out of the water. Evidently, they were all soaked through and caught tidy colds, but the thing of it was that they had some unknown ailment on board their ship, which is why they had come up on the rocks, because half the crew was abed. Who knows where they had taken this sickness up? However it was, two days later there was not a single Turk left among the living, and then the pestilence spread among the old folk. A priest came and held a service. He fumigated the building with incense, but all to no purpose. In a week or so, every last old man in the entire almshouse was clean dead and gone. They buried them all together in one pit, and sprinkled them with lime too, like plague victims. From that time the house stood empty. None of the old men wanted to be sent there, and if anyone's kin would start pestering him about it, he would peg out in fright, sooner than be packed off to Santa Clara.

'And so the house was vacant for some ten years, until Tommazo, who had been exiled from the island by the English because of his foolish tarradiddle about politics, returned from the mainland. During that time he had travelled the wide world over, and had seen how people lived in other lands. It must have been there somewhere that he had come upon his new notion. He petitioned the community for permission to use the vacant almshouse, and really, who could begrudge it? He put new windows in—coloured ones for the most part—and went and opened a school, and that school was to win no end of renown, but also brought not a little harm. He named it himself, called it a trade school.

'Of course, Tommazo was not doing all this out of charity. He had more need for that school than anyone, the reason being that when the English exiled him, Tommazo forfeited the right to inherit what was left to him by his parents. It's the shortage of land that's the cause, of course, but on Minore we unbendingly observe an ancient custom—even the English could not shake it. According to this custom, any man who has left the island to live in foreign parts cannot return to his portion, even if he were to crawl from the sea on his knees. It matters not whether you go of your own accord or are sent by force.

'But a man must have something to live on, so Tommazo started his trade school. He had been a fine carver in his younger days, on wood and on stone alike, and there on the mainland, I daresay, he saw how they could squeeze money out of any trifle, and so, amid our poverty, he took up a profitable pursuit. The children he brought into his school were mostly from the plateau. They had big families up there and were abidingly glad to have one less mouth to feed. He taught his charges the skills they needed and set them to work. The boys fashioned boxes and chests out of wood, painted them green, red or yellow, decorated them and on the lids painted pictures of brown cliffs by a blue sea or goats on a hillside. They collected shells on the shore as well, and stuck them onto the little caskets as a border. Something instructive was inscribed on each box, like "Santa Clara is my love" or "In Antafagusta your sorrow the sea dispells on the morrow". To prevent the children from making mistakes, he taught them to read and write somewhat, and that is where this here enlightenment came into it, because until that time only our priests and merchants could write. The girls spun goat wool and knitted jackets and jerkins. They raised the goats themselves, at the school. The seaweed grows thick in Santa Clara, in the shallows by the shore. It dyes wool brown when boiled, and that is why all the jackets they knitted were white, black and brown. Little by little, we came to consider those as our national colours. The done thing was to decorate them across the front with a picture of goat-kids. That's where our famous Minoran goat jackets came from. They were sold in every shop in Antafagusta afore the war, and even in London too. I hear tell that folk paid two pound apiece for them. That's not so easy for me to believe, but they do say that it's the plain truth.

'Every Friday, Tommazo would load his two-wheeled cart with

finished chests and jackets, harness up his donkey, take two of the older boys with him as helpers, and set off to Antafagusta, to the bazaar. There used to be a big bazaar in Antafagusta on Saturdays. They would usually return on Saturday evening, singing aloud, and at the school they would have macaroni from the town instead of boiled potatoes for supper, while Tommazo himself would make off for the inn, to get pickled. He wouldn't come back until Sunday evening, which gave his pupils a chance to rest.

'Sometimes no one would be that keen to buy his goods at the bazaar, and then Tommazo would have to resort to trickery. He would send his helpers away for a while and a little bit later they would come back pretending to be customers. They had agreed in advance which chest or jacket they were both to snatch hold of. There would be proper to-do, the boys would be grabbing at each other's lapels, and trade would start to pick up. The goods must be worth something, people thought, if there's a fight over them, and so they would come up and start asking prices. And sometimes the artful Tommazo would hide a lot of his goods and would get something out from under the counter for a customer, making out to be doing him a great favour. And so all his chests were sold, although the purchasers later racked their brains, wondering what to use them for. There weren't that many who had wealth enough to store in chests and boxes.

'And so it went on. There was no cause but to rejoice. After all, because of Tommazo's solicitude, many children were getting their bed and board free and on holidays they were even given a few minares for pocket money. He was teaching them clever things into the bargain. In those days, the folk here were not spoiled by wealth, and their gratitude to Tommazo for what he was doing for their children was heartfelt. They called him the Teacher, and would bare their heads when they saw him coming in the distance.

'The troublous times began after the school had existed to general satisfaction for three or four years. By that time, the first pupils had grown up. The girls started making eyes at the boys, while the lads were getting a good look at the lasses. The folk from the plateau are sprightly when it comes to that. I've always said that while they might be lacking a wee bit in other ways, they're handy enough at getting babies.

'Tommazo himself in his younger days had been a great one for the girls. There wasn't a place on the island where he didn't have a lady-love. And so it never came into his head to keep an eye on his charges or to put his foot down. He reckoned that mischief is what youth is for. So it happened that a number of the older girls in his trade school all turned up in the family way at once. Well, the to-do that was made, you'd have thought they were the first lasses who'd got knocked up on the entire island since Adam and Eve! The priest in his pulpit railed at the young folk for wallowing thus in lechery. The Archbishop of Antafagusta himself went to the Governor, demanding the immediate closure of that vile sink of depravity.

'What could the Governor do? He had no desire to quarrel with the clerics, and Tommazo's sharp tongue had long ago brought him under suspicion. Like I told you, the English had exiled him. So the Governor upped and closed the school. It was a mere bagatelle to him. He didn't even have to inform London. Tommazo got angry, went down to Antafagusta, and made his faithful donkey deposit a big pile right in front of the Governor's mansion. The guards seized him, gave him a drubbing, and tossed him in the clink, and then they had the celebrated trial about the donkey droppings. People remember it still. Now they put out flags on the day when the jury came in with its verdict on the Tommazo affair and said that he was not guilty. For you can never prove that a man can influence an animals' natural functions. Perhaps you can't prove it in good form, but I, for one, know that Tommazo's donkey was trained better than any circus horse that ever was. On a word from its master, it would bray and kick and who knows what else?

'Well anyway... They closed the school all the same. The pupils were sent home and carried on doing a little bit of handicraft, and the knocked-up girls bore their babies, as they have down the ages, and started to feed them mashed potatoes...'

It would not be true to say that this story is well remembered on Minore to this day. The years in their passing have obscured the details, but the reputation of an enlightener is invariably attached to Tommazo Oon's name, like a title, and that reputation just grows with every passing decade. Most of his former pupils are no longer of this world, and those who are still whiling away their remaining days have a persistent memory of a distant youth that was all sunshine and rainbows.

In any case, I was more than certain that one could act in the interests of the memorial without fear of incensing Ron Eldon's Christian Liberal government. No one could take me to task publicly, because the Herald had been officially declared an enlightener, the forefather of independence, and a national hero. It was not important that the present government did not completely share all his ideas. One would, for instance, be hard put to claim Tommazo as a good Christian, even posthumously.

Half an hour or so after my conversation with Ambassador Leverkühn, a figure wrapped in a flowing white burnoose approached me in the thickening twilight, inconspicuously and without a word. A black and white plaited cord, like a dappled snake, was bound about the stranger's head.

'Allah be with you,' the stranger said softly.

By the large almond-shaped eyes and jet-black beard, I recognised the First Secretary from the Embassy of the United Emirates. A secretive man he was, much like his embassy and all its dealings. I could never work out what interests of state were served by maintaining such a sizable staff in the UE Embassy on Minore, but it was more likely than not a matter of prestige—and a profusion of petrodollars, that goes without saying.

The Arab drew me aside, and glanced around in a suspicious manner that was so Middle Eastern. When the naked eye failed to turn anything up, he placed a finger on his lips and took a small black box from the folds of his voluminous robe, raised the antenna, and swept it around himself in a circle. I had recently seen a similar gadget—a new pocket detector from General Electronic Systems—advertised in a technical journal. According to the advertising blurb, it could locate any electronic listening device within a half-mile radius. Having completed this procedure, he put away his little miracle of modern science, and only then began to speak.

'Tell me please, Mr. Yanno, does this rumour about the memorial have any foundation in reality?'

I answered in the affirmative.

'You are an informed person. Could you perhaps tell me your opinion as to the possible reaction in Minoran government circles if my government were to offer a modicum of financial support to this undertaking?'

'I think that they would certainly be gratified by such a friendly gesture.'

'My thanks to you. And would it be appropriate, in your judgement, to donate so trifling a sum as fifty thousand?'

'You know, I am of the opinion that the size of the donation is of less importance than the deed itself.'

Well, brother Damian, you can book a church for the day. Your memorial is as good as paid for.

The Arab bowed, handed me his visiting card, and departed soundlessly. And all the best to you, Khaleb Mokhietdin al-Nasr...

I signed myself into the clinic, in the firm determination of kicking the drugs and the entire awful life I was living. And all the same, it was inhumanly difficult—an organism inured to poisons was crying out, in its every cell, for another hit, and there they were, trying to break me of the habit. There were times when I was on the brink of insanity. If I had had the tiniest opportunity to get to the poison cupboard, I would without doubt have thrown myself greedily on whatever was inside, even at the risk of my life. Just to lose consciousness, just to be free of the neuralgia that was coursing through my whole body, to be released from unbearable torments that defy description. The agonies gave ground slowly, returning at times, and then I began to understand why they were keeping me so long in the hospital.

And yet the greatest danger was awaiting me after my discharge, when it seemed that all was behind me.

About a week after I came home, I went one evening for a walk on Britannic Boulevard. Every day thus far I had gone there with Murana, but this evening she stayed at home with our little girl, who was poorly.

By the time I got to the Festival Hall, the sun had set. Mercury lamps were shining high up in the palm trees. I wandered slowly, avidly drinking in the motley comings and goings. After the white hush of the hospital wards, this was a delight. I was having great fun even with the more dotty side of life. I used to have no time for fashionable females in pants with ankle straps, hung about with bracelets, languishing in the heat under piles of mink furs. Now they all seemed funny and cute, these fragments of a regained world.

I did not notice where the two of them came from. They were both dressed in tight black leather jackets and black shirts. Their Christly beards bespoke some connection with the leftists, my obliging friends of yore. I personally had never shown much interest in their world-view. They had simply paid attention to me, had sympathized with me when I was suffering without my drugs. Perhaps it was those same two lads. You can't really tell them apart—they've all got the same face, are all identically hairy, and all have a fervid glint in their eyes.

'Where have you been keeping yourself?' asked the one who was walking on the right. 'I haven't seen you in ages.'

'I was in the clinic.'

'Want a smoke?' said the one on the left, getting out a packet of Winstons. That was how they carried the joints.

'No, I don't do drugs any more.'

But he seemed not to hear. He lit the cigarette and shoved it at me. It scorched my hand like fire. I was scared, as though the drug could get into my bloodstream by the merest contact, and I dropped the cigarette onto the pavement, where it lay, sending up a thin wisp of smoke.

'Look at that—he doesn't want it any more, he doesn't give a hoot!' the one on the left said in amazement.

'You wouldn't have been sucking up to the bourgeoisie, would you?' The one on the right turned his thin face toward me.

'Pack it in, will you?' I said. 'I haven't been sucking up to anybody. I just don't do drugs any more. I'm clean.'

I noticed them making signs at each other behind my back, and the next instant they grabbed me under the arms and dragged me toward the street, where a Land-Rover stood, all spattered with brown mud.

'Stop clowning about!' I yelled. 'Let go! I'm in no mood for jokes today.'

'Quiet!' hissed the one on the left, and tightened his clawlike grip on my arm.

'Or you're going to get badly hurt!' the one on the right said, in a dull, menacing voice, and gave my arm a deft turn that sent a sharp pain searing its way up into my shoulder.

In better days I would, perhaps, have torn myself away, but I was a lot more helpless with the prosthesis. And the drugs and the long treatment had sapped my strength too. There was no way out; I was obliged to go along with it. I had a momentary thought of calling for help, since there were plenty of people around, but I immediately dropped that idea, and not just because I was afraid of humiliation or pain, either. I simply could not believe that I really was in any kind of danger. It was just one of their crude jokes, and nothing else. That was why I did not feel right about making a racket.

They pushed me into the Land-Rover. The lads in leather jackets got in after me, and a third, dressed in the same way, got us moving.

'At least tell me where we're going.'

'Where we should be,' the one on the left snapped.

The vehicle, bouncing in the potholes, left the town, then turned toward the plateau and jolted along a cart-track that led into the hinterland. It was already completely dark, so I had no way of keeping track of where I was. My attendants were ominously silent. I tried to start a conversation a couple of times, but they acted as though they were stone deaf. For the thousandth time, I asked myself what they wanted from me, and could find no answer. Were they about to call in some old debts? But if that was it, then why take me anywhere? It would have been simpler to shake me down at home. They knew very well that I would hardly take any cash with me when I went for a walk.

The vehicle finally stopped and they told me to get out. I saw a somber, deserted place, like a gaping pit engulfed in darkness. In the slope nearest to us was a cave mouth, feebly lit from within. My companions pointed wordlessly in that direction.

Halfway there, I suddenly realised where I was. This was the dry bed of Lake Nakhan, in the very center of the island. When I was a child, before the war, a stream—actually a rivulet—flowed from here. It came off the tableland in a waterfall and ran into the sea between our village and Antafagusta. In those days, that rivulet supplied the town's drinking water. The lake was fed with rain and freshwater springs, and the water in it was always clear and chill.

The lake perished during the war, when the English got the idea of starting a phosphorus industry on Minore. There were just too many losses when the raw material was transported on supply ships trying to run the Axis U-boat blockade. Almost every other vessel went down somewhere out there, yet the war effort needed more and more phosphorus for munitions. Then the military decided that pure phosphorus could be transported in small quantities by cargo planes, and that would be a great deal less dangerous. So they sent in a New Zealand sapper battalion to build a phosphorus factory.

The New Zealanders were grand lads. I remember them really well. They were affable and cheerful, and much more sociable than the English, but not at all like the noisy, loudmouthed Americans. And they didn't get so raging drunk, either. They were the reason we started raising sheep. They were so used to having lamb chops at home that they couldn't live without them, and they paid well for lamb. So that was when we joined in and got our three ewes. But the New Zealanders were not to blame for drying the lake up. It was just that the electric furnaces needed electricity and there was nowhere to get it from. The low-capacity electric power plant in Antafagusta was scarcely capable of giving a reddish glow to the few light-bulbs to be found back then in the town and the surrounding areas. Besides, it shut down for weeks on end, every time the Germans managed to sink a collier on its way to the island. There wasn't even enough electricity for the air base, so the Americans had their own diesel generator. The English then arranged to have a new hydroelectric station built on the north side of Antafagusta, next to the phosphorus factory. They laid three full lines on, to bring the water down from Lake Nakhan. And the factory was started up.

The summer of forty-three was dry and hot. Though the water level fell rapidly in the lake, there was a fair hope that the winter rains would see things right. But even during the winter, the hydroelectric station took more water from the lake than the skies put into it, and the springs were unable to make up the shortfall. Come the following autumn, there was nothing but a tiny pond at the bottom of a depression which had once been a lake. The intake was above the water level, and the hydroelectric turbines stopped. But by then the allied war effort could do without our phosphorus, so they shut the factory down too.

We hoped that the lake would fill up again, little by little, and that's what happened at first. The water plane kept growing and even the rivulet revived. But the war had ended by then, and hungry Europe needed fertilizers. We were languishing in poverty, while the price of fertilizer went sky-high. We signed a big contract with the Consortium, and it started the first of the huge quarries that now cover the entire island like pockmarks. When the excavators broke into the aquifer, water began to seep into the quarry. Big machines worked day and night, pumping it out into the sea, so it would not hinder the work. Only later did we realise that we had slashed the lake's life-line. What little was left of Nakhan quickly began to dry up, until in the centre of the island there was nothing but an ugly stone bowl with a cracked bottom where even weeds had a hard time surviving for a long while afterwards.

At first, they arranged religious processions, led by the Archbishop himself, and held services to save the lake. Then they took to demonstrating against the government. Ares Damian's government was in power in those days. Every week, he signed yet another agreement with foreigners, giving them—at a price, of course—the right to search for, mine, or build something. In the papers they called this cooperation, the internationalization and democratization of the economy. But after the death of the lake the government found itself at a critical pass, and in the following elections Damian could get no one but his relations to vote for him. He fell, with a mighty crash, and Ron Eldon's Christian Liberals have governed us since then. It seems to me that they have stayed in power this long simply because we don't have another lake to destroy, and all the other obscenities that the government gets up to are not quite such eye-openers.

Tankers have brought us our drinking water ever since. It is pumped into huge silvery reservoirs in the port, like oil. Water on Minore is more expensive than beer, beer being useless for washing clothes or making soup.

And so it was to the dry bed of Lake Nakhan that they took me that evening.

The cave was lit with a few gas lamps. Behind a bare table were seated four bearded men in tightly buttoned jackets; they flanked their ringleader, a man with unkempt gray hair. Looking more closely, I saw two submachine guns and several pistols on the table.

The gloom of the cave made it easier to visualize than to see the rest of the leftists standing back against the walls. Some were dressed in black leather jackets. I later found out that these were the street-fighters, who were usually dispatched when a brawl was in the offing. Right in front of the table several figures crouched, perching on boxes or squatting on the floor. I was taken toward them. Eyeing them more closely, I saw some familiar faces. Most of them were people I had often spent time with down at the port, before I went to the clinic. They were junkies; their weak, flabby lips and trembling hands gave them away. An inspired hunch told me that they were evidently as much in debt to the leftists as I.

So were they going to try us? Fear began to creep into my soul.

The gray-haired ringleader stood. He was an entirely colorless thing: he had a grayish complexion, a gray waistcoat, a gray suit.

'Brothers in arms!' he yelled vehemently. 'This is the hour! The accursed bourgeoisie on Minore and in the entire world shall know, as they should, in whose hands rests the power over life and death! And very soon! The people has passed sentence, the people will enter the field, and then will the black mongrel blood flow forth from the satraps of capitalism!'

He explained the job on hand. As he put it, the bourgeois government was working up a new and shameful farce designed to hoax the people. The ashes of the Herald were to be moved, with much pageantry, to his birthplace of Santa Clara, in order to divert the people from revolt, which was the sole sublime and truly worthy act. Therefore the planned cortege must never reach its destination.

We ten junkies, I being the only one to have shaken free from my self-destructive mania, were given ten identical black attaché cases containing explosives, and a safety-fuse apiece. Each was assigned to a bridge on the road to Santa Clara, under which he was to lie in wait until the cortege arrived. When it approached, we would be

76

given a sign, after which the fuse must be lit, and then it would be every man for himself. How to get away was a matter of no particular interest to anyone in the cave. If the explosion at one bridge was badly timed for some reason, the next one would go up. It was a tenfold foolproof arrangement, all the way to Santa Clara.

When I had the cheek to remark that the safety-fuse looked a bit short to me, the ringleader jumped up and roared, 'Do you think we make our own here? The amount expropriated from the bourgeoisie in the quarries is the amount that has been cut up! And don't even think of trying any monkey business, or else...' He rapped his pistol butt on the table, threateningly. 'It is, all in all, a great honour to be allowed to lay down one's life for the people!'

That was when I recognized the leftist leader. He owned a wine shop on an alley near Britannic Boulevard. I had been there a very long time back, before my motorbike accident, looking for some wine for Murana's birthday. I remember being made to wait quite a while. There happened to be a rich customer in the shop, possibly a visiting director from the film festival. The assistant was taking a case of whiskey out to the car, while the owner, bowing deferentially, was opening the door for his client and blowing some nonexistent specks of dust from the latter's sleeve. After the customer had got into the car, the gray-haired shopkeeper tripped forward, let out a gusty breath, all but spat on the windscreen, pulled a checkered handkerchief from his pocket and took to rubbing the glass zealously. He stood for a long time, bent at a deferential angle, in the cloud of exhaust fumes, and returned to his shop only after the car disappeared around the corner, not slowing down at all.

I was allocated a bridge not far from where I was born, close to what used to be the village of Bonegripe. The bridge was the first on the route, which eliminated all my hopes that the cortege would never reach me. At the crack of dawn on the day that the ashes were to be moved, I was to hide under the bridge. I began to search feverishly for some way out of it, because the last thing I was prepared to do was blow anybody up. The only thing I could come up with was to leave the attaché case under the bridge, without lighting the safety-fuse, and make myself scarce. Then, when they asked me for an explanation, I would announce to them that they had given me a rotten charge and how was I to know why it hadn't exploded? By that time the police would certainly have found the briefcase and taken it away. True, if they got it into their heads not to take their eyes off me, then God help me, for they were pitiless. Their cave looked like a munitions cache.

Having got back into town but before going home, I disgustedly hid the black case in an unattended vault in the nearest cemetery.

Every evening, a motorcyclist in a black leather jacket appreared under my windows. He would brake, put his foot on the asphalt, gun the engine a couple of times, which was the signal, and wait for me to show at the window. I absolutely had to show, so that they would know that everything was O.K. and I was waiting for the order.

All those days I was not myself at all. I was tormented with fear that my masters would vent their malice on Murana and the child. They would definitely do that if I tried going to the police for help. I was in their hands, in their trap, and I had not the foggiest idea of how to get out. I became edgy and irritable, and any little thing would set me off. It was lucky, though, that Murana attributed all this to my recent stay in the clinic and did not plague me with questions.

Four days later, a pair dressed in leather jackets rode up on a motorbike and gestured at me to come down. The lad on the passenger seat informed me that the operation had been cancelled, and demanded that I return the bomb. We went together to the cemetery, and I handed the case over to him. I was so happy, I wanted to shout; but I kept a firm grip on myself.

That night, I was able to sleep soundly again. Later I found out that the authorities had decided not to go ahead with the reburial. Instead they had got the idea of raising a memorial on the Herald's tomb in Antafagusta.

And still, one of the junkie fraternity—a homeless vagrant who lived during the warm weather among the huge rocks which rose up like retaining wall at the very end of Britannic Boulevard, close to the port—made a bad end of it. The leftists had given him a whole packet of joints as an advance payment. No one ever found out if, after holding out for a long time, he had toked himself into a stupor and had lit the safety-fuse himself in a moment of craziness or if he had got so stoned that he didn't see how close the burning cigarette was to the fuse. In any event, there was an unexpected explosion and flying squads of policemen went charging down to the port. The morning papers wrote about a mysterious diversionary action in a deserted spot, while the evening paper published a photograph of a collapsed pile of rocks scattered with rags and plastic debris. The reporters made all sorts of wild guesses about a technologically impeccable suicide and a Mafia vendetta, but nobody got anywhere near the truth.

The next day I went to look at the place itself. It was very easy to see the hole among the rocks, as if some great huge hand had cleared a little space there. The rubbish had already been blown away by the wind; the debris had been carried off by the police to be examined. All signs of a junkie having lived in the area had vanished. It was as if he had never been there. I thought what negligible traces humankind leaves here on earth. And it clicked that I, of all people, could not even remember his face.

A few meters below, the waves were dashing noisily against the rocks, just as they had the day before, and the day before that.

6

'Artur, can you hear me? Are you listening?'

There was something odd, something unfamiliar in Delia's voice—a certain overbearing timbre that made me wary.

'Yes, of course I'm listening. What's going on?'

'Artur, we have to meet right away. Come to the polder at twelve. I'll drive there.'

'You might explain what's the big rush. What's up?'

'Be there, then you'll find out,' came the impatient response, followed by a click.

Typical female trick—turning simple things into some big mystery, I thought. If it had been anyone but Delia I would have had no compunction in not showing up at all, if only to make an educational point. You can't let women mess you about. But my relationship with Delia just happened to be at that stage where hope is always mingled with the fear that something could come between us and spoil everything. As yet, I wasn't a bit fed up; I hadn't even begun to get sick of it.

Somewhere in my subconscious there was a lurking astonishment that this woman—beautiful, experienced, and clever in her own way—had settled on me. I mean, as far as she knew I was only an obscure newsman—certainly not a hot journalistic property, not yet. Delia came from a good family. Her father was a doctor, the most famous gastrologist in Antafagusta. And, since the older folks were often troubled with stomach catarrh, liver disorders, and all that sort of thing—due to an excessive fondness for mint liqueur and eating habits that had once been below par and now were intemperate—he was doing very nicely, thank you, and making money hand over fist. Delia had graduated from college and got involved in the fine arts for her own amusement. When I met her she was into cinematography and was writing articles in which she tried to trace a parallel between the French 'new wave', which was now old hat, and the later American hyper-realism. She was perfectly capable of sitting through all the festival screenings, even those which were notoriously tedious, and she dragged me along too, so that I got a solid dose of cinetoxemia which would last me a good six months. Delia had been married when she was very young, but they hadn't wasted much time getting divorced. She didn't like to talk about that part of her life, but once she did let slip that her ex-husband was a toiler-moiler, a philologist by education and a failure by specialty, that he was warming a chair in a lexicographical department somewhere, earning a measly handful of minares by tossing file cards out of one box into another.

Set against a background like that, I couldn't help feeling rather superior.

I was quite surprised by the place where we were to meet. The polder is a deserted, desolate scrap of land without a single cafe where you can sit and chat or even a bench, for that matter. Lovers never rendezvous there, and the reason for that, perhaps, is the polder's inhospitable cheerlessness, which is so thoroughly dispiriting and turns the mind willy-nilly to thoughts of eternity. Even vagrants feel out of place there. An unpaved, badly graded road leads out to it. Heavy lorries had beaten that trail out once upon a time, and so it had remained—dust to the heavens in fair weather, and mud to the knees in rain.

The origins of that scrap of land were rather peculiar. At the height of the phosphate fever it was suddenly discovered that Antafagusta had run out of space for new offices and homes. At the same time, the government and the Consortium kept taking on more and more administrative personnel and on top of that people were pouring in from the plateau, driven out by the yawning quarries, and they all needed somewhere to live. On the land side, Antafagusta is pinned in by the steep drop from the plateau. Of course it would have been perfectly possible to start building up there, but the quarries would probably have got that far within a few years anyway and it didn't make a lot of sense to build over a phosphate deposit.

The town authorities hoped to make the problem go away by ordering the demolition of all buildings more than forty years old that were of no particular architectural value. As a result, the suburbs filled up with look-alike housing and every evening people were reluctantly dragged into dramas involving muddled apartments, which were meat and drink to the professional cartoonists. Then the authorities went after the parks, and the fun and games started. There's a conveyer in the port—it's been there for years, and it goes striding on steel struts two hundred or so meters into the sea, where deep-draught ore transports anchor to take the phosphates directly into their holds. Ever since it was built, the entire town has been positively plagued with the phosphate storms that blow up on those days when the wind carries the yellow dust into town from the sea. The phosphates irritate the respiratory passages and the whole town resounds with the hacking coughs of thousands of people. Bronchitis has been the predominant ailment here as long as the conveyer's been around. In view of all this, the townsfolk are particularly sensitive to any situation that calls for tree-felling. Quite to the contrary, in an effort to keep the dust back, people plant saplings in any empty patch of land they lay eyes on. So once again—for the umpteenth time—there were furious protest marches, a good number of windows in government establishments got smashed, and the town council was obliged to reverse its position on building in the parks.

So it was decided to lay down a polder in the bay off Cape Cataracta, some ten-odd hectares of it, as a site for a new district. The entire Republic was supposed to benefit from this, since it would bring that much more territory under Minoran jurisdiction.

The government already had sufficient funds on hand. A contract was signed with a Dutch firm, which promptly shipped in large excavators and suction dredges and set to work without delay. Cape Cataracta became a favourite place for the inhabitants of Antafagusta to take their walks: they even built a promenade. People came evening after evening to see how the work was progressing. The Dutch started off by piling the boulders that lay along the shoreline into huge sea-walls and then they began pumping sand up from the bottom of the bay and pouring it inside those embankments. First the portion of the bay that was enclosed between the stone dikes gradually grew shallower, the green water turned bright blue, and then the yellow sand started showing through. Finally, the surface of the polder rose above the water. This event was marked with great pomp and circumstance—a new piece of Minore was, after all, being born. A big rally was held on the flag-bedecked shore right by the polder, with choirs and orchestras and a tear-jerker of a speech by Serdik Amora, the mayor of Antafagusta, whose keynote was that 'our future is rising from the sea'. I can imagine it vividly; I have had occasion to look through some newspapers that were published around that time. A short while back, my agency commissioned a piece on dubious ventures in the Minoran economy for which the little man had had to pay through the nose. There are times when my agency's predilection for stories on things that turned out to be a washout for someone somewhere simply astonishes me.

The Dutch were near to finishing their job—they only had to raise the polder a meter or so—when all hell broke loose. Apparently someone had directed the attention of Consortium functionaries to the rather unusual and highly uniform sand that lay on the beach and all along the shoreline. In utter secrecy, and without asking the government's permission, the Consortium had its chemists take samples and run analyses which gave some unanticipated results. The sand along the Minoran coastline was found to contain a large percentage of titanium magnetite, and, since many of the world's advanced nations had rapidly developed their space technology and that sharply jacked up the going price for titanium and vanadium on the world market, the Consortium immediately sniffed some prodigious profits in the air.

A whole barrage of machinations was set in train, starting with bribes to newsmen and political figures and ending with diplomatic manoeuvres. The Consortium ran true to form, giving no thought to dropping a million on lobbying when there was a hundred million to be made. The result was not long in coming: the government capitulated. The Dutch firm was paid off and collected its compensation for breach of contract as well, then was given the old heave-ho. Mayor Amora made a nationally televised speech in which he announced that according to the latest research the former sea-bed which lay under the polder had begun to subside in a most unexpected and dangerous fashion and therefore, in the interests of public safety and for the general good of the municipality, it had been decided not to build a new residential area on the polder. Certain tatty old neighbourhoods in the center of Antafagusta were to be torn down instead, so that new buildings could be put up in their place.

A week later, the bulldozers started demolishing some lovely late colonial buildings which bordered the town park. The first high-rise went up a year later, and now you can hardly make out the trees in the park through the concrete boxes.

But the polder stayed—a bleak, whitish plain rising two meters or so above sea-level, set against the rocky promontory of Cape Cataracta. Stormy weather sends the waves rolling over the stone dikes, licking their crests away little by little. When the waves are high, the sea around the polder seethes and foams, and the deposited land inside the dikes is dotted with puddles large and small which never dry up and whose tepid waters teem with microscopic algae. And because they die and decompose there too, the place reeks with an acrid odor of rotting things. The gray plain is framed with something that looks just like a greenish strip of mold.

The Consortium did not start extracting the titanium magnetite from the polder straight away. There were tactical considerations involved, since rumours about kickbacks to the authorities had started making the rounds in the way that only top secret information does. Less confidential particulars are not so interesting.

Meanwhile, though, a lot of the townsfolk had got the word that the shore sand was extraordinarily valuable, so they started toting the stuff away in baskets and sacks under the cover of night. And in less than no time Antafagusta was raided by marauding fleas, hatched from the innumerable eggs that people brought home along with the sand. People scratched themselves silly and waited patiently for someone to come and offer them hard cash for the sand they were hoarding. The sharper ones took the risk of working the sand over themselves by rinsing it in a sieve and calcining it with bone char and sulphuric acid in a crucible. No one actually knew what to look for, and the untutored experimenters were to blame for several explosions and blazes, where spilled chemicals invariably made life more difficult for the firemen. The only thing the government could do was to order a modern foam extinguisher for the Antafagusta fire brigade. But, as time went on and nobody contrived to extract any gold from the sand, the alchemical fervor slowly died down.

The Consortium, however, had not abandoned its plans.

The sages in the Consortium public relations department had some practical advice to offer: start the work some distance away, and move step by step toward Antafagusta. After everyone had got used to it, the polder's turn would come. And that was how it was done. They took the excavators off to what used to be the village of

Bonegripe and started loading sand into lighters which ran it to Serana where it was transferred into goods wagons.

The shoreline was a disheartening sight after the top stratum had been taken. I stopped by there once myself. The jagged edge of the island's bedrock rose up out of the water like the submerged jawbone of a prehistoric monster which over the years had lost most of its teeth and had kept only fragments of the rest. In the distance, beyond the rim of the plateau, the engines snarled in the phosphate quarries and the buckets rose and fell. If they finally break through this cliff too, I thought, then that's the end of that. The sea will certainly burst inland and it'll be time to redraw the map of Minore. No force on earth will be able to push the sea back, and Minore will end up as a pathetic little atoll.

The polder was listed as part of the town's green belt, regardless of the fact that the only growing things there were weeds sown by the wind or by birds. The disconsolate whitish plain gradually acquired a ground cover of goosefoot, nettles and burdock, and its only regular visitors were kids from the town who caught fish and went diving off the dikes. At first there were even some decent catches to be had, but then even the fish, apparently, lost interest in this neck of the woods. Perhaps they were scared away by the synthetic detergents which flowed in ever increasing quantities into the sea down the urban sewage outlet that ran between the polder and Cape Cataracta. The water there was always topped with foam.

And why had Delia wanted to meet me here, in this woebegone, evil-smelling place? I could have simply gone to her house, or, if she was bothered about what the neighbours might think, she could have arranged to meet me in a cafe in the town center. No, women really are completely illogical creatures.

'Stemo! What have you done?'

The piercing cry burns like the lash of a whip. And even I am hard put to decide for sure if those words are something I heard once while I was awake or if they came in one of the nightmares that I have been having so often of late. My nerves are not what they were: the drugs have really done a number on me. Often I shudder with fright for no reason at all, as though afraid of some disaster which is about to happen at any moment.

But no—I can see figures there in the distance, by the machine. One of them is being propped up on both sides and that person is dragging one leg. It's Kolo. He's the one who shouted just now.

They showed up toward evening, as twilight was falling. There were five or six of them, and they were all carrrying crowbars or lengths of piping. While they were still some way off I saw that Kolo was with them, so I suspected nothing untoward. Nor did I waste time wondering what the lengths of piping were for, or what these people were meaning to do. I mean, I had known Kolo for ages. He was my

83

friend, and I had nothing to fear from him. And anyway, all the time I had been working there as a guard no one had ever tried to intimidate me.

True, I hadn't seen much of him recently. Kolo's life had not taken the best of turns. The phosphates quickly ran out on his holding, and he hadn't been paid a farthing for many a long day. No one could have seen it coming, but when the mining was well under way, they discovered that there was only rock on his land, not ore. Long ago, in times beyond recall, there had apparently been a tremendous earthquake, and a giant crevice had opened up in the sea-bed. The magma had risen almost far enough to breach the sea crust and then had solidified. A little further, and a live volcano would have been born. The crevice reached Minore and it lay, as chance would have it, exactly under the plot of land which Nikanor, Kolo's father, had bought. By stripping the top layer of phosphates, they had laid bare the dark grey basalt underneath. An excavator bucket went swinging down into it and buckled several teeth, the engineers came running up, took one look and said, 'That's enough of that. If we try for any more, that dab of ore could cost us much more than it's worth.'

The Consortium's accounting procedures are horribly precise. All data on changes in ore mining rates are promptly fed into a computer and so, beginning in the following month, not a red cent was deposited in Kolo's account. He had a crack at protesting, saying that he wasn't to blame if the earth had once seen fit to come apart and that there was not one whit of difference between his holding and everyone else's. But no man can argue with a machine, and what is the Consortium, if not a gigantic money-making machine?

At first Kolo got by, because he had something put away. The first blow was that he had to give up his habit of buying new shoes every week. Kolo was infuriated, not so much by the fact that now he had to wear the same pair of shoes for weeks on end, but rather because everyone else was still throwing money about without a care in the world, buying stereo sets and sports cars and endlessly trading them in. Yet that was just the beginning. A few months later Kolo's pockets were empty, and hunger was just around the corner. That well and truly shook him up.

He did try to adapt to his fate. He went to work in the quarries, where they paid well. But in return for the money they demanded honest-to-goodness work and strict discipline—things which Kolo had parted company with long before. I think he had come to believe what he had yelled that day at my door, 'We'll soon be millionaires yet!' Now that was the least he would accept, but the Consortium had no intention whatsoever of making him a millionaire. Kolo was increasingly vexed by the fact that others, for no good reason he could see, were still getting as much as before or even more, without the least inconvenience. He was offended to the depths of his soul and, having taken offense, he promptly chucked in his job and started hanging about with the Own-landers, who were ranting and raving at every street corner that the Consortium should be tossed out on its ear, that we should return as quickly as may be to fishing and goat-herding and live as our forefathers had lived. Kolo was right out of temper with the phosphates: what good were they to him? He sold his motorcycle, his television, and three sumptuous tape recorders, lost weight, became resentful, dressed in second-hand clothes and worn-out army boots dug out of the rubbish tip on the old air base, and the things he said when I was around finally made me start avoiding him. He had evidently got it fixed in his mind that I was to blame for his troubles.

I hadn't seen him for a long time before that evening, and I didn't have the foggiest idea what he was living on. After my disaster with the motorbike, I had spent a long time looking for some way to occupy myself. It hurt to think that I was now a hopeless cripple, and the aimlessness of my existence lay heavy on me. At that time the Dutch had just begun laying the polder. They put out an open call to fill the auxiliary jobs. I hemmed and hawed for a long time before I went down to the office. I was scared that they'd send me packing, like 'Where d'you think you're going, gimpy?' But I finally got the better of myself and went to inquire, and it was immediately obvious that they really did have something for me. I became a guard on the work site. They gave me a whistle and a rifle and told me that my job was to go on duty every evening, after the last shift ended.

I got the hang of my new job within a few weeks. It was fun. I would start off with a stroll along the dikes that loomed over the water, then continue across the scraps of artificial land that sloped up out of the sea. It was very quiet there in the evenings. From the harbour, beyond Cape Cataracta, you could sometimes hear a deep-throated hooting when the *Maltese Cross* was casting off or a water tanker was entering the port. All the rest of the time I was alone with my thoughts and with the seagulls that circled indolently over the water or sauntered around the dank polder with me. No one bothered us there, and little by little I taught myself to lift my legs up high and jerk my head to look behind me, like a seagull. I enjoyed doing bird impressions.

In point of fact, the polder didn't need anyone to keep an eye on it. I was really standing guard over the equipment that was left there overnight. I had to keep away any kids with an urge to break windows and stop derelicts from coming and swiping machinery parts to sell for a dram or two. I would have to drive kids off now and then with my whistle, but the derelicts must have reckoned that there would hardly be much of a market for the vehicle accessories to be had there, so they did most of their pinching in town, where they could wrench antennas and side-mirrors from parked cars.

And so I did not suspect that there was any particular danger in store when a bunch of men with crowbars and lengths of piping showed

85

up that evening around the furthermost excavator. Perhaps I would have been more upset if Kolo had not been among them.

This time Kolo was decked out in a heavy canvas jacket and pants. His outfit was too big for him: it bagged clumsily and hampered his movements. He shuffled along, dragging his feet, as though he were weighed down by an invisible burden. I couldn't help remembering how light his step had been during the new shoes era, now lost irretrievably in the mists of eternity. He was giving me sullen, searching looks.

It all seemed pretty strange to me, but it was, for all that, none other than my old mate Kolo...

When I got there, the polder was exposed to my view in all its desolation and despondency. Delia hadn't arrived yet. It was unusually stuffy; the sun's rays were having difficulty penetrating the solid yellowish haze that hung like an inverted bowl over the island. There was a dead calm; the fine phosphate dust which rose from the quarries and the ships' holds floated, canopy-like, in the air, mixing with the water-vapour. The dike which encircled the polder separated two completely identical flat gray surfaces: the one over on the other side glittered dully like the oxide coating on a lead mirror, while the one closer to me was matte.

It was a wasteland, a dreary place. The polder lived a life of its own, with puddles full of seaweed and birds that paced across the sandy surface, smooth as a table-top, in search of food. It didn't need people at all; it was sufficient unto itself. I suddenly felt quite superfluous here. There was not the slightest shelter and I was exposed on all sides to anyone who cared to look. I might as well have been translucent. This vitreous state was not pleasant, and I wanted to get out of there, on the double, and go under cover somewhere. But I had to wait for Delia.

I drove out onto the gray plain and stopped the car near a yellow plastic sheet which was stretched close to the ground on four pegs. I was curious to find out what this was—a hideout built by little boys from the outskirts of town, maybe, or perhaps a hippie encampment. Hippies are O.K. to chat with, especially if they aren't phonies and trendy poseurs but honest-to-goodness opponents of all civilization.

Three pairs of legs were sticking out from under the sheeting in various directions, clad in identical pairs of denims and sneakers which gave no clues at all as to the sex or age of their owners. As I got closer, I also noticed thin blue and white leads emerging from the sheet and running every which way. Following the leads with my eyes, I saw that they all terminated in funny little white suction cups.

My approach went unnoticed. I coughed. Nothing. I coughed hard and blew my nose loudly.

There was a quiet commotion under the sheeting. A man crawled out, rump first, and I saw that it was Professor Umbermann. The other two pairs of legs belonged to young men with droopy moustaches. They squatted down on the ground and observed me with a glum kind of look on their faces. It had struck me some time previously that droopy moustaches give young men rather a pathetic air. All three were thoroughly bedaubed with sand and clay; they looked like they had been crawling on their stomachs for quite a while. An unaccountable buzzing came from under the plastic.

'Hello there, Professor!' I greeted him, rather perplexed by all this. 'What clever stuff are you up to now?'

'Shhh!' Umbermann hissed, glancing rapidly under his awning. We're looking for earthworms.'

I bent down and took a look under the canopy. There on the ground stood some spanking new matte-finish gadgets, their nickel-plated knobs glittering. They were buzzing quietly, their dials were shining, and their coloured needles trembled, as if registering a suppressed flow of electricity. Those blue and white leads were hooked up to them.

'Well, what's this contraption?' I asked, my interest piqued.

'State-of-the-art earthworm detectors from General Electronic Systems', Umbermann remarked with unconcealed pride. 'They were developed from a line of military locating devices and are just fantastically sensitive. Only the very largest universities have them as yet, but I managed to get hold of one through UNESCO.'

He stopped talking and gave a sign to his assistants, who ambled off in opposite directions, and, checking with the schematics they carried, began to position the suction cups.

I looked closely at the dials. The trembling needles were pointing, one and all, to zero.

'Have you found any of your mutants yet?' I asked.

Umbermann shook his head sadly.

'Could the instruments be to blame for that?'

'Oh no,' the professor said with a sigh. 'You can see for yourself that their lowest reading is 0.05 EW/m^2, which means five-hundredths of an earthworm per square meter, to the depth of a meter. And I can't complain about my aides, either. They're second-year biologists from Serana University. The department head is an excellent man. They're competent lads and they're willing to go looking for worms at any moment, day or night. The only thing is, we can't find any.'

'Listen, why exactly are you looking for them here? This land has been laid artificially. Why would there be any worms here? They don't fall from the sky now, do they?'

'No, but there are none anywhere else,' Umbermann declared plaintively. 'At least there's no one to bother us here, so we can work in peace. You know, these people are a dreadful lot. They just have to walk right into you, and won't go around for anything. Look, one imbecile on the plateau drove his donkey over my hand!'

The Professor waved a hand bound up in a soiled bandage.

'I don't get it,' I said. 'Hasn't even one of your colleagues turned up to help you? I counted several dozen of them myself at the IEA meeting. You'd get on better if everyone pitched in.'

Umbermann let out an uncharacteristically sarcastic laugh.

'You actually think that those were serious scientists? My dear man, ninety percent of the people who attend scientific congresses all over the world are nothing but the adipose tissue of science. At the very best they did something constructive in their dim and distant youth, and at worst they got on a roster of scientific delegates straight from school. And so they charge about from one symposium to another, go home just to pick up clean underwear, sit in meetings with a learned look on their faces, and in fact care about nothing but the grade of hotel they'll be staying at and the activities programme. And they make contacts just for the pleasure of quoting each other in their publications.'

'That's a pretty harsh judgement. Things can't be as gloomy as all that—or can they?'

'Since you ask, there was just one serious chap at the IEA session, an African called Ababu Waldde Haled. He has written a staggering monograph on the earthworms that live in the salt-saturated soils on the Red Sea shore, to the north of Massawa. No one had ever studied them before. I think that at some point those worms will be a real help to us in our efforts to rehabilitate saline soils—and that's a problem which gets increasingly serious as more and more people go in for artificial irrigation. But I say again, he was the only one in that whole coterie who was worth the time of day. He's a brilliant fellow, only twenty-six years old, and he hasn't got blasé about his work yet.'

'But what, then—did he decide against joining you?'

'My grant isn't large enough to support the two of us. Besides, he had to get home in a hurry. He's set up some biological experiments with those worms of his, and not in a laboratory either, but out in the field. Can you imagine how much nerve that takes? So he was in a rush to get back to Asmara before the flood waters begin rising on the Anseba River, or else the whole thing will be washed away, and he'll have to start all over again next year. And every scientist's years are numbered. Let him do what he has to do out there, and I'll go after my earthworms on my own here.'

There was nothing I could say to comfort him. Umbermann took off his panama hat and wiped a handkerchief over his glossy bald spot.

'How did you get on at the Figaro?' I inquired, changing the subject.

'There's a two-month wait, an incubation period, or so the owner assures me. He tells me that with a bit of patience the hair will start growing like anything... I don't know, though—my grant runs out in two months, and then I'll have to be off. I said as much to him, but he's adamant that there's no way to hurry the process along...'

At that point I saw Delia's stylish car turning on to the polder in a cloud of dust. It's a highly recognizable shade that puts one in mind of bull's blood. The colour scheme is offered to vain and shallow-minded customers under an awesomely resonant name—'Corrida', no less. Delia actually is infatuated with all that smacks of hispanic passion and mystery. I cut Umbermann short and hurried off to meet her.

Her gaze was tense and her lips were dry with agitation: she had to keep wetting them with her tongue. Either because of that or because of the cigarette that she was shifting from side to side in her mouth, the lipstick had smudged on her lower lip, making her mouth look lopsided. But the self-confident smile never left her face.

We moved away from the car. There wasn't a soul near, if you don't count the seagulls.

'What's going on?' I asked.

Delia stopped and gave me a probing look.

'The thing is, my lad, that we're going to have to put on a wedding.'

'Going to have to?' was all I could find to say before the next surprise knocked the breath out of me.

'Yes, sad to say. You understand, of course—I mean, you're not an idiot. It's all very simple. I'm pregnant. And don't go to all the trouble of wondering what else it could be—it's all been weighed and discarded. I don't much care for the idea of an abortion. My nerves are too sensitive and my imagination's too lively. But I don't fancy bringing up a child alone, either. Besides, you've sworn a good twenty times that you love me. In that case, it's all turned out for the very best. I dare to hope that I'll make you a reasonable wife—I mean, I am rather fond of you. I don't doubt that you understand that, because otherwise things wouldn't have gone as far as they did. I'm no tart.'

Her beautiful face was mottled with agitation. It was difficult to tell if she was levelling with me: her emotional state ran conspicuously counter to her logical and well-considered arguments. So I was all confused at first. 'A trap,' was what flitted through my head. To that point I had looked on our affair as a pleasant interlude, an adventure, and I was in no way prepared to take on any sort of responsibility. That scared me. 'A trap,' I repeated doggedly, and then my defence mechanisms kicked in. My brain started looking for ways out. Procedures for extricating myself zipped one after the other through my head. I didn't even take the time to think what a heel I was being—I was, after all, seriously attracted to the girl.

'But it can't be done,' I said, as gently as I could. 'I'm on temporary assignment to Minore, I'm footloose. Any day now I'll get a new posting, I'll pack my bags, and perhaps I'll never come back. You've got a home here, your parents live here...'

'I'll go with you,' Delia announced decisively. 'Would I be the first woman to follow her husband? Perhaps I would have left anyway—it's hard to breathe here. But you know how complicated they make it for us.'

That's it, then—a wedding ring guarantees an exit visa. It's a trap with long-range sights, I insisted to myself, still working hard on believing it.

'I hate to tell you this, but I've never even thought about getting married. I'm incorrigibly footloose. It's always seemed to me that in this day and age there's nothing more normal than a no-strings relationship between a man and woman.'

Delia's thick black eyebrows pulled in over the bridge of her nose.

'And I was stupid enough to believe that you really did love me!' she exclaimed bitterly.

'Of course I do,' I hastily assured her. 'But as for getting married...'

'Stop repeating yourself!' Delia interrupted my pathetic burbling. 'Now I see. You thought I was one of those flighty pieces, of whom you, I wouldn't doubt, have had plenty in your time. All you know about love is what happens between the sheets!'

'Now that's not fair!' I tried to object.

'No, it's not. And I intend to keep that up. I'll teach you a lesson, and do you know how? I'll go to a newsman in some other agency who thinks you're as much fun as a hole in the head, and I'll just happen to tell him quite a remarkable story. Something like this, perhaps—there is in Antafagusta a certain sex-mad correspondent who travels around the world under the protection of an official passport, and all he ever does is doublecross the trusting citizens of friendly countries and all he really wants is to make unmarried mothers of them. Do you think anyone would pass up on the chance to cramp your style? I'm even sorry for you. It'll be goodbye Charlie, the end of your career. But what's to be done? It's your own fault.'

'Your're not serious.'

'Why not? After what you've said to me, why should I make it easy on you? I didn't think you could be this callous. Obviously, I don't know much about people, or I'd never have let you anywhere near me.'

'But, I mean ... couldn't we come to some kind of agreement?' I was still trying to wriggle out of it.

Delia pursed her lips.

'Possibly. But only if you have second thoughts. Curiously enough, I still seem to have a thing about you, although you're not worth it. But anyway, think it over. You might just find that you have a shred of humanity in you somewhere.'

Play for time, you've got to play for time so you can finesse this, I told myself: just so long as we don't actually break up, because then she really will carry out her threat. She'll have cooled down tomorrow and she'll be able to come to a more sober judgement, if only on what's best for her.

'I have to think,' I murmured.

'Very well,' Delia agreed. 'I can see you're not at your best right now. Isn't it strange, though? I make you a proposal and you ask for time to think! Shouldn't it be the other way round? But there's all this role reversal going on these days, whether we like it or not. Chickens are crowing and roosters are clucking—and I'm not a bit keen on it. I suppose I must be old-fashioned. Too bad. But please don't drag it out—I have feelings too.'

She gave me her hand in passing and went towards the car, stepping lightly. Delia's tall, shapely figure in her dark brown suit stood out sharply against the diffuse gray background of the polder, as if she had been placed there by an artist's hand. I suddenly felt such loneliness, bathed in the light of that unframed painting, as I had never before felt and for a moment I had a flickering urge to chase after Delia, to call her back and say, 'Yes of course we'll get married, we'll be together for ever, but don't let's have any more of this loneliness!' But a calculating level-headedness immediately overcame the turmoil inside me, and I stayed put. Delia got into her car and sped off, raising clouds of dust.

In the distance, Professor Umbermann was crawling on his stomach under his yellow canopy and prayerfully looking at his instrument readouts...

'Stemo! What have you done?'

That outburst rocks me again and again. People are swarming about by the bright yellow machine. Someone is being propped up on both sides, and he's dragging one leg. That person is Kolo.

First I told them that unauthorized individuals were not allowed in that area, and that my job was to keep things in order around there. They had no business being on the work site. There were lots of different pieces of machinery left all over the place, because the work would be continuing tomorrow. An ignoramus could accidentally damage one of the tools, and I was responsible for them all.

True, I had read in the papers about the Own-landers' campaign against the letter of intent to have the Dutch come and lay a polder. They were perhaps right, in a way, to insist that we do all the work ourselves. That would have employed a lot of people who didn't know what to do with themselves and were idling their days away on the proceeds from the phosphates. It would have employed people who were struggling to make ends meet, too, and those with an axe to grind, like Kolo. But the government was of the opinion that it made no sense to wait while earth was brought to the bay in wheelbarrows, nor were they going to buy expensive equipment for this one project. And anyway, where would we find people who knew how to operate those machines? It would be different if we were meaning to turn all of Minore's bays into dry land. The Dutch were a different kettle of fish altogether: they had reclaimed half of their country from the sea. They had all they needed to do the job, and it was just a question of getting the things there and starting them up.

I had chanced to see some Own-lander demonstrations on Britannic Boulevard. They usually carried big placards that read, 'Dutch go home! Our sea is ours!' My first thought now was that they had just come to wave some of their placards. I also thought that it was a lot of rubbish, and that I'd have time to get rid of them before people showed up for work. Everything would be fine and the Dutch would know nothing about it.

'Shut your noise, old son!' Kolo said in a voice I didn't know.

The others paid me no attention at all. They had dispersed among the excavators and bulldozers, scattering like peas out of a pod. A moment later there was a metallic clang, then another. I heard the jingle of shattered glass.

I hurried to the machines. Two Own-landers were bashing at a bulldozer with crowbars. One headlight was already broken.

I jerked the rifle from my shoulder.

'Back!' I roared. 'Back! Now!'

The strangers froze for a moment, and glanced in my direction. Then one of them hefted his crowbar again.

Raising my weapon, I fired into the air over their heads. The shot thundered out as deafeningly as a cannon round. The echo came straight back from the nearest cliff.

The one who was wielding the crowbar dropped it behind his back in fright. They both doubled over and ran for it. I grabbed my whistle and a piercing sound tore through the silence that had reigned after the gunshot. I could hear footsteps on the other side of the bulldozer too. There you go, I thought: you've pulled it off! Now they'll skedaddle. A nervous shudder went through me: it finally sank in that these were really vicious people. They could have laid into me at the drop of a hat.

Good thing I had fired straight off. Who knows what they might have got up to—setting out to cripple the machines with neither rhyme nor reason, blasted maniacs that they are! Surely they don't imagine for a moment that this is the way to influence the government?

I stood motionless by the bulldozer and listened to the footsteps receding into the distance.

Suddenly I heard more banging and again there was the jingle of glass. That got me going. My artifical leg stumping heavily on the ground, I hoofed it in the direction of the noise.

Kolo had clambered up onto the big wheel of a huge, brand-new yellow excavator and was belabouring the cab windows with a length of piping. Once again huge wheels, shod in thick black tires, started whirling before my eyes.

'Get back, Kolo!' I roared. 'Get away right now, do you hear?'

He made a brief turn toward me.

'Push off!' he barked malevolently, and stove in another window.

'Back, or I'll give you a taste of lead!' I yelled, sliding back the bolt.

'To hell with you, peg-leg!' Kolo howled in fury, still working the machine over.

A dreadful, unbearable pain struck my left leg, the leg that was gone. I always feel that pain when I'm very upset. My jumbled up nerve endings literally start striking sparks and leave me groaning and gritting my teeth.

Hiking my rifle, I aimed at Kolo's straddled legs—at the left one, just below the knee—and squeezed the trigger. I didn't hear a report; I don't know whether there was one or not. Perhaps something odd happened and the bullet came flying out without a sound. I know only one thing: I heard, and can still hear to this day, Kolo's piercing cry,

'Stemo! What have you done?...'

The doctor gives me a serious look, rubs his chin ruminatively, and asks, 'Sometimes you feel that you're Artur Yanno and sometimes that you're Stemo Kulamar? Don't force yourself, you're still a bit rocky. If it's true, just nod your head. And now that you're wide awake, you definitely feel that you're Artur Yanno? You're nodding, that's good. This means that your brain generates the sensation of being Stemo Kulamar only during periods of rest. I hope this will help us with the treatment. That bothers you? Don't be afraid. There's nothing much wrong. It's not the first time this has happened. You've just had a bad concussion and that's all it is. Now try to calm down—completely calm now—relax and get some rest. You have nothing to fear. Try to stop yourself as much as possible from remembering unpleasant events. Don't go dredging up from your memory anything that has ever shocked or scared you. Keep your mind working on little details, so that your brain will more quickly come to grips with the trauma it has suffered...'

He says more, he's still talking, but I'm in no condition to listen. I seem to be drowning in something very ethereal, something beaten to a froth. Doing as the doctor told me, I calm down completely. My feet and hands suddenly become warm and very heavy. My whole body is flooded with heaviness. I start to feel good. Nothing worries me any more. The difficult questions are gone, and this is my chance to stick with life's little details. But they keep getting mixed up with all sorts of terrible things—and I'd like to know why, I'd so much like to know why ...

7

Without a shadow of a doubt, it's the best report I have ever filed. I am well aware that my things rarely have that touch of immediacy. They're often airy-fairy in style. You get the feeling that I'm making a big deal of my intellectual superiority over the reader, and that, of course, puts people off. I mean, these days our readers don't take kindly to being preached at—which is not to say that anyone has ever found it all that enjoyable. And who can blame them? There really does seem to be an inordinate number of preachy people about just now.

This report, though, wasn't like that at all. I am pretty good at judging my own articles dispassionately—though not until after they're finished. If I could do it while I was writing, it would be a piece of cake to step into the shoes of a Walter Lippmann or a Sulzberger, who are syndicated in at least eighty major and minor newspapers every single day, and who, I wouldn't wonder, view any fellow newsie with anything less than a Nobel prize as a talentless workhorse eking out an existence in some belletristic backwoods.

Thanks to my contacts in the administration of the Antafagusta police force, whose pub crawls I have lavishly financed, I got to the scene sooner than the other reporters, only twenty minutes after it happened. They had just taken the headliner away and all the secondary personages and eye witnesses were still on the scene and still rather upset. They turned out to be all women, and they were milling about on the pavement under the large gold-framed letters MNB, this being a branch of the Minoran National Bank. In the evening those letters were also outlined in bright lilac neon—the Minoran National Bank has quite a thing about lilac; its cheques and teller tokens are lilac too—but in daylight those ponderous letters exude a dull blackness, for all the world like a bank safe with its door ajar. The noisily agitated women seemed out of place against those mirror-like windows adorned with their golden monogram but I had an immediate hunch that women had played the central role in what had happened.

Some distance away, a white motorcycle lay on its side by the kerb.

It all started some thirty minutes after the bank opened, at about half past nine in the morning, when the place was drowning in customers. The bank outlets on Minore always have more business than they can manage. Ever since the Consortium began mining in several large quarries simultaneously and thousands of erstwhile farmers began receiving monthly royalties for the phosphates mined from their land, and especially after the government had accumulated sufficient funds to start handing out pensions, allowances, and various welfare supplements, almost every Minoran has had to go to the bank once a week or so. Many people started spending huge amounts of time there, and monetary transactions became a favourite occupation. The former paupers, who had suffered for ages on the barren plateau where the plots dried into dust and the goat pastures shrivelled in the heat, got no end of fun out of watching the amounts in their savings books grow week after week. They weren't at all put out by the fact that minares were declining in value and bought less as time went on. The numbers in the accounts still went beyond their wildest dreams.

At about that time, the bank started running short of personnel. While more and more people were receiving money, no one was interested in grinding over columns of figures any more. When the old tellers—those who had been trained by the English during the Protectorate—began to retire, windows started going unmanned. Some of the branches had to be closed altogether and then a veritable howl went up: people were being deprived of their favourite pastime, and no way did they want their money sent by mail. There were sporadic rebellions to defend the people's banking rights, and they were impossible to quell since the police wanted the branches reopened too. The government, struggling to keep itself in power, had no choice but to start hiring mainland workers in Serana. But, while the Consortium's generous wages attracted brawny and willing workers and well-trained machinery technicians for the phosphate quarries, the only ones interested in becoming bank clerks were illiterate girls, too stupid or lazy to finish school, who weren't exactly career-minded. They were forever getting their numbers wrong and, because of their shaky command of the language, couldn't always understand what the Minorans were telling them. The customers had to rewrite their cheques over and over, and endless queues became a permanent fixture in the banks. Thousands of people spent hours lined up in front of the windows, with a book or some knitting.

Anyway, as I was saying, at about nine thirty that morning, a strange-looking man who seemed to have no face entered the branch on Adomar Street. Unceremoniously elbowing through the queue in the doorway, he pushed his way inside. The people at the tail of the queue immediately started muttering their disapproval. The newcomer ignored them completely. He raised his hand over his head, and in a loud, jangling voice cried out,

'This is a holdup! Nobody move, or I'll shoot!'

Everyone turned toward the sound, and saw a pistol glittering in the robber's upraised hand. He gave everyone a minute to scrutinize the weapon, then started pushing toward the barrier. At that point it became clear what was wrong with his face: he had a nylon stocking over his head, which sort of erased his features.

But if he thought that his firearm would scare the customers, he had another think coming. The only people who went stockstill, their faces pale, were two tellers on the other side of the counter.

The rest of the densely packed mass of people jammed into the room began to sway in agitation and showed no particular desire to let him through.

'Stop monkeying about!' a big-nosed old woman in a black kerchief yelled piercingly. 'You want to skip the queue, eh? Crafty, aren't you? Well, you can whistle for it—we were here first.'

Another woman—elderly, burly, and obviously a mother several times over—made toward him, her eyes glittering with fury. Face-to-face with the busty matron, the robber suddenly looked scrawny and pathetic.

'Hush up!' the matron flapped a hand at him, as though driving away a tiresome cat. 'We know your tricks! Last week we had one come running in, whining that his little 'un was poorly and he needed cash in a hurry to get the child to the doctor. And afterwards I saw him with my own eyes in the bushes behind the market, carousing with his mates. That's what he needed the money for!'

'This is a holdup!' the man cried again in a strained voice. 'Everyone get back, and give me the money or I'll shoot!'

He was waving a massive great bag around in his free hand, but, try as he might, he couldn't get to the counter. He hesitated for a moment, then slung the bag over people's heads, and it landed with a loud slap on the barrier. He was still brandishing his pistol uncomfortably over his head, because otherwise no one would have seen that he was armed. Besides, he probably couldn't stomach the idea of poking the barrel right into the crowd. You can only aim a firearm at a person from a distance: if you touch your target with the barrel, it's not a bit different than killing with your bare hands.

The old woman in the black kerchief, pushing her way nimbly through the crowd, grabbed the robber's raised arm.

'Stop your clowning! Get cracking—into that queue, before we throw you out!' she roared angrily, dragging with all her might at her victim's sleeve. The pistol held aloft in the robber's hand made big circles high in the air. 'You think you're so smart—yes, but we're not falling for your fairy-stories about bandits.'

'This is a holdup!' the stranger tried again, but his voice broke, and it all sounded pretty feeble.

At that instant, a shot rang out. The bullet hit the ceiling, sprinkling plaster down onto people's heads. Either the robber's nerves had given out or the combative old dear had overdone it, but for whatever reason the pistol went off in his hand.

An elderly woman with a child in her arms was standing by the door. When he heard the gunfire, the little tyke began to whimper. He had a unique way of being scared.

'Gra-a-anma, I wanna wee-weee!'

'The rascal, he's frightened the child!' the grandmother wailed. 'I'll be back in a jiffy—don't take my place.'

She elbowed her way to the door. Then the women really got cross.

'Hooligan!' the cry went up all around. 'To the clink with him! Give him what for! There's no peace with 'em, day or night!'

Women were closing in on the robber from all sides. He was so hedged about that he couldn't even lower his arm. Someone hit him in the back with such force that he dropped his pistol, and a forward little chit took his massive sack off the barrier and, with vociferous approval from the crowd, pulled it down over its owner's head.

Dragging the bag off his head and lashing out in all directions with his arms and legs, the disarmed thief began to fall back toward the door. The shouting and general hubbub among the women grew louder. He beat a hard-fought retreat under blows that rained down on him from right and left. One of the tellers, shaking herself to life, phoned for the police.

Having finally got out into the street, the thief manqué jumped onto a motorbike, a big white Suzuki, that was parked by the kerb. He had left the engine running, evidently expecting to make a quick getaway. But the engine was dead.

The fugitive tried to start his bike, but he couldn't get a peep out of it. Seeing the infuriated women pouring out after him like a swarm of irritated wasps, he knocked the Suzuki off its stand and tried to get it going by running it down the slope. But every time he let the clutch out, the motorcycle stood as if rooted to the spot, not giving a single solitary 'putt' to cheer him. He had just stopped after his third unsuccessful run and flopped weakly onto the seat, gulping air through the thick brownish nylon stocking, when a blue and white police car came into view round the corner, its siren wailing. The stunned felon made no attempt to get away or resist. As the policemen jumped out of the moving car and approached him, their pistols at the ready, he obediently stretched out both hands to them. The handcuffs clicked on. He got off his white Suzuki, which slowly began to tip sideways. He gave it a look full of despair and then, suddenly furious, kicked it so hard that the motorbike jingled plaintively and the thief himself almost went flying.

The old woman with the little tyke in her arms stood on the pavement chortling, with a pleased look on her face. She was obviously having a good time, and was in no hurry to get back in the queue. By the time I arrived on the scene, she had already bored everyone else with her story, so she buttonholed me to explain what she found so amusing.

'I came out on the street and wasn't I just vexed to death with that hooligan! The little lad was that frightened he nearly wet his pants, and he's nervous enough as it is. So I come out and there's his chatterbox rattling away, confound him. I saw him riding up myself. I was surprised, too—just look, I says to myself, what some folk will squeeze themselves into, just so they can outswank everyone else!

Well, I'll show you a thing or two! I went up to it, unscrewed the cap, and I tells the lad to wee-wee into his petrol tank. "Go on," I says. "Do as much as you can." The little fellow was that glad, and he starts going. Then I put the cap back on. The motorcycle was still rattling a bit, and there was a smell of steam from the back end. Then not another whisper. Serves him right, I thought. Now he'll have to wheel his old jalopy home and let him puzzle out there what's to do with it. But that wasn't the half of it—the police caught him, confound the man. And praise be for that—what kind of law and order is there when any scoundrel can come banging away with his shooting iron in a public place and frightening the children?'

I had never written a report like it. It was colorful, it had psychological sidelights... If that wasn't front page goods, I thought, then something's gone thoroughly awry in the world. I was already relishing the idea of Avik Nersesyan going green with envy and wiping that omniscient grin off his face. Not to worry, let him tough it out. Haven't I had to shrug it off enough times when I was pipped at the post by other people? Now my luck's turned.

Oh, the naive self-delusion! The following day, when I was putting the final polish on my story, top management got onto a new hobby-horse. It was all to do with some thrice-be-damned shellfish—glutinous muck which I personally cannot abide. Some con artist from the scientific world was making all sorts of racket about how he had raised shellfish of record-breaking size by introducing warm effluent into shallow bays, which put him on the brink of solving the protein supply problem that our overpopulated planet, under constant threat of famine, presently faces. No two ways about it—he must have had a relative or at the very least a close acquaintance on our agency's board of directors. Publicity like that doesn't come easy. For ten days all the front pages had nothing but shellfish, under banner headlines, and my piece just couldn't compete. Then somebody discovered that the shellfish were unfit for human consumption because they stank of sewage and went off a few hours after being gathered. So it was all a lot of fuss over nothing.

Unfortunately, my brilliant report had gone stale too in the meanwhile, and Avik Nersesyan, of all people, consigned it to the round file without turning a hair.

I won't write another like it, not in the foreseeable future...

I sat on the balcony, surveying the shore for want of anything better to do. Our building faces west, and the balconies are in the shade until dinnertime, but after that the devilish heat drives people indoors. The building stands right behind Cape Cataracta and it used to have a staggering view over the sea. Besides, it's quieter and more peaceful here than on the other side of the cape, on Britannic Boulevard. The view has been completely spoiled since they laid the polder, but I didn't have far to go to work while the project was still on. Now the gray polder stretches out before me, flat and unbroken, except for a strange yellow plastic canopy which had appeared the week before and the three mysterious figures that pottered around it from morning to night. At first I kind of thought that they were surveyors who had come to slice the polder into pieces like a pie. But then I saw that they hadn't brought a tripod with them and that they spent most of the time on their hands and knees, not walking upright like anybody normal. Once I was on the point of going to see what kind of people they were, but somehow I just couldn't find the time. That's my story, at least. It looks like I don't even want to admit to myself that I've been avoiding the polder since that night when Kolo was there, yelling, 'Stemo! What have you done?'

I was sitting on the balcony in the cool of the morning, looking down at the deserted shore and the little boats beached high on the whitish sand. They belonged to people who lived nearby. The white, red and gray rowing boats—pair-oars and four-oars they were—looked to be taking a breather, each in its own spot beyond the breakers' reach. To protect them from the wind, their owners had built sandbanks up between them, but with time the banks had been flattened and now were visible only from up here, on the second floor, from where they looked like barely noticeable hillocks, and only when the light was falling aslant, at that.

One of them—the little bright blue craft in the row nearest the sea—was mine. I used to enjoy rowing out to drop a line or two. Rocking on the waves without a care in the world, pulling up the hooks ever so often, and getting a bite now and then, with any luck—there's never a dull moment. But ever since they laid the sewage pipe out there, the little inlet they left between the cape and the polder is always full of soap suds and all kinds of rubbish, especially when the wind is from seaward. It's disgusting to row through and there's not a fish within miles, so my boat stays on the shore. I noticed that its paint was already starting to fade.

So there I sat, my gaze wandering over the polder. Those little strangers were darting here and there in their unaccountable enthusiasm, dragging wires behind them; I had seen those wires once when I had bestirred myself to go and get my binoculars. Then there was a ring at the door and Murana appeared with the news that a young man was asking to speak to me.

The lad was thin and very young. He was obviously going to a great deal of trouble to grow a stylish droopy mustache, but the results of all his hard work left something to be desired. He was dressed as they all are nowadays—in a blue canvas blouse with an indescribably grimy shirt showing under his unbuttoned waistcoat. It took some doing, but you could make out that it had once been chequered. The lad's lack of confidence showed in the earnest way he was trying to chew gum and smoke a cigarette at the same time. There wasn't much room in his mouth for words, and I had to concentrate hard

99

if I wanted to make anything out.

'I'm Roxy's boyfriend,' he announced, to start things off. 'You can just call me Tell.'

I nodded, more or less automatically. This bolstered his nerve.

'You know, man...' he began, then the smoke sent him into a coughing fit. Pulling out of it, he continued, 'Roxy and me would like to cut loose a bit. You can't sit about for ever, get me? You need to cut loose while there's time and you're still of a mind to. Because later on you go stupid, you get rocks in the head, and then you're stuck, get me? Right, then, so we need wheels. You don't get far on Shanks' pony these days, get me? You just slip us the ready for a chopper and we're off. Deal, is it?'

He tilted his head to one side, lifted the tiny cigarette stub to his mouth and enveloped himself in a thick cloud of smoke. The boy's barefaced impudence actually tickled me at first, but then I felt my temper rising.

'Roxana!' I shouted into the next room.

Murana appeared in the doorway.

'She isn't here. She's been gone since morning,' my wife said, with a helpless gesture.

'She's at my place,' the lad announced coolly. 'And not since this morning but since last night.'

I looked at Murana. She lowered her eyes.

'And what exactly is she doing at your place, my young friend?' I inquired.

'We're going together,' he replied, not batting an eye.

A sharp pain stifled the flash of anger. How had I missed it? Roxana had grown up. But when? How quickly the years sneak by! I had been all wrapped up in myself, my motorcycle, my accident, my boat, my money and my drugs, and I had not noticed life going on its merry way and passing me by, as though I did not exist.

'And precisely why should I give you money for a motorbike?' I asked, staying very calm.

'Who else would?' the boy exclaimed in surprise. 'I mean, you're Roxy's old man! My old man's a ragtag, works like a carthorse in an office—he doesn't make enough to buy a pedal-bike.'

I gave the scrawny kid the once-over. He looked to be about sixteen. They were still children: Roxana herself was only fourteen. What was all this? For a moment I imagined my tender little girl in the company of this grubby guttersnipe with his insolent stare, and everything went dark before my eyes. I stood up so abruptly that I knocked my chair over. The boy bounded to his feet and took up a defensive judo stance. Murana imploringly stretched out her hands to me from the doorway.

'You scram, sharpish, and stay out of my sight. And tell Roxana to hustle herself home right now or be ready to suffer the consequences!' I bawled in a voice that made the lad flinch.

A second later he was looking at me with the evil glare of a rodent backed into a corner and screeching, 'Then they're surprised that young people don't like them! What's there to like when you're a miserable pinch-penny and a mope with rocks in your head? The slightest thing and you start bellowing and waving your arms like clapping in irons and being deported's too good for you! As if that money's worth anything to you—you're too far gone to enjoy it.'

I let fly sharply in the boy's direction. He started back and disappeared through the door.

'Why be that way about it?' Murana whispered. 'I mean, Roxana...'

'Never mind, she'll come,' I snapped irately. I could not admit that it was gnawing at me too.

But she didn't come. All day, until evening, I paced to and fro in the flat, like a caged animal, went outside three times to look, and was very sorry that I had not kept a better grip on myself. I should have come on all friendly at first and got him to tell me where his hang-out was—that's where I would have found Roxana.

At dinnertime on the following day I had a phone call from Heaven's Orderlies. They told me that they had Roxana. Was she safe and sound? I yelled down the phone. She was safe and sound, a weary female voice replied, but there was so much unspoken meaning between the lines of the answer that my heart grew heavy as a rock.

Roxana was in the open ward at the shelter, deep in an unwholesome sort of sleep. She was flanked by seven companions in misfortune. Murana and I scarcely recognised our daughter in the pale, dishevelled creature we saw sleeping on that iron cot. They had found her early that morning by the port, drunk as a skunk on alcohol and on drugs too, quite possibly. They had picked up three other teenagers, almost children, along with her. No one could explain how they had got there, or who had thrown the party they had left to go and get some shut-eye between the containers down by the berths. It just so happened that there was a receipt or bill in Roxana's pocket with the name 'Kulamar' and our phone number on it. The rest were still unidentified.

They asked us to look at our daughter's friends, in the hope that we could give some idea of who they were. The lady on duty was a little surprised when it turned out that we didn't know them. True, one of them was Tell, but we knew nothing about him except what he called himself, and perhaps that was a nickname. The lady looked at us with unveiled sympathy.

Heaven's Orderlies started their work here quite a long time ago, when it became obvious that the police and other authorities were simply lacking the manpower to clear the drunks and vagrants off the streets and send them somewhere where they could sleep it off and pull themselves together without offending the sensibilities of their fellow citizens. The drug addict problem gets worse by the year. I think that the Orderlies are somehow connected with the Salvation

Army; in any event, they get support from the Vatican and the occasional hand-out from our government. And they're irreplaceable now. It's just awful to think what would go on in the streets without them. Their dark gray ambulances with shaded windows show up all over the place, staffed by men and women in gray outfits cut in a style that makes you think of a monk's habit and an army uniform both at once. There is one of their nondescript shelters in just about every town and village, housed more often than not in an old stone building from the colonial period, and over the exit, all day and all through the night, the letters HO burn like a token of charity, picked out in cherry-red neon.

They let us take Roxana. She didn't wake up when we carried her to the çar but came round later at home in her own bed. Murana and I had decided that when she woke up we would not say a word about what had happened. None of it could be changed, so the less said about it the better. A little later, when she had recovered from all of this and raised the subject herself—that would be different. No point in rushing things.

But the conversation came sooner than we expected. Toward evening, when Roxana had slept all she wanted to, she suddenly presented herself in the soiled denim rags she had been wearing the night before when she had taken her tumble in the port. Murana had hidden them in the bathroom so they could be washed and disinfected, but the girl had turned them up and put them on again.

'Where did you find me?' she asked, as if we were the ones at fault. 'And where's Tell?'

'Child,' I said, 'there's something we need to agree on. Keep your questions to yourself and your mother and I will like it very much if we never hear Tell's name mentioned under this roof again.'

Roxana's bruised eyes glittered.

'If I'm a child, you're another!' she bawled, repulsively shrill as any fishwife. 'He's my boyfriend, and you can just stop lecturing me! I'm ashamed enough as it is that you're so grabby—you just couldn't part with the money, could you? Poor Tell was going out of his mind—he wanted a motorbike so badly. We could have gone on trips. And now he's going to have to lift it!'

'If he wants a bike all that badly, he should work and save some money.' I was staying very calm.

'Work!' Roxana mimicked me sarcastically. 'Aren't you the clever one! How hard do you work for the money they give you? Knock yourself out from morning 'til night don't you, poor thing? So why should Tell be anybody's pack mule? And did anyone even take the trouble to think how psychologically sensitive he is?'

'Love, your father has worked hard enough in his time.' Murana was trying to smooth feathers.

'Oh sure, when he was a kid, feeding goats out on the plateau. I've heard it a thousand times!' Roxana taunted. 'And the whole world is supposed to make that up to him until the very end of his days. And that's his only advice to everyone—if at first you don't succeed...'

'That's enough!' I said. 'Among all else, I've paid your way all your life, so don't go fouling your own nest. Everyone should build his own future—but better not do it on borrowed money, or it'll all collapse before you know it.'

Roxana was unstoppable by then. She wasn't about to listen to anything I said.

'But you see I know that you call my generation the Little Sharks. You're always giving us a bad time, saying that we want it all but we've done nothing to deserve it. Maybe that's true. Only didn't you bring us up like that? We know how short life is. There's not enough time for anything if you start from nowhere. Maybe we want everything that real people have. You're old—all you have to do is keep a hold on what you've got. And we need the whole world! And everything in it. We want all those neat things that the foreigners bring in. What makes us worse than them? Why don't we have them? Because you've grabbed all the money and written your daft laws?'

There was more than a bit of truth in all this. Quite some time back our government set down some very tough restrictions which turned everything that isn't an absolute necessity into a luxury and put it under embargo. And on the rare occasion when things of that sort are imported they always cost the earth. But it's for our own good, after all, so we won't fritter away our vital foreign currency reserves. The special government accounts have to keep growing. According to estimates based on birthrate and mortality figures, twenty years down the line, when the Consortium has finished up here, there will have to be five hundred thousand dollars stashed away for every Minoran citizen. With that money, any one of us who has not turned up his toes by then will be able to begin a new life on this devastated island. Or, if that proves to be impossible, we can start afresh somewhere else.

I had a crack at explaining all this to Roxana, but got nowhere. She simply wasn't listening to me.

'I want to live now, like everyone else—not in twenty years when we're all old and doddery and can't tell sour from salty. We're not about to become manure for our children to grow on! Go on, call us Little Sharks if you like—but we have the right to live any way we want!'

She was carpeting us, apparently, instead of the other way round. It suddenly dawned on me why the port is always thronged with people when the *Maltese Cross* docks, why there's always that incessant whisper—'Are you selling anything? Anything to sell?'

To tell the truth, nothing we could have said to Roxana would have made her stop and think. But everything was still going along relatively well until I told her that she was no longer allowed out in the evenings. The girl went beserk. She screamed that she'd have the entire building on its ear if she was locked in. I very nearly swatted her, but my instincts told me that if I were to hit Roxana right then she would have to be dragged home forcibly, and that was a revolting prospect. Our family suddenly fell apart. Roxana flung some ugly words into our faces, mine and her mother's. Murana was weeping soundlessly, as any good but not very bright woman would when she stands powerless before the complexities of life. I was pathetically trying to maintain at least a semblance of family unity. Otherwise, I thought, it'll all go to hell in a handbasket.

Roxana left, taking her victory with her.

Until darkness fell, I sat on the balcony in the fresh air and bit my nails. I was overwhelmed by a mad craving for a cigarette, but I had stopped smoking in the drug dependency center and I was not at all sure that if I started again I could stick to ordinary cigarettes. I'd just have to tough it out, no matter what. The sun was taking an aggravatingly long time to set. It just hung suspended over the sea, a glowing ball that was belting out heat and making the whole universe unbearably stuffy. On the other side of Cape Cataracta, by the port entrance, a water tanker was hooting lazily, gratingly. Evidently it was waiting for the pilot to come out, while he, as often happened, had a broken motorboat to contend with or was soused to the gills, but for whatever reason he just couldn't seem to get under way.

The polder was already engulfed in twilight, but reflected sunshine the colour of molten copper was glancing off the windows of our building. Those crackpots down by the yellow canopy were still pottering about, but now they were carrying lamps—pretending to be fireflies, probably.

Going back into the room, I brought out the rifle with the range-finder. I had not touched it since the day I had pulled the trigger out there on the polder. But before that I had often taken it down to the target range because I liked to shoot a bit, just to keep my hand in. I had once been a pretty good shot.

Hoisting the rifle, I aimed at the yellow canopy. A boy dressed in jeans was the first thing that appeared in the eyepiece. My finger trembled on the trigger—wasn't that Tell? With one stroke I could rid myself of all troubles—he was the evil spirit that had turned Roxana's head! I raised the rifle barrel and a stranger's face, framed by a dark beard, came into the sights. Gripped with disappointment, I lowered the rifle. So much for my terrifically simple solutions. Again I hoisted the rifle. The lenses caught reflections from the sun that was now hugging on the horizon, dazzling me. When my sight came back, the eyepiece held a bald-headed man—certainly not a youngster, although he was dressed like the first one I had seen. He was waving his arms and jawing away. I would have laid any odds that he had a disgusting womanish voice and everything that came out of his mouth was damn stuff and nonsense. That man irritated me. He looked exactly the part—a trendy sermonizer come to bamboozle our children.

I aimed at him for a long time, and relished it. At the head first. I imagined what would happen if I squeezed the trigger—the bullet would smash his egg-like skull into large yellowish pieces, which would flake away like slate. He would fall silent in the middle of a word, and would no longer be able to trot out those idiotic lectures of his that resembled nothing so much as the doleful hooting of the tanker beyond the cape. The hooting would stop too, no doubt, because they were Siamese twins. Next I moved the crosshairs to the eggpate's chest, to the left breast pocket of his denim waistcoat. If I squeezed the trigger now, the force of the bullet would throw him two steps back, would pitch him backward onto the yellow canopy. Then everything would get snarled up—the wires would tangle and get twisted, and they wouldn't go snaking across the polder any more. Bloody denim freaks—they're all sickening but the most sickening of all are the old codgers who trick themselves out like snot-nosed kids, try to butter them up, and fill our boys' and girls' heads with all sorts of foolishness. Our children wouldn't act so daft if they weren't around. They're the ones who hunker down in front of our kids and then start chuntering on. They're the ones who take a thick-witted delight in getting kids too young to know any better all up in arms, so as to turn them into cretins just like themselves—in a world of their own for the rest of their lives.

My finger wrenched the trigger.

There was a loud clack that seemed to rattle right through me. I stared stupidly at the rifle with the rangefinder which I held in my hands, and felt the sweat breaking out on my forehead. Slowly, laboriously, I turned my eyes to the yellow canopy. I was afraid of what I was going to see, yet at the same time I couldn't stop myself from looking. What I saw astounded me. They were footing around the yellow canopy, as if nothing had happened.

Not too sure what was going on, I slid back the bolt. From the chamber popped an unexploded round, a brass cartridge case with a bronze-coloured bullet. I carefully took hold of it, as if it could go off at any moment.

The firing pin had made a deep dent on the percussion cap.

It's what we call Russian roulette. There's one bullet in the revolver cylinder and you spin it without looking, and then pull the trigger. I had noticed that life is often nothing more than a game of Russian roulette. The last time, on my Honda, I had lost. This time I had been lucky. Everything was all right, and there was justice in this world...

The telephone was ringing insistently. I didn't want to pick it up, but the jangling finally got on my nerves.

'Artur Yanno speaking.'

There was a rustling noise in the earpiece, as if someone was taking a deep and noisy breath. Then a coarse, rather husky male voice said,

'You're a son of a bitch, Artur Yanno! A stopper for any barrel and a bourgeois stooge, and a putrid revisionist as well.'

'I don't find your obscenities particularly hilarious. Do you have anything to say to me?'

'Just wait a bit, you stinking swine. This is for the good of your health,' the stranger declared, quite unfazed. 'If you want to know what's in store for you, first listen while I tell you what you are. After all, greetings are mandatory in polite society, aren't they?'

My caller chuckled, pleased with his own joke. Something prompted me not to do anything rash so I didn't hang up.

'All right, listen carefully, you stinker,' the stranger continued, serious now. 'You will jack out of the memorial game and try to fix it so that the whole business is forgotten. We don't like it, understand? Run through town starkers if you must, but give the papers something to think about rather than this business of lumbering a dead man with a statue! Or else we'll find a quiet little place for you where no one ever goes, and we'll set you in wet cement up to your neck, and we'll have a spitting match into your left eye while we're waiting for the cement to harden. You with me? Then get on with it before our patience blows. Ciao, bambino!'

The last bit was evidently designed to start me thinking about the Sicilian Mafia, and that was supposed to scare me. I sat by the phone and thought. Who could be so put out by the memorial? The caller's vocabulary range seemed to point toward the leftists, but that wasn't cast-iron proof. It could just be an attempt to muddy the waters. What could I do? There was no point in bothering the police. The Antafagusta police are none too keen on cases that don't come clearly marked 'this end up'. A corpse and a knife—now that they understand. A corpse is material evidence, so to speak, and a knife can yield fingerprints. And who were they going to go after here? Besides, he more than likely called from a public phone. Even rank amateurs and underage extortionists are careful about that these days.

I was almost a hundred percent certain that my telephone was bugged. They like to keep abreast of things here on Minore. That being so, the authorities would sooner or later be told that I had been threatened. What more could I want?

At least one thing had come across with absolute clarity. There were those who very much disapproved of Damian's notion about building a memorial. But all the same it would have been useful to know who they were. My only option was to go and take some soundings in the Figaro salon.

And still that silly phone call had left a bad taste in my mouth. People have an unwholesome habit of not forgetting rotten things that are said to them. Without that habit we would be a lot stronger, but unfortunately we're stuck with it—that and a lot of other things in human nature.

As it happened, I was in no position to ponder those telephoned threats for long. I was almost at the end of the time that Delia had given me to think. All the while I had been racking my brains, trying to find a solution, and had just come up with what I thought was a very astute stratagem but one that would need some fancy footwork to pull off properly. And so I quickly forgot about the husky stranger and his cannibalistic sense of humour.

8

The next morning I ran into an unusually sunny Damian in the Figaro salon doorway. He gave me a conspiratorial wink and tapped a bent finger meaningfully against the newspapers in his jacket side-pocket. I didn't have to go round the houses to know what these signs meant: the morning papers had announced the formation of a committee, headed by Ares Damian, to raise a memorial to Tommazo Oon, and had listed the more prominent contributors, beginning with Ambassador Leverkühn.

I had hardly taken my seat when the proprietor himself came tripping up and started fussing around me. Eldon seemed unusually agitated. At first, while he was preparing his razor and wrapping cloths around me, he just huffed and puffed wordlessly, as though bursting with unspoken tidings. I let him suffer for five minutes or so, then I asked,

'What's the matter, maestro? You look like you're chock-a-block with news.'

It popped right out then.

'Oh, Mr. Yanno, how can you even ask? You just had to get mixed up in that business. You're new here, after all—you don't know how complicated all our ins and outs are. The premier is hissing with fury, like an overheated hair dryer. He's going to have to clean this whole mess up now.'

'What d'you mean—is a memorial to the Herald so hard for him to take?'

'But that's not it, my dear Yanno. You're thinking that he's miffed bacause you've spoiled his carefully prepared campaign to have Tommazo's ashes reburied? But my precious brother is not that much of an egoist, although as a child he was reckoned to have the biggest head in the family. No, no—you'd do better to ask why he wanted another reburial, as if the Herald's remains hadn't been trundled about more than enough as it is.'

'He 's hardly going to explain all that to me.'

'Mr. Yanno, you are an experienced journalist. Your profession obliges you to catch literally everything on the fly—except what you get from official sources, of course. I can't believe that you could have failed to guess that there's more to this than meets the eye. My brother and I are at a loss to understand exactly what your interest is in pursuing your present course of action.'

'And if I assure you that I never had an ulterior motive?'

Dan Eldon covered my face with foam, laying it on with quick and angry strokes of the shaving brush, then stepped aside to strop his custom-made Solingen razor.

'In that case, you're the most naive newsman ever to set foot in Antafagusta. You kick up such a shindy and you don't have the slightest inkling of what you're about! You might have asked first, you might have listened—are there so few intelligent people around here?'

He sounded so profoundly hurt that I automatically began to make excuses for myself.

'Well, if truth be told, I didn't have time for that. I was sufficiently ingenuous to assume that any nation would appreciate it when others also showed respect to its notables. The very evening I arrived on the *Maltese Cross,* Ares Damian tracked me down...'

'Damian, of course!' Eldon interrupted me loudly. 'Who else? Well listen, you impossibly naive newsman, and let's not hear a sound from you, or my hand will get trembly and put a nick in your valuable hide. The premier's plan to rebury Tommazo was engendered not by sentiment but by stern necessity. Howling necessity, at that! The eastern end of Antafagusta, where the tomb is located, will be standing in the way of a quarry before twelve months are up. And that's not so bad in itself—after all, the quarry could simply be diverted. But the unfortunate thing is that those bean-counting geologists who work for the Consortium and stick their noses in every nook and cranny have got wind of the fact that the thickest seam on the entire island—seventeen metres deep—starts right under the town. And they have to get to it fast, while prices for phosphate fertilizer are still high on the world market. In two or three years they could plummet. The story is that the Japanese have discovered extremely rich deposits on some godforsaken islands, and the Russians might respond to the demand by putting up a portion of their reserves for sale. The Consortium is asking us to sign an exceedingly profitable contract as a matter of urgency. They're actually insisting on it, and they're threatening to fold up the mining operations on the island altogether if we turn them down. But how can you tell people that we're moving those beloved bones because the Consortium is going to start mining for phosphates on this very spot? That's absolutely mind-boggling! There's no government in this world that would make an announcement like that, not unless it was looking to get thrown out within the day. The only alternative was to return the ashes, with all honours, to Santa Clara, the Herald's birthplace. Down by the sea there's a solid sandstone cliff. If the tomb is carved in that cliff, then no one will ever disturb the dear departed. But now Damian... Why has he made this whole thing his business? Well, simply because he hopes that if he can ruin this deal for Ron, then the Consortium really will shut down its cranes. The government will be financially embarrassed, the public payments will be cut, and he can turn the general discontent to his advantage and try to overthrow the Christian Liberals and clamber to the top of the heap. As ideas go, it's not that stupid. Now do you see?'

I suddenly felt jaded and uncomfortable: jaded because all this manoeuvring was so petty, and uncomfortable because I had been dumb enough to allow the silver-tongued Damian to feed me a line. But the most mortifying thing of all was that my bosses, it turned out, had had more foresight than I when they told me not to butt in. I had got myself into this idiotic situation—there was no one else to blame. Now what was the best way to untangle myself? I must have been looking crestfallen, because the barber started trying to console me.

'Don't take it so much to heart! After all, if you really didn't have a clue that there was more to it than met the eye, then you can't be faulted. You were tricked, that's all. And I was just about to start feeling bad about it—such a nice man, but a Damianite.'

'I'm no way a Damianite,' I observed, pulling myself together and acting slightly insulted. 'I thought I was making a friendly gesture that would impact on Minore's self-image. How was I to know what a perfect web of intrigue you have here?'

This made Eldon titter, with pride and a touch of malicious glee. 'The smaller the nation, the more intrigue you'll find! That's long been a fact of life in politics.'

I decided that as of then I really would have nothing further to do with the memorial. When all was said and done, I was not the one who had dreamed up this comedy. I had just played a bit part in it, and that could be overlooked completely, if one so wished. I would become an interested bystander. That was how I tried to soothe myself, but I still felt a tad guilty—I had, after all, put my shoulder to their wheel. There was just one thing for sure—no one in the agency was to be tipped off on the mess I had made. That would put the finisher on it; they would never let me live it down.

That day I raced straight from the Figaro to Ulla Stenmark's press conference. I was far from sure that I would be able to get anything worth my while out of it, but nothing more substantial was going on in Antafagusta, as usual, and my conscience sometimes chafed me for loafing about week after week without putting out a single story.

Ulla Stenmark, once a world-famous actress known to cinemagoers as the Scandinavian Iceberg, had announced that she would be holding a press conference during the last week of the film festival to publicise a return to the silver screen, her proverbial come-back. In her heyday, Ulla's chief claims to fame had been her sumptuous bust and her dazzlingly white skin. The projectionists in some southern countries had to put their hands over the lens when her bedroom scenes came on-screen, so that hot-blooded audiences would not feel compelled to make matchwood out of the auditorium furniture. Ulla had been perfectly content with that sort of distinction back then. But she had eventually outstayed her welcome. Younger stars began to appear and Ulla Stenmark's name vanished from the film credits.

Now she wanted to break back in. To tell the truth, every fading star wants to twinkle again, but very few of them manage to carry it off. The grapevine said that Ulla had hit lucky and found a producer who was prepared to take a gamble on her after such a lengthy hiatus. I was interested to find out if anyone really believed that the days of the buxom blonde were due for another go-round.

The venue for the press conference was a bit of a surprise too. It was to be held on the polder. Was Antafagusta so short of decent locations? The choice was evidently supposed to be deliberately outré. What would do for a mere mortal would not satisfy a star.

The polder was ringed with floodlights which were absolutely unnecessary in the bright sun. But the people from the TV companies, who were busy aiming their distance lenses like the barrels of recoilless guns, seemed to know what they were about. They were snapping orders to their assistants, while half-stripped lighting crews hauled ponderous stands half a meter there and a quarter of a meter back until one or other of the camera moguls got fed up and signalled 'let it go' with a dismissive flip of the hand.

Ulla appeared in a fluttering, diaphanous dress the colour of barely sprouted grass. She was wearing green eye-shadow and on her feet were green evening shoes with long straps that twined round her legs. A pair of huge, green-tinted, owlish glasses topped off the ensemble, concealing her famous dusky gaze. So Ulla Stenmark's green period was beginning. In the old days, everything had been eminently tight and trim, whereas now her clothing—and even the very skin on her shoulders, it seemed—drooped, while her shoulders and hipbones jutted out at some pretty sharp angles.

A man in a white dinner jacket with a slightly sunburned bald spot and a black toothbrush mustache did not leave her side for one moment. The impatient gestures with which he shooed away the photographers who were getting under the feet—that and everything else he did—said he was the boss. Every now and again the actress would give him a fleeting glance, as if canvassing approval. There wasn't much guesswork needed—that was Rolf Ladansky, Ulla's new producer. The bags under his eyes made one think that at least some of the care which had been lavished on the pressing of his impeccable white dinner jacket would have been put to better use in smoothing out his face.

Some swarthy, spry little men, evidently Ladansky's minions, pushed the reporters back into a large semicircle, so that Ulla and her companion could strike an attitude against the background of the polder, smooth as a table-top. They had a pretty monumental look about them as they loomed over the man-made plain. A lone yacht was cruising out on the ocean. It raised a multicolored spinnaker as soon as it came into our line of sight, then kept tacking about so as to stay in view. The boat had evidently been hired in a none-too-subtle attempt to make the background more photogenic.

The shutters clicked and the reels of film whirred. Ulla, shifting from one foot to another, froze in a languorous half-face pose for the cameras. A gentle smile, filled with sympathy for humankind and touched with mild suffering, never left her face. This was a completely new role for the celluloid boudoir queen.

The producer waited for the excitement to die down a little before calling for silence with a wave of his hand and declaring,

'Ladies and gentlemen! Next week Ms. Stenmark will begin shooting a new film which we, judging from the artistic merits of the screenplay and the cast we have signed, can comfortably predict will be a great success and, perhaps, one of the highlights at next year's Antafagusta Film Festival. For this reason, Ms. Stenmark has agreed to meet with you today, in order to share with you her creative thoughts. Ulla, if you please.'

He nudged the actress' elbow slightly and she playfully flashed her knee under the fluttering dress, but immediately thought better of it and gracefully set her foot down, toe first.

'I spent a long time preparing for this role—the role of a romantic,' she said in a rather drowsy voice. 'I think the screenplay's awfully good. It might almost have been written for me. A very romantic story, a little melodramatic—the sort of thing that's done these days. I don't see anything wrong in that, although some critics frown at melodramas. In my view people should be able to cry in the cinema if that's what they want to do—I mean, tears are cleansing and ennobling, wouldn't you say? Perhaps everyone won't cry, but those who will are foremost in my mind. Truth to tell, my dream from the very beginning was to play romantic roles. But none came my way until Rolf happened by and saw through to my innermost being...'

'Where have you been all this time?' an impatient reporter interrupted her. 'Is it true that you were planning to end your film career and open a restaurant at some health resort?'

Ulla had not had time to react to that question when another newsman called out,

'Is it true that you went to Switzerland to have a baby and then were busy bringing up your unannounced love-child?'

Ladansky felt he had to intervene.

'Gentlemen!' He raised his hand. 'I would ask you to confine your questions to artistic matters. Ms. Stenmark will be happy to answer any question with a bearing on art.'

'I spent a whole year in the Schwarzwald, in a private *pension*,' Ulla confided dramatically. 'It's the best place in the world to get oneself into shape. During that time I lost twenty-five kilograms. You ask me how? A crash diet and exercise. Very few calories and a lot of walking. My goal was to prepare myself for the role of a romantic.'

She lowered her head, plucking at her belt, while her eyes gazed meekly at the ground. Some novice photogs couldn't stand it and snapped her again. The experienced newshounds weren't about to buy such an unsophisticated ruse.

'How do you feel about lesbian relationships with actresses you work with?' an elderly, curly-headed man with the flaccid face of a rakehell inquired, thrusting a microphone under Ulla's nose. 'Who do you get on best with—Liza Minnelli? Lea Massari? Liv Ullmann?'

'Yes, I know them all,' the actress replied in some perplexity. 'Of course I do—we've worked together.'

The curly-haired man smirked maliciously.

'Which of them do you think is most fun to be with?'

Ladansky dragged at the actress' elbow and, screwing up his face, whispered something in her ear. Ulla, furiously angry, turned to the curly-headed man, leaned towards his microphone and almost spat one solitary word into it,

'Creep!'

'Gentlemen—questions about art, please!' Ladansky shouted, his right cheek twitching nervously.

The newsmen livened up a little.

'How do you feel about the new bottomless beach fashion? Would you wear it in a film?' someone at the back asked loudly.

'Oh, it's ever so romantic!' Ulla smiled, and cast a playful glance at Ladansky. 'But that all depends on the contract I sign with my producer.'

'Do you consider a romantic role difficult to play?'

'The greatest difficulties are already behind me. You know, the first week I was on a complete fast, just drinking tea. Then five hundred calories a day in the second week—that's next to nothing— and seven hundred and fifty calories a day in the third week. Tea, juices and fruit, believe it or not. I was actually dizzy yesterday evening when Rolf took me to a restaurant at the beach, but I allowed myself only half an oyster with champagne...'

People started lurching about for no apparent reason at the back. The newsmen were being jostled from behind, and the entire crowd began to sway as if it were about to surge over Ulla and Ladansky and swallow them up. The photographers in the front row were jammed right up against their subjects, far too close to take any more pictures, and they started saying uncomplimentary things about whoever was shoving them. Soon the reason for all this became clear. The leftists had arrived and had begun barging forward with all their might, bumping against the reporters and the lighting technicians, getting all tangled up in the cables, knocking the lights over, stumbling and swearing. They were dragging around a banner on which was written in uneven letters, 'Floozies are Stars and Stars are Floozies!'

A troublesome bunch, I thought. They just have to be center front, can't bear to miss any of the limelight. The Own-lander pickets who had shown up in time for the start of the press conference were perched quietly on the Cape Cataracta parapet, swinging their legs and leaving it to the wind to billow out a banner which flaunted their latest run-in with a foreign language: 'Minor Art for Minore!', it said. Although who knows—maybe this time they really did know what they had written.

8–1298

One ebullient leftist got completely wound up in some cables and upended a lamp assembly. The lamp exploded with a crash and hot shards of glass spritzed over people's feet. It made me jump.

At that moment, somebody grabbed my sleeve. Turning about, I recognised the woman in octagonal spectacles who had dragged me from the Archipelago corridor to the IEA meeting. Now she was hauling on my sleeve and directing a loud, breathy whisper into my ear.

'Thumb your nose at this vulgar nonsense! What happened to the story on the peripatetic session?'

'They're sitting on it at the agency,' I said, ineptly trying to extricate myself. 'They haven't said a word to me about it. They've probably come across something more important.'

'Brainless idiots! Look, there's a man who'll save the world.' She pointed into the distance, where Professor Umbermann was poring over his detectors on all fours.

The researcher was unperturbed by all the fuss and bother around Ulla Stenmark. He and his assistants were just trying their best to reel in the leads from under the feet of the crowd.

'But he still hasn't found a single mutant,' I observed. 'Perhaps there are none. Maybe they went on a phosphate binge and turned their little toes up.'

'But at least he's looking. Or do you suppose that those who don't even take the trouble to look stand a better chance? But he definitely will find them, here or somewhere else, and that's a fact, a definite fact. People who are so painstaking always find what they're looking for. You could get onto him before he's a world-famous celebrity— that would be a great honour for you!'

Meanwhile, the leftists had managed to capture the high ground. Their beards jutting, they were crowding around their banner, assiduously trying to make sure that the photographers got a good look at it. But—with the exception of some omnivorous photoscavengers, who take pictures of absolutely everything in the hope of making a sale to the local evening paper if nowhere else—all the journalists, who were heartily sick of the leftists' antics, pointedly ignored them and instead went haring off after Ladansky and Ulla.

One particularly zealous photographer, with a meter-square aluminium box containing his back-up equipment slung over his shoulder, was manifestly bound and determined to outdo himself that day. Not letting Ulla out of his sights for one moment, he had been performing the incomprehensible trick of taking photographs with both cameras at once. When his subject began to leave, he pelted after her, brashly elbowing his colleagues aside. He was far too busy to keep an eye on his box, which was swinging perilously from side to side. He pounded past the yellow canopy just as Professor Umbermann was looking out. I suppose all the drumming feet were shaking the polder and producing some astronomical readings on his detectors, as though myriads of earthworms—his long-awaited mutants—had suddenly materialised out of nowhere.

The Professor's egg-like head, covered with sparse hair, was right in line with the gung-ho photographer's aluminium box. There was a dull thump, and the Professor went limp. The photographer felt the jolt and flashed a look backward, but the huge box hid the unconscious Umbermann from his view, so he raced on.

The leftists were kicking up their own racket, surrounded by a dozen loiterers whom they obviously took to be journalists or else what was the good of showing off their banner like that and shouting their slogans? The Own-landers on the parapet were pointing at them and chortling sarcastically. A little further away, against the gray backdrop of the polder, the interview was continuing, though Ulla was looking rather wan now that she was out of the spotlights.

'Is Ingmar Bergman the father of your child?'

Ulla gave a determined shake of the head.

'Dino de Laurentiis?'

'Jean-Paul Belmondo?'

'No, no, no!' Ulla, hysterical by that time, cried, 'Leave me alone! My child has no father at all, do you hear? He has no father and doesn't need one!'

She dashed off, teetering in her high-heeled shoes and dragging Ladansky after her, while he tried ineffectually to bring her to a halt. Like a green comet, Ulla tore across the gray plain with the reporters in full cry after her. The puzzled leftists realised, a little belatedly, what had happened, shouldered their spangled banner and tramped off in high dudgeon after the newsmen. No matter how hard they tried, though, they couldn't make it to the front so that they could form up for the cameras again.

I deliberately lagged behind the rabble. The whole thing was wearing pretty thin. It had been fun while it lasted, but I couldn't use it. Our agency is a sober-minded place, where they take a dim view of ballyhoo and dirt-dishing. And if any should be needed to spice things up, Avik Nersesyan can take his foreign correspondent friends to a cafe and pump them, or can dig it out of the gutter press, to which the agency subscribes precisely for that purpose. Seeing that they had let the story on the bank heist dry up and blow away...

In the distance, a group of Heaven's Orderlies were bustling around Umbermann. They lifted the Professor onto a stretcher. His body was rubbery, as though there wasn't a bone in it. A dark gray ambulance with gray curtains at the windows was parked some way off. Scraps of blue and white leads lay scattered across the ground.

And beyond the yellow canopy stretched the polder, as solitary and cheerless as it had ever been.

So it happened that I, Stemo Kulamar, a citizen obedient in every respect, rose in revolt against my government.

They had to be brought to book for the way that young people had turned their backs on their parents. How else could it be? I mean, we had raised our Roxana with a great deal more care than had been our lot when we were growing up, and the outcome was that the girl all but despised us. Later on, I will say, the thought occurred to me that there could be some undisclosed reason for this disgusting state of affairs. It's not just here in Minore—you hear tell that young people have got out of hand all over the world. Some scientists even suggest that nuclear explosions and insecticides could be at the bottom of it. The world, after all, had enough and to spare of both by the time Roxana was born. I don't really understand it, but since somebody has said that there could be some kind of link, then there probably is.

That was not my line of thinking back then. No, something was out of kilter on this earth if the basic sense of gratitude toward one's parents had vanished. And who was to blame for this, if not the government? I had long stopped holding God accountable for everything. So let the government shake in its shoes, since it had made such a muck-up of things!

That was just around the time that the Own-landers staged a mammoth anti-government demonstration on Herald Square. It was sparked by Ron Eldon's secret agreement with the Consortium to sell all the sand on Minore's shores, when titanium magnetite was discovered in it. In fact, lighters were already taking sand from where the village of Bonegripe used to be, and there was very little to-do about that, but no one knew at the time that all our shoreline sand had been sold.

It's one thing when they simply start a quarry somewhere—who wants to be stingy about sand, no matter how big the quarry is? But when they sell off all the island's sand on the sly, then there has to be something underhand about it, which means that we've been swindled again. Fair play says that Minore belongs to all Minorans, not just to the government. It had taken us a long while to tumble to the idea that the excavators would be gnawing at our island from the inside as well as from the outside. And so we were all the more furious when we found out that the entire island, end to end, had been sold and we couldn't do a thing about it.

It all came out, as usually happens with secret deals, because somebody slipped up. A functionary from the Foreign Ministry, who made a bit extra working as an inside man for the security service, had got nabbed on one of his moonlighting jobs. He was following orders to install a microphone in the swimming pool of a country-house that belonged to Ares Damian, the former prime minister. The gardener caught him, boxed his ears soundly just in case, and phoned the boss. The police, understandably enough, wanted to hush the whole business up, but instead a noisy scandal erupted which even the chief of police couldn't smooth over, and the spook was brought to trial.

The poor blighter had obviously been promised protection and a light sentence. He guilelessly told the court that some stranger had recruited him for twenty-five minares at the Antafagusta market.

He had seen the stranger only one and a half times, and always under heavy make-up and a big peaked cap, so there was no way of recognising him. This man, allegedly, had said that he had hated Ares Damian since his schooldays and was now collecting a compromising dossier on him. The court ignored Damian's snide rejoinders, was quickly satisfied by the explanations offered by the accused, and gave the poor thing eighteen months' suspended sentence, for trespassing on private property. And that appeared to be the end of it.

But that's when the fatal blunder was made. The undercover man, who had got away with nothing worse than a scare, turned up at the security service offices to collect what was due to him, and he was told that they did not know him from Adam and that they had never laid eyes on him before. The door was slammed in his face. And it would not have been so bad if the matter had been allowed to rest there, but the botched job was still rankling the security service functionaries, who never had got their microphones installed in the swimming pool at Damian's place in the country. So they telephoned the head of chancery at the Foreign Ministry and gave him such a thorough going-over that he had the unlucky bloke sacked from the Foreign Ministry too. They forced him into an early retirement which deprived him of his long-service bonus and debarred him from working for the government ever again.

That was the straw that broke the camel's back. Having tried to get a fair shake from his superiors and coming up against a brick wall there, the brand-new retiree went into a slow burn. While working for the Foreign Ministry, he had edited the text of the secret 'sand' contract, so now he stomped off to the editorial office of *Our Own Land*, demanded to see the editor-in-chief, and spilled everything he knew—and probably not for free.

The next day a special edition hit the streets, with huge stand-out red headlines: 'SELLING THE VERY SAND FROM UNDER OUR FEET * WHY THE POLDER WAS REALLY ABANDONED * RON ELDON GETS A GOOD PRICE FOR ALL OF MINORE, OUR ISLAND TO BE DRAGGED UP BY THE ROOTS'.

Three days later there was the demonstration on Herald Square, and I went along to show how disgruntled I was with the government. It was not just a rally of Own-landers and their cohorts: literally hundreds of townsfolk, infuriated by the news of the government's double-dealing, had gathered on the square. When duplicity comes to light, any decent person will try to show how he feels about it. That's one way you maintain a sense of self-worth. I doubt that anyone gives a hoot about how much real good it will do.

You live and learn to the very end of your days. Looking back, it's clear to me that many protests are completely pointless. But it's still hard to come to terms with the one fact of life that applies to absolutely everything in this world, which is that anything capable of change can change only for the worse. As soon as you have that straight, it gets easier. There's no longer any need to get angry at anything. Quite to the contrary, you should just be pleased that things used to be better. The only pity of it is that it's unbelievably difficult to make yourself look at life that way.

There were so many people that the authorities had sent extra details of police to the square. In addition to the ordinary policemen, the special constabulary had turned up and the police reserves had sent an armoured car, one of the three which the English had foisted on us at the very end of the protectorate. They were old Saracens. During the protectorate they had put in so much time careering all over the island on the trail of those who were campaigning for independence that now they were fit for nothing but a complete overhaul. As usually happens, the English had cracked down particularly hard on the independence advocates about five minutes before the protectorate ended, when everyone on Minore could plainly see that not only the days but the very hours of the English were numbered here. When independence was declared, the last British High Commissioner figured out that it was a lot better to sell the old armoured cars on the spot than to take them back to England for repair. And so they rumble about to this day, and the transport buffs in the police reserve just keep on making up new spares for them, welding their silencers and changing their tires. It's a good thing that Antafagusta does not cover much ground and that extra police detachments are not often used, while our Saracens have not been out of town for a very long time. However, those in charge of the police department hold to the opinion that the repulsively blocky look they have about them helps to inspire a fitting respect for authority.

The square was filled with people. They had rolled a barrel out into the middle and were using it as a podium for rabble-rousing speeches, but I couldn't get close enough to recognise any of the speakers by sight. The speeches were being piped through an amplifier, and that was how I found out that they were demanding a referendum on the cancellation of the secret agreement.

'The shamelessness of the Christian Liberals has reached its apogee!' yelled one of the orators who impressed me more than the rest. 'It's not enough that they have sold their native soil. Now they are turning the very sand, where our poor deprived children play with their little buckets and spades, into an export commodity. The tears of innocent children are but a sprinkle of rain to our unscrupulous rulers. Shame on them!'

Suddenly someone gave me a nasty clout in the side. I turned round in surprise. Kolo stood there, his face twisted in a scornful grimace.

'Come to snoop have you, you yard-dog?'

'From whose yard?' I muttered in reply. I was still burdened with guilt about Kolo.

'Why didn't you bring your gun?' Kolo went on. 'You could have

118

done the police narks a good turn. My other leg still works, you know—I only limp on one!'

His eyes burned ominously. I instinctively pulled back.

'Just drop it, Kolo,' I implored him. 'I gave notice for keeps after that.'

'Well, of course you did. What else did you have to do there?' he said derisively. 'I'd just like to know what your game is, stiffing your way in here.'

He was advancing on me menacingly. I thought that I could more than likely have fended off Kolo, underfed and lame as he was, but I had noticed that there were two sullen individuals with him, one who was a head taller than I and another who was well set-up and strong. I was in an unenviable fix.

'I've come to the demonstration, like you,' I said, trying to take the edge off things.

'Sure, sure—to give the narks some back-up,' Kolo nodded with an evil smirk, and added, more to his companions than to me, 'Well, not to worry, pal—it's a good thing that you've run into me. We'll give you such a back-up that you'll see stars.'

The sullen individuals started toward me, pushing people out of the way. They were coming from both sides, cutting off my line of retreat. The people around me, made wary by what Kolo had said, were eyeing me with leery hostility. Suspicion, once planted, grows rapidly.

The people let Kolo through. Limping on his left leg, he came nearer. There's no easy way of getting out of this, I thought. A thirst for revenge was written all over his face. It wouldn't be so bad if they just slapped me around, but they might be out to do permanent damage. There was not an ounce of sympathy in the crowd around me, and I, with my prosthesis, was not exactly a warrior bold. And there was no way of sloping off, because I was hemmed in by a solid wall of bodies. The sun beat down, sweat broke out all over my body, and my head spun from the heat.

The hopelessness of it all made me desperate. I had a sudden urge to scream aloud and lash out, bite, kick at everyone round me—anything to break the tightening ring of fear. Kolo's friends were close now. Another step and I would need to start taking them out before they decked me.

In that instant the crowd grew agitated. The police were on the move, coming in behind the armoured car. The demonstrators in the front rows were retreating from the steel box that was bearing down on them, the ones at the back were getting squeezed, and the whole mass of humanity started heaving to and fro. Those at the back had not yet realised that they should make room.

'Break it up!' a tinny voice barked from the police loudspeaker. Warning shots were fired into the air.

Everyone was suddenly in a hurry to be somewhere else. People absconded in all directions, and the crowd grew thinner with every second, as if an enormous vacuum cleaner on the edge of the square was sucking up the human dust specks. I glanced at Kolo. For a moment he hesitated, then shook his fist at me in disappointment and hurried away, limping. The sullen individuals had already done a vanishing act.

I was overwhelmed with reckless joy.

'Where are you going?' I called after him 'We haven't had our chat!' He turned and shot me a furious glare.

I was quite alone. The ground was strewn with all sorts of rubbish, as usual after a demonstration, and a Saracen was slowly crawling straight at me across the littered asphalt of the square. Its thick, snake-patterned tires seemed to be coiling downwards with the relentless motion of thick, black boa constrictors.

'Break it up! Don't obstruct the police! Let the police vehicles through!' The commander yelled his orders through a jangling loudspeaker.

I heard behind my back the gusty breathing of the crowd and the pounding of feet, and an incredible stubbornness suddenly awoke within me. Was this how it was all going to end? The government was going to get off this lightly? The armoured car was still advancing on me in first gear. I stood motionless. When the Saracen had crawled to within about three meters, a dull, low-pitched warning signal came from a klaxon that seemed to be rusted solid with long disuse. I held my ground. Then the upper hatch was flung open with a clang, and a policeman's head in a steel helmet poked out.

'You damned plateau donkey, you lame-legged devil, get the hell out of here. Don't you see that I can crush you?'

I did not budge, and I even permitted myself the small pleasure of spitting through my teeth onto the asphalt right in front of the armoured car.

Its machine gun fired a short burst into the air. I'm not all that plucky when the bullets start flying, but this time, evidently, I was mad enough to be brave. I played deaf. I truly didn't think about it, but deep inside I was no doubt convinced that they would neither crush me nor shoot me.

The armoured car stopped about a meter away. Two policemen jumped out of it, their boots clattering. They grabbed me and dragged me aside. The armoured car went on its way.

I was steamed up now. Oh-ho, they think they're all done with me, do they? I wrenched free from the two chubby policemen and threw myself into the armoured car's path, before the broad-beamed coppers knew what had hit them. The Saracen had almost gone by, but I contrived to get my left leg, the one with the prosthesis, under the wheel. Then I started roaring my head off. It was awful to see those black wheels rolling over me, but after all I had to take them on at some point or that haunting vision would never release me. In the next instant the wheel rolled over my leg. The people in the armoured car most likely did not notice. An invincible force threw me aside onto the dirty asphalt and a fearsome pain skewered my knee and my hip-joint, which were being pitilessly twisted by the prosthesis suspensions. I think I passed out for a while.

A crowd was churning around me when I came to. They pulled me carefully out from under the armoured car, which had come to a standstill. Then dozens of hands seized hold of the Saracen and began to rock it furiously. There were shouts of 'Blood-suck-ers! Blood-suck-ers!'

Panic-stricken policemen sprang through the hatches. Our police have never been conspicuously courageous, but then I guess fearlessness isn't the strong suit of any police force. They took to their heels under a shower of pummelling fists. A moment later, the armoured car toppled over with a terrible crash.

'Blood-suck-ers!' the crowd breathed.

Gray figures were fussing around me. They all seemed to have the same face, but I realized later that this was because they were all wearing the Heaven's Orderly uniform. While they waited for the stretcher to arrive, I was able to watch what happened next, despite the fiendish pain in my leg.

Petrol, clear as water, was streaming from the armoured car onto the asphalt. I don't think that anybody deliberately put a match to it—more likely someone simply lit up or threw a burning cigarette butt onto the ground, not noticing the cloying smell of petrol. But that was all it took, and the armoured car alongside me burst into brilliant flame. The fire seemed to drive the crowd crazy, and the police found themselves under attack. I was around long enough to hear car windows being shattered and some thudding shots. That was the police firing rubber bullets into the crowd in self-defense. Then the people dressed in gray carried me away from the fire and put me into an ambulance which was dark gray on the outside and silvery inside. I tried to kick myself free. I was scared stiff. The starkness of it reminded me very much of the expensive silvery-gray coffins that are used to bury rich people on Minore. No one paid any attention to my futile floundering. They just slid me into the ambulance on the stretcher, like bread into an oven. Before they slammed the back door, Kolo appeared momentarily in the doorway. He was completely transformed: a fanatic fire burned in his eyes.

'Good for you, Stemo!' he cried. 'I knew you were a straight arrow deep inside! Hang on, I'll find you. We'll make it hot for 'em after what they did to you!'

He actually did turn up that evening in the hospital, and brought with him a correspondent from *Our Own Land* whose job was to make a hero of me. I was in a lousy mood. The excitement had subsided, the pain-killing injection had apparently worn off, and my leg ached unbearably. I was lying there exasperated, wondering what

121

had made me do it and why I had seen fit to stick my poor leg where it wasn't supposed to be and land up in hospital. I wanted to tell my unexpected visitors to get lost, but Kolo set to work calming me down. He did the talking on my behalf, and told the newsman how we had herded goats together as children, how we loved our land, and how even as a youngster I had suffered at foreign hands, when the Flying Fortress wheels razed my home. It turned out that all my life I had done nothing but fight for my own land, although that was the first I had heard of it. It was a story that plucked at the heart-strings. For two weeks after it appeared in the newspaper my ears burned with shame.

The demonstration had put the wind up the government. A few days later, the newspaper published an article written by the Minister for the Economy which was so long that I doubt anyone could have ploughed through it. That article did a fine job of muddling everything up. The minister said over and over that irresponsible elements were misinterpreting the government's economic policy, which was quite straightforward and universally beneficial, that by no means all the shoreline sand had been sold, and that from the coming January all allowances, pensions and other payments would be subject to a twenty-five percent across-the-board increase out of the proceeds from the sale of the sand. That did more than anything else to quieten people down.

Since I was being touted as a hero who had suffered blamelessly during a nationwide demonstration, the government compensated me generously, and even ordered a new bionic prosthesis from London, which they paid for. It let me move my foot by tensing my thigh muscles, so I didn't limp any more. The armoured car commander was summarily dismissed from the police force, and the poor thing had to go looking for another job.

When I came home from the hospital, I found a mass of faded bouquets and lots of boxes of stale chocolates. The chocolates had developed a white coating, but they did come in useful. Tell had moved into Roxana's room while I was in hospital. The girl announced to me that they were going to live together until she was sixteen. Then, if all had gone well, they would make it legal, but otherwise why bother? Murana, having no one to side with her, had been unable to stop them. So they would come home in the evenings, would pounce on the boxes of chocolate, and then listen to caterwauling music turned up unbearably loud. They claimed that music to be very relaxing and restful, and I am altogether convinced that they're right, because when it's on there's absolutely no point in trying to do anything except sit there and tap your foot to the rhythm...

'And I never knew what a swine you were, Artur Yanno!'

Delia flung out those words and they hung—stickily, gummily—in the air. I could hear them in my room for several days afterwards.

If truth be told, she had no business getting so worked up. All I had done was meet her ploy with a counterploy. You have to get the measure of your opponent, but it's a rare woman who can do that. At one point I was even wondering if Delia had really seen our relationship as somehow different, somehow deeper than it really was. But I dismissed that idea pretty quickly. It was, no doubt, nothing but pure calculation.

I had found Landa the mother-to-be down in the port district, where she sold lobster meat fried in sesame oil—a delicacy among the shore folk which was also a matter of great curiosity for most of the tourists. Landa was plump and rosy, and she smelled ineradicably of fish and onions. She cried up her wares at the top of her voice, trying to outholler the other lobster vendors. The port district and the suburbs abound with peppy women like her. The size of her stomach told me she was at least seven months pregnant. I offered her ten minares if she would come to my place for an hour or two that evening. She would have nothing to do except back me up in everything I said.

That was the evening that Delia came to hear my decision.

At first I left Landa in the kitchen, and only called her in after Delia, so sure that she had carried it off, was seated in an armchair, her legs crossed. 'There, you see,' I said. 'Man is weak and I'm guilty round and square. This is Landa. She's also carrying a child of mine, and, as you can see, she has no alternative but to have the baby. I can't cast her on the mercy of fate, the poor girl—she has no mother and no father, she's got no money and she's uneducated. Left alone, there's no way she can bring up a child. She has told me that if I leave her she will throw herself off Cape Cataracta and drown herself and the little one.' At this, Landa took on a martyred expression and nodded her head. She was a slyboots, and no mistake.

Perhaps Delia's intuition was telling her something. She tried to grill me on how this had come about and when I had found time for it, but Landa and I didn't give an inch. It was a pity, of course, I declared dolefully, but since things had turned out this way I considered it my duty to stick by the one who was in the worst extremity. Surely Delia didn't want to push a poor girl into suicide!

That was when she shouted those words, loading them with all her exasperation, all her rage. I'm still surprised that the door of my room stayed on its hinges after being slammed like that.

I had hardly caught my breath when my attention was drawn to an odd change in Landa's behaviour. The big-bellied girl, who to that point had been silent and submissive, was suddenly transformed. She was lounging in the armchair with an unaccountably cheeky look on her face, and seemed to be sizing me up.

'Well, what are you lolling around for? Do you have plans to stay the night?' I asked her, my voice trembling slightly. Rummaging in my wallet, I placed a ten-minare note on the coffee table in front of her. 'Thanks for your help. You can go now.'

'Just you wait a minute,' Landa said, her searching look not leaving me for a moment. 'Do you reckon that's enough to set you straight with *your* child?'

'What child?' I roared. 'What are you rattling on about? Have you gone bananas? I don't know anything about your child, nor do I want to. I'll pay you what I promised, and you'll be a good girl and toddle along!'

I felt completely frazzled. The nervous tension was getting me down.

'But you just said yourself that you're the father of my child and you promised to marry me.'

'You've gone mad!' I shouted in a rage. 'Don't you understand that it was a trick, and that's what I hired you for?'

'That's splitting hairs and I can't make sense of it. I'm a simple girl and easy to fool—that's probably what you thought. But I can find that lady again. I know her, all right. She lives in a side-street near Britannic Boulevard. And hasn't she got it in for you! What we could tell folk about you, me and her ... if you don't give me money ... or something else. And do you know what—if they pay me at the paper too, I'll let them photograph me with my bare belly showing! Why shouldn't they pay for something like that? The way they do it, they put a black strip over your eyes afterwards, if they don't want people to recognise you—that's right, isn't it? I wouldn't mind doing that...'

I was literally suffocating with fury. I felt that if I had to spend five more minutes listening to her chatter and not understanding a word she was saying, I would croak. I had to get rid of her, fast.

At last I managed to get her through the door, but it cost me a hundred minares, a bottle of Scotch whisky and two cartons of foreign cigarettes. On the way out, the beady-eyed female glanced in the corner and noticed a brightly coloured plastic shoulder-bag decorated with a picture of a backside in tight blue jeans, the kind of bag they sell for three minares apiece on the black market. Nor did she miss the casual shirt with the orangutan's face on it that I had bought on a Malayan market in Singapore. I had to sacrifice them both. Hurriedly tossing all this booty into Landa's arms, I bundled her off.

With the click of the the dead-bolt, I almost collapsed. My lord, I thought, it's enough to make you think kindly of chastity belts. There's literally nothing that can't be bought and sold here!

The doctor by my bed is rolling two broad paper tapes to and fro. They fall to the floor and, rustling, try to loop round his feet. When he saw that I had opened my eyes, he dropped the tapes he was comparing into his lap and asked,

'Yanno, do you hear me?'

I nodded. I wondered how I could fail to hear him, since he was right there talking to me.

'Right now you feel that you're yourself, Artur Yanno?'

I nodded again. A baffling, bulky device stood close by, clicking and endlessly reeling out paper tape. The doctor compared the tapes again, and seemed to be pleased with my answer. Then I felt that something was attached to my head. To check it out, I turned my head sharply, first in one direction and then in the other. There was an unseen wire somewhere, and it was pulling my hair.

'Don't jerk your head,' the doctor warned. 'Those are electrodes. We're taking an encephalogram. We need it to start your treatment. Tell me something, though—did you feel that you were Stemo Kulamar just now, a short while ago?'

I strained my memory so hard that my head buzzed. Stemo Kulamar—that name seemed very familiar to me, but no matter how hard I strained, I could not remember a single person with a name like that.

'I don't remember...' I said, working vocal cords that were stiff from lengthy disuse.

The doctor nodded understandingly. Then his attention was caught by a strange noise coming from behind my bed-head. He glanced to the far end of the ward, and it was a while before he settled down again. I gathered that there must be someone else back there.

'Who's that?' I said, working those vocal cords again.

'It's him—it's Stemo Kulamar,' the doctor replied.

'What's he saying?' I asked.

The doctor sighed.

'That's the whole point—he isn't saying anything. He just tosses about and groans with every blip on the encephalogram. He's permanently semi-comatose, if that means anything to you. It seems that you're the only route whereby his conscious mind can break through the block that's been thrown up.'

'Who is this Kulamar? The name's sort of familiar ... but I can't remember.'

'Just someone who lives round here. But whether you know him or not, I can't say.'

The long conversation had wearied me.

'Then what's wrong with him ... with that Kulamar guy?' I asked, mustering all the strength I had left.

'He was concussed in the explosion, just like you,' the doctor replied. 'Only he has some serious head injuries as well.'

I suddenly vanished somewhere and heard no more. Once again there swam up before my eyes, as if emerging from a thick mist, pictures filled with colors and sounds which I had already had time to forget.

9

'Kulamar? He'll live...'

The words reverberate as if they had been spoken in a huge resonant room whose vault was hidden somewhere in the darkness far overhead. I can see nothing, can feel nothing, I just hear those echoing words and they seem to crowd out all other sensations and even thoughts. I do not know who said them, or to whom, or why they were said. I take them in quite separately, as though they have a look and a heft of their own, and a color, too. They're brown—golden-brown, like ripe chestnuts.

Every now and then, from somewhere outside of me, a blue welding flame beats restlessly in the corner of my eye. It trembles like lightning frozen in place. Lightning makes you instinctively look for shelter, but I cannot feel my own body, I don't know where I am, and much less am I able to do anything about it. The bright, hissing flame that feeds my anxiety just goes on burning and burning in the corner of my eye.

The tale of woe, of course, began with the demonstration on Herald Square, when I shoved my prosthesis under the armoured car. Or maybe before that—on the gray polder in the desolation of evening, amid the slumbering equipment, when I hoisted my rifle and aimed at Kolo as he clambered on the yellow excavator. Or suppose it was back on the coast road, when those miserable hippies, who have long ago forgotten the whole thing, popped up in front of my Honda? And why shouldn't they have forgotten it? I mean, they escaped with a mild scare and had made tracks even before the dust had settled on the road. Why should they care if I lost a leg? No, no—it *was* the demonstration. Arguing it any other way could bring you to the pretty pass of deciding that the seed of misfortune was sown at the very instant when, out there on the edge of the plateau, I gave my first cry. I mean, all the events of my life, from that moment on, are somehow strung together on a single thread.

If it hadn't been for the demonstration, which ended in such an unexpected way, I would never in my life have had enough money to buy that expensive sports car. Had the government not gone to the trouble and expense of getting me a bionic prosthesis, which did wonders for my self-regard, I would most likely never have taken the risk of slipping behind the wheel of such a powerful machine. And then nothing would have happened. So I know perfectly well how it all began, although that doesn't make it any easier on me.

But then I start wondering—is it really all that simple? Of course I can pull together all the links in the chain, but then images from my distant childhood, befogged by time, suddenly drift up from the depths of my memory. Besides my pants and my shirt I had one other item of clothing, which was just for showing off in and which belonged to me and me alone—my grandfather's comforter-jacket. At least, that was what I called it, though really it was a sheepskin waistcoat which by that time had turned an indeterminate brownish-black color. The decades had worn it slick on the outside and bald on the inside. The armholes and neck opening had stretched so much that the waistcoat didn't offer much more than comfort, which is probably why I called it a comforter-jacket. The threads that held the scraps of sheepskin together would give way ever so often, and I had to close up the seams with a big curved needle. Grandfather had willed the waistcoat to me. I remembered him vaguely, but my clearest memory was of a motionless doll with an auger-sharp nose that they had carried to the village cemetery when I was four years old.

My grandfather's comforter-jacket was the only thing I didn't actually need in my day-to-day life. It wasn't for eating and I had just about enough to cover my nakedness without it, but perhaps that's exactly why it was so dear to me. In the evenings, when I brought the flock in or came home from school, I would put it on and furtively stroke it with my hand, which made the waistcoat even shinier, but that didn't trouble me a bit.

Later, during the war, the loss of that waistcoat grieved me more than the loss of our entire house. All I could find amid the ruins were scattered scraps of brownish-black sheepskin. Those huge wheels had bashed the masonry blocks about and got them so mad that they had torn into the garment pitilessly and flung the scraps around like large black butterflies, so that there was nothing I or my curved needle could do about it. Sitting among the ruins, wiping the tears away with the back of my hand, I tried to patch something together, until my father got angry with my fiddling about. He snatched the scraps of sheepskin out of my hands, threw them away, and told me to start picking up the rubbish and the stones so that we could begin building another place to live.

I was heartsick over my waistcoat for a long time. When it was gone, I had only the barest necessities—a shirt, a pair of trousers and a mattress with a goat-hair coverlet, which my mother used to sew up when it tore. That's probably the secret reason for my great fondness for all sorts of material things—good, expensive, lovely things.

It often happens that a person who has to deny himself a lot as a child never recovers from the experience all his life long. I had another friend in Bonegripe besides Samuel Arbis and Leo Neckarborn. His name was Uriel Veldar. Uri's family were appallingly poor. His father had died of tuberculosis in the first spring after the war. Our consumptives always died in spring when the sun started beating down mercilessly. More than usual passed away during that first spring after the war. It was as if they had been doing everything humanly possible so as not to let go while the war was on, and by the time it was over they were altogether spent. Uri was just a little thing back then. They lived on whatever he and his brother Yessa, who was two years older, could catch with a hook and line, and on what his mother raised in the garden. There were three little girls in the family too, and in those days they didn't understand anything, couldn't do anything to help, and just fretted for something to eat. Once Uri crossly blurted out, 'The nitwits, you can't make 'em understand why there's not a crust of bread in the house, but they're smart enough at scrounging food...' The family went hungry for years, and when they started giving free porridge twice a week to the poorer kids in school, Uri always stayed behind to scrape the bowls.

Now he gets regular payments on what used to be their garden. He weighs a hundred and sixty kilograms, and he still goes on stuffing himself in a morbidly gluttonous manner. Samuel Arbis met up with Uri on his most recent Antafagusta trip. Flabbergasted, he said to me,

'Good grief, Uri Veldar should be put in a cage so people can pay to go and see him! No European would ever believe that there are such tubs of lard in this world.'

Uri really loves to go bowling. He can't bend down to pick up a wood—he has to squat with his knees apart and everyone watching him is always afraid that the skin over his knees and buttocks is going to split. Uri will wheeze his way through a game or two and then hurry off to get some hors d'œuvres before dinner. No one can credit that he was once a thin little boy with willowy hands and feet. All that remains of that time in his life is the greedy glimmer in his eyes.

It came out differently with his brother, Yessa. Yessa was the head of the family, and the main thing he had to worry about was putting bread on the table. His mother always slipped something extra into his bowl, even if there was nothing else in the house. But he too bears the stamp of unimaginable poverty. Yessa's a bachelor as well, but, while Uri is prevented from marrying by his freakish obesity, which stifles all passions in him except the desire to stuff his face, Yessa's problem is his incredible stinginess. He doesn't want to spend his money on anyone but himself. Sometimes he gets so bored that he goes to kick up his heels in one of Antafagusta's best restaurants, provided that Uri isn't gorging himself in the same place. Yessa can't handle that. He has his own frailty, though: he carries his money in one-minare notes and pays by handing out a thick wad of them with an expansive gesture. Then he will hire ten taxis, put his hat on the back seat of the first in line, and walk home, while the taxis file slowly behind him. When he is so inclined, he will hire a taxi to go in reverse. He meets his obligations generously and refuses to take his change, but always pays only for himself, so his friends have stopped having dinner with him, and Yessa invariably eats in restaurants alone. He is particularly afraid of women, because he thinks they're only out to fleece him.

That flame from the welding torch hits my eyes again, sending a sharp pain down my optic nerve. What are they welding? Or perhaps it's the sun glancing off my disastrous car, my silvery Firebird. Her metallic sheen caught my fancy straight away, and I saw something cosmic in her long, glinting chassis. I had the sudden thought that this powerful, arrowlike car would help me break out of the dust and confinement of the day-to-day. There would be new meaning in my life, and time and space would be mine to command. When I bought it, I thought contentedly, 'All this thanks to what happened on Herald Square.' Strange as it sounds, I was almost grateful to fate for the gift she had given me. Buying that car immediately raised me in the world and set me among the chosen.

The silvery Firebird parked under my window instantly brought on the sensation of being born anew. Murana and I would go tearing along the ring road, which had been surfaced by then; we circled the island as we had long, long ago, before Roxana was born, when I still had my ill-starred Honda.

It all started when Roxana got pregnant. Mind you, it had always been just a matter of time. I only found out about it when it was beyond concealing. That was when I noticed that Tell was going missing in the evenings more and more often. Once I caught him on Britannic Boulevard with a disreputable-looking bunch. They were sprawled on the unswept steps that led down to the sea, and the boys were all over the girls. Tell himself was draped around a young girl I had never seen before. I pretended that I had noticed nothing.

I tackled him that evening at home. To my amazement, the damned brat didn't think he had done anything wrong. Quite to the contrary, he screamed at me as though I were being atrociously unfair to him.

'You think I made Roxy start a kid? The heck I did! If she'd taken the pill like she was supposed to, none of this would have happened. What do I do now, then—sit at home and stroke her paunch?'

'Listen, old son,' I tried reasoning with him. 'Don't you get the idea that it's at least partly your child too? It wouldn't hurt you to take a bit of responsibility.'

'There you go again—responsibility, responsibility! I still haven't worked out what life is supposed to taste like, and you want to stick me with responsibility! Life's over soon enough as it is. A few decades—that's peanuts. You have to do something to get some fun out of it! What can I do about it if Roxy isn't much good for sex any more? You want me to castrate myself because of that? And, you know, I am a completely normal man!' He stuck out his narrow chest.

I flew into a rage.

'Listen, boy!' I yelled at him. 'If you don't stop blathering on, I'll castrate you with my bare hands. I've got better things to do than shoot the breeze with you!'

9–1298

So Tell had a tantrum. He started keening like a woman, in a revolting, reedy voice. Then the tears came, and he smeared them across his cheeks with his grimy fists. The tattered sleeves of his jeans jacket rode up when he did that and I couldn't help noticing how bird-thin his arms were. The eternally hungry Uri Veldar of my schooldays was standing right before me.

'You're all the same!' Tell roared. As usual at times like this, he made his accusations in the plural, speaking for no less than an entire generation. 'What do you want from me? Have I been raping Roxy? Am I supposed to do an injury to myself now, just because she's been so sloppy? It's a medieval idea that you're only supposed to worry about the women. In actual fact, men are a lot more vulnerable and do you know that not being your natural self makes you neurotic, and incurably neurotic at that? And neuroses completely destroy the human personality and no two personalities are ever alike... But what do you care about that?'

Shaking with sobs, he ran out of the room. The front door slammed a little while later. Then Roxana came and had a tantrum of her own, wading into me as though I had come along and rudely broken up their happy home. For a time our flat turned into a regular madhouse. I was sorry I had interfered at all—I mean, all I had been trying to do was straighten something out that had gone manifestly askew.

We couldn't go on living this way. Finally, with an enormous effort, I managed to drag out of Roxana who Tell's parents were and where they lived, and I went to see them. Tell's father was a Consortium pen-pusher, an accountant. They had lived in Antafagusta since the year dot and had never owned so much as a shred of land, which meant that they were not eligible for any payments and were very badly off. I had too quickly become accustomed to always having plenty of money, and I took it as read that everyone else had the same lifestyle. Tell's father was a thin, bent man with a yellowish face. I didn't like him at all, especially because at first he tried to brush me off.

'All this is their business. I know nothing about it. I have never interfered, and I advise you to do the same. Let them live as they see fit, just like we do.'

'But there's going to be a child soon. A child!'

'There have been other children born in this world. It'll get along all right, I dare say. What do you want me to do—return my offspring, like a lamb on a lead, back to the bosom of his family? What right do I have? He's a grown man.'

Even before this, I had never trusted these damned intellectuals, who are forever prating on about democracy and whining about human rights the minute anyone starts insisting that we get things into any kind of order. This sallow accountant was definitely the snivelling, prating type. Instead of giving his son a well-deserved paddling, he was just blowing out all that hot air... What a line—he's a man too, you can't boss him around! You certainly can, you liar!

I realised that this was going nowhere, so I decided to lean on him a little. In words of one syllable, I pointed out that I happened to know some bully boys who for two hundred minares would pulverise his kiddiwink so badly that he'd spill out of his skin if you tipped him upside down. That unnerved Tell's papa. He started stuttering and giving me crazy looks, but at least he stopped being obstinate and said that he would try to get everything sorted out. Just don't get upset, he said, for goodness' sake don't get upset.

Tell turned up the next day, as quiet and meek as a lambkin. He did everything possible to avoid me, and never said a word. Not that I wanted the pleasure of his conversation. I was just pleased that he was back and that when the time came we would get him and Roxana married, the little dears. And after that they could decide for themselves whether to live together or separate. It would be no skin off my nose either way.

The birth of Roxana's baby put a stop to my jaunts in the car with Murana. It was suddenly obvious that she was the only one available to take care of the child. Roxana, with all sorts of fanfare, started waiting on Tell hand and foot and was far too busy for anything except the feedings. Tell accepted her attentions as his due but as for actually doing anything—nothing could have been further from his mind. I felt in the way again, as I had once before, when my own child was born. I was ill-at-ease in my own home—a grandfather at thirty-five!

Speed was my only consolation.

I can't complain that fate didn't give me fair warning. No, she wasn't that rotten about it. The final ultimatum came about six weeks before the ill-omened day, but I didn't see it for what it was. I didn't want to think about it, called it a coincidence. I was so self-assured, it wasn't even funny.

It happened on the way into Antafagusta from the east, where the quarry stopped and the Herald's tomb and the first houses could be seen across the open field. I was coming rather riskily out of a long right-hand bend, cutting across the centre line. I didn't want to lose the good burst of speed I had going, not until I got to the built-up area. I had driven this way before on the same stretch of road. Everything was deserted and completely quiet. Then suddenly, from a ditch by the side of the road, as if appearing out of thin air, there arose a figure with a long, egg-shaped head. A loose blue sail-cloth garment, like something a scarecrow might wear, was flapping round the figure as it dashed across the road, eyes pinned to the ground. My visual recall immediately told me that I had seen this egg-pated man somewhere before and that he irked me but I did not have a spare second to put a time or a place to it.

I sensed that it was too late to brake. The best I could do was decide exactly how I was going to get by this blind booby—in front of him or behind him. I chose the latter, since, looking intently at the road under his feet, he was crossing from right to left at a fairly rapid clip. I only hoped that he would not notice me and jump back in fright. That would really put the kibosh on it. I steered to the right, slap up against the grass verge: we have driven on the left ever since the English were here. Now I would skim past him and then I could heave a sigh of relief—honestly, what chuckleheads there are in this world!

As I drew level with the great dope, I suddenly saw a phosphate tip-up clanking toward me at a horrific speed. The drivers are paid per kilometer-ton, so they belt from the quarry to the port like raving lunatics and cause at least an accident a week on our narrow roads: one or another of them concertinas his lorry and goes to join the choir eternal. But the new hires want to make good money too, so they refuse to draw the obvious conclusions and belt about like their predecessors did. We call them the infernal draymen.

The phosphate tip-up with its trailer—bigger than anything in an aeroplane bomb bay, ten tons and then some—was coming straight for me like an express train. I was in its lane, and in another instant we would butt foreheads with such force that we would be smashed to smithereens, to molecules, and that would be that, for good and all.

I don't know what instantaneous, subconscious response made me swing the wheel. My car bounded to the right from under the tip-up's very nose, left the road, sprang goat-like over the ditch and carried on across the waste ground, jolting madly over the scattered rocks, before coming to a stop some ten meters from the Herald's stone burial-vault, fancy columns and all. When I got out of the car a few seconds later, my hands were trembling so hard that I couldn't feel the handle, so I pushed the door shut with my elbow. My legs were like cotton wool.

The tip-up was rumbling off into the distance. Otherwise I might have thought that I had gone deaf, so complete was the silence that hung over the level tableland. I started seething at the blasted oaf who had almost put me six feet under. Trying to stop myself shaking, I dashed unsteadily toward him.

The egg-pate was leaning over a worm that had been squashed by the side of the road. He didn't pay the least attention to me until I shook him by the shoulder. When he straightened up, I saw on the lapel of his sun-bleached jean jacket a white badge inscribed 'Doctor Umbermann, Vice President, IEA, UNESCO'.

'What the hell are you doing roaming about on the road?' I started into him. 'Life no fun any more, or what?'

The doctor looked up at me, his eyes brimful of infinite despair.

'And why do they go so fast—can you tell me that?' he exclaimed, taking no notice of my question. 'Why? Do they really think they're going to get anywhere? Or fly off into the air? Just look here—this is the one and only mutant I have ever found. Perhaps it's the last one in the entire place. And they've crushed it like the merest wood-louse! They squash the life out of everybody—and they'll squash the life out of each other as well! Too late, it's all too late...'

I backed off. Who wants to mess with a loony? And the egg-pate was waving his arms all over the show. But then he forgot about me and squatted down again by his slug, as if I had ceased to exist.

I spat irately and went back to see if the car had been badly damaged. I also waited another half-hour, until that nasty trembling in my hands stopped. Fortunately, a few dents were the worst of it, but I didn't feel too great for the rest of the day. The next day I had the redeeming thought that I had actually been lucky—I had, after all, avoided a major disaster. As soon as this notion came to me, I calmed down and gradually began to forget the whole thing. The only up-shot was that I began to take the turn near the burial-vault at a rather more sedate pace.

It was a big mistake to forget it all so easily. I should never have forgotten that tip-up which rumbled past me with a dreadful sound like the tolling of a funeral bell. I should have remembered it to the end of my days. Else what's the point in being forewarned at all?

If I had been going just a little slower, I would probably have been able to swerve away from the bright red BMW which suddenly jumped out on the right-hand side of the road, coming straight at me. Maybe I would have had to go up the verge again, across the rocks and over the hummocks. But I would still not have maimed myself.

A band of young people, boys and girls, their eyes round with hor-ror and their mouths opened wide, shouting—all that behind the slope of a windscreen. I saw them for no more than a fraction of a second, but they will be there before my eyes until the very day I die. Where were they coming from? Where were they going in such a hurry? Ask away, with your twenty-twenty hindsight! What's left of them? People are always in the most tearing hurry when they are rushing to nowhere in particular.

A split-second before that, I had seen plainly that the car was out of their control. With an unquenchable thirst for speed, they had been hurtling down the road for so long that they had lost any sense of danger and the driver, without even realising it himself, had gone beyond the point where he could make the car obey him. Catastro-phes like that, collisions on an open road in broad daylight that are inexplicable at first sight, have been happening more and more fre-quently here of late. In many cases the accident victims either die or are so badly crippled that they will never be able to explain how and why it all happened. Even when the doctors' hard work pays off and they get better, they are usually unable to provide any real informa-tion on the causes of the accident. The moment is erased from their memories, as if they had not been fully conscious at the instant of the crash.

They say that what we are dealing with here is an unstudied phenomenon known as high-velocity magnetism, which draws speeding cars toward each other. True, that makes about as much sense as talking about divine providence, but at this stage I'm far from sure that something otherworldly might not be behind all these accidents. I mean, normal people should not go smashing into each other for no apparent reason on an open road. Or do we all go crackers at certain points in our lives, and if we happen to be bowling along behind the wheel of a car at the time, then an accident's bound to happen?

I myself was in an unusual state at that moment. The engine was roaring with a sense of its own boundless power. The wheels, with no obstacles to stop them, were scudding along the dark-gray asphalt, and through the steering wheel my palms could feel the pleasant, unthreatening roughness of the road surface. It made me want to hit the accelerator a little—just a tiny bit—harder. I seemed to have unhitched myself from the loop of the ring road. My speed had torn me from the ground and was carrying me away into earth orbit, and the terrain that swept past me, gliding endlessly, became spine-tinglingly unrecognisable. There was no more room in my thoughts for my everyday problems: not for Roxana, Roxana's child and Tell, who by that time had taken over most of the flat, not for the Own-landers, who had been to visit me again, to talk to me about something they were planning that interested me not at all, to slap me on the back and resurrect for the umpteenth time the business with the armoured car, nor for the leftists, who also hadn't forgotten me. At least once a month, in some secluded spot, a messenger with a beard would collar me and, with menace in his voice, would remind me that I should be ready at any moment to let the goddamned bourgeoisie feel the fist of a true revolutionary, because revolt is the only just cause. I was fed up to here with it all, and the only thing that could release me from all my unpleasant memories was a good fast spin in the car. Here, no one could get to me. I was in sole control of my situation, and had space under my sway.

Murana had never understood that, which is why she was so daunted by high speeds. Perhaps nature has made women that way? It was all the better that her grand-daughter kept her tied to the house.

The red BMW leapt out from behind the corner like a blazing meteor, going not at an ordinary earth-borne speed but at something approaching take-off velocity—around a hundred and eighty, I should think. My own hundred and twenty just complicated matters. There was an endlessly long moment before I grasped that the red car coming toward me was already halfway across the center line and was pulling further and further to its right.

I had only an instant in which to act. I did not dare to go right myself, so as to get round these nameless suicides by taking the wrong side of the road. I had no way of knowing whether or not there was anything following them round the bend, for me to crash into head on, or whether the driver of the BMW would realise what he was doing and pull the car back over to his side of the road. It was useless to brake at that speed and that distance. What I did was not much good but it was, I think, the only thing I could have done. I dragged the car to the left, off the road. All that remained was to hope that there were no trees, stone walls or abandoned quarries in the way.

That was when I saw the faces of those children, contorted with mortal fear, behind the BMW's windscreen. More and more teenagers are getting expensive cars on the strength of their parents' easily-won affluence, and it seems that they're not expected to take care of them. Their minds are not yet mature and it's all just a game to them, although they are playing with life itself. True, they say that it's not only children who are that way—they say that it's a national calamity. We have gone too quickly from the donkey to the car, and we are every bit as obstreperous and giddy when we gad about on the roads in our tin cans as we were ten or fifteen years ago, when we would set out to leg it to the market in Antafagusta. Folk in the know go one better—supposedly we're making up for what we've been missing, because for centuries we couldn't even gallop to church on Sundays as people did in so many other places, since horses were given very special treatment on Minore. And besides, only the very well-to-do had a horse. There were no more than two or three of them to a village.

Now any one of us can have a car with several dozen—count 'em—horses under the bonnet. How could anyone hold back, not make the most of a chance like that? At the very least I'll outdrag anybody I see ahead of me on the road and let's not hear a word about being careful and all that road safety stuff. This is mine from the ground up, paid off to the last farthing, so I can do what I want. Accidents happen to dolts who shouldn't be allowed on the road. They'd be better off at home, staring at the boob tube. The lords of the highway are the real men around here!

I was two-hundredths of a second short. The red BMW clipped my back wheel. It was like an explosion. The side windows seemed to buckle out with the force of the impact, and I felt the car leave the ground and fly off the road. There was a leaden crunch of breaking springs, and then it was as if a giant, invisible hand had rolled the car end over end, all accompanied by a horrendous crash and the sound of iron grating on iron.

I did have time to be pleased that, because I had my seat belt on, I was in no particular danger. I could not be flung out of the car and it was going to stop sometime or other. But then I took a terribly hard, jarring blow, everything flattened out around me, and my body was speared by an unendurable, searing pain. And on the instant everything disappeared.

Time ceased to exist. I had no sensation of myself. There was only that dazzlingly blue flame out there, beating into my eyes and hissing

135

tiresomely. I don't know if that began at the moment of the catastrophe, or an hour later, or maybe even on the following day. Whatever are they welding? That endless, tedious hissing wearied me so, right up to the very moment when—under the invisible, reverberating dome, perhaps in the underworld itself—those words were said whose meaning penetrated into my conscious mind.

'Kulamar? He'll live...'

He'll live, he'll live? That's odd. I *am* living!

'Artur Yanno, can you hear me? Do you understand what I'm saying to you?'

My eyelids seem to be glued together. With an immense effort of will, I open my eyes. There's a doctor standing by the bed. I know him and I can't remember his name at all, although I am convinced that I have been told what it is. Behind him, leaning forward, is someone else dressed in a white coat, that's all puffed out, evidently by the street clothes he's wearing underneath.

'Artur Yanno, the encephalogram shows that you have just been in contact with Stemo Kulamar's brain activity. Did you feel that you were Kulamar?'

I nod. Dammit, my neck's all numb. Have they been doing something to it? I never get a quiet moment so I can ask them about it all, not while this infinite weariness keeps pushing me toward sleep.

'The inspector wants to know if by any chance you've remembered anything connected with the explosion.'

'Not with that, with the car accident,' I reply in a hoarse voice I don't recognise.

The man in the coat that is stretched awkwardly over his clothes leans toward the bed, so as not to miss a word. Now there's a black police uniform showing where his coat bulges open. The policeman is discussing something with the doctor and I can't make out a word. The doctor nods and says loudly to me,

'The inspector asks you to please do your best to remember anything that might have any bearing on the explosion in your car. Of the survivors, Kulamar was closer than anyone else to the scene of the incident. Perhaps he noticed something that could help the investigation.'

The policeman nods and tries to get something across by gesturing at me. But I'm exhausted again, I'm at the limits of my strength, and I can't make head or tail of anything any more. My eyes close and my ears start ringing again with the disgusting, metallic clangor that's been going on since the moment of the explosion, rising and falling under my skull.

'Oh, Mr. Yanno, that business of yours is still spreading like a blob of ink on a blotter! You just can't imagine how far it's gone!' Dan Eldon rattled out as he combed my hair. His eyes brimmed with distress. 'My poor brother's about ready to give up. Being honest with you, when your name's mentioned his chin begins to tremble, and that's a bad sign. You're a nice man, but he could well use the first convenient pretext to expel you from Minore. Ron is a kind sort of person, but there are limits even to his patience. Thus far he has had no wish to pick a quarrel with your esteemed government, because otherwise you would have been fingered as a spy long ago and thrown out...'

'Give me a break! I've had nothing to do with that for I don't know how long—ever since I found out, with your help, that the point at issue was not the Herald at all but the Consortium.'

'Too late, my dear Yanno, too late! You can't backtrack on this one. Do you know what happened yesterday?'

'I can't imagine.'

'The Ambassador of the United Emirates asked for a private audience. He didn't fudge about in the usual Eastern fashion—he took the bull by the horns straight off. They've evidently started adopting American ways. His Excellency the Emir, according to him, has long been on the lookout for a summer residence, because of the trying climate they've got at home. In the hot season it's about as good for the health as an overheated Finnish sauna. So the Emir has cast his eyes upon places where summer temperatures are more moderate and also where the sea is cleaner—not covered with oil slicks, that is—and his regal gaze has lighted upon the island of Laote, which is off Minore's northernmost tip, opposite Santa Clara. He would like to buy it, if someone will just tell him the price. He intends to build a summer palace, a moorage for his yachts and a helicopter pad there.'

'So sell him the island. Why hold onto it? You can get a decent price—he's got petrodollars to burn, so he's not going to haggle.'

'Yanno, Yanno, stop pretending to be simple-minded. A government that sets about selling its own state is a government in collapse.'

'What nonsense!' I responded scornfully. 'You're selling your whole island to the Consortium.'

'That's a completely different thing—the place is still ours and that is the crux of it. There are some pundits researching the history of Minoran colonization right now, and, believe me, its roots stretch back time out of mind. It's been discovered that some remote mountain tribes perform exactly the same ritual dances for a goat wake as used to be done in ancient times on the Minoran plateau. That's a thread, you see, which will finally lead us to the ancestors of our forefathers and to our distant kinsmen. But one thing is already clear—Minorans have been living here for at least three thousand years, so there's no way we could give this place up to anyone.'

'Three thousand years, you say?' I couldn't resist poking fun. 'Since the Egyptians were building the pyramids, right?'

That stoked Eldon up.

'Of course! Did you know that they've found petroglyphs in the

137

sandstone quarries of Santa Clara that are three thousand five hundred years old? Archaeologists have established that those pictures were carved into the cliff face by the ancestors of the Minorans. And do you know why they say that? There's a hitch-knot shown in those pictures which is exactly the same as the knot used to tether goats on Minore to this day!'

'A knot!...' I couldn't hold the sarcasm in. 'What proof is that? I should think that there aren't, in the nature of things, enough knots available to allow one for every national group on this earth. Following your line of argument, all the world's white, yellow and black strands are traceable to a single source.'

But I had obviously overstepped my mark. Dan bit his lip in an aggrieved manner, started breathing heavily through his nose, and for a while did not say a word. Then, after a lengthy pause, he declared, 'It's *our* land, all the same, and you can pooh-pooh that all you like!'

'Then don't sell it—do you think I care? I just thought that making money was the be-all and end-all for you people.'

'At first Ron tried to decline politely, and do you know how the Arab reacted to that? He screwed up his eyes in the nastiest way and announced, "My government, in contributing so generously to the memorial to your national hero, did not expect you to take such an ungrateful attitude!" '

'Insolence typical of Eastern potentates,' I remarked. 'No need to let it bother you.'

'That's easy for you to say. The Emirs of the United Emirates have become wealthy in recent years and have invested their capital unstintingly far and wide, in the Consortium among all else. No one knows exactly how many shares they hold, but it's more than likely enough to affect Consortium policy. Supposing they started edging Ron's government out, to get even? You know—well, any schoolboy knows—that every premier we've ever had has sat confidently in his seat while the Consortium was holding that seat steady.'

'Try and get them to sign a long-term lease. After a few decades, no one will remember when the Emir was supposed to return the island to you. So it will be sold on the quiet.'

'Ye-e-es,' Dan said pensively. 'But what if the worst-case predictions turn out to be correct, and after the phosphates and titanium magnetite have been removed from Minore there isn't an iota of land fit to live on? In that case, we still have the hope of setting up a mini-Minoran civilization on Laote, using the money we've been saving. It is, after all, the only one of our islets that has room to swing a cat. I mean, they won't all want to close their bank accounts and emigrate to the mainland. You come across such a diversity of pigheadedness in this world.'

Having run out of suggestions, I had to leave the shavester alone with his troubles. I tried to ward off the thought that I had been suckered into playing a bit part in this business. It was too late, anyway.

I drove to the plateau, to see old Ossian. I wanted him to tell me more about how Tommazo became the Herald. Tommazo's hundred and twentieth was coming up, and I hoped that if I could get out a decent discursive piece in good time, it might be run in the weeklies. I had to have some fresh reminiscences, and they were available only from Ossian. As far as I knew, he was the last of the Herald's contemporaries whose memory and intellect were still unclouded by old age.

Ossian was sitting outside, as usual. A hole yawned immediately beyond the stone wall, and part of the wall had tumbled over the edge, into the quarry.

'You've come here for the last time,' Ossian said, not stirring—he could for all the world have been the chieftain of an extinct tribe. His gaze reached far into the distance. 'I'm going to have to move. They've got a flat ready for me in town.'

There was no life in his voice. He seemed to be aloof from everything.

'How can you do that?'

'Who's asking? I talked with them and urged them not to touch the strip that remains between here and the slope, while I live. I mean, they won't have long to wait. But their boss said that there's a whole steamerful of ore here and it's more than his job's worth to leave it. They promised me money, but what do I want money for? If they'd offered it me fifty years ago, I could have bought a flock of goats. There's one good thing—the machine that's gnawing at the mountain under my house broke down yesterday. Now it'll be Monday before I have to move, even though they wanted me out of here today. And who knows what can happen between now and Monday?...'

The lunar landscape of the quarry floor stretched in the distance. Excavators and tip-ups crawled across it. The endless roaring of their engines came up like peals of volcanic thunder that was inexorably descending on Ossian's shack from the quarry side. And who has the power to stop approaching thunder in its tracks?

It was no better on the opposite side, by the sea. Far away, where the village of Bonegripe used to be, there were more excavators pecking at the ground. There suddenly seemed to be untold numbers of them. No matter where you looked, the shoreline was mangled and the sea came up almost to the edge of the plateau. The coastal plain was all gone, except for the road. The Consortium needed it, which was why it was still there.

Just then, a lighter loaded to the taffrail cast off from Bonegripe. It was riding very low in the water; a wave could have swamped it at any moment. Some weeks previously, a boat like that had been lost with its entire crew during a sudden storm at sea. The opposition newspaper, *Our Own Land*, published a report which said that the skippers, who are mostly former fishermen from Bonegripe and Santa Clara, deliberately overload their ungainly craft so as to earn more, since they're paid per mile-ton. The Consortium turns a blind eye to it because the more ore brought in one trip the bigger the profits. The newspaper demanded that a commission be set up to conduct a public investigation of the accident, but the government wriggled out of it, blaming the lighter sinking on a late storm warning and bad navigation by her skipper. It was obvious that nothing had changed since then. After all, the port inspectorate was also on the Consortium payroll.

We were silent for some time. Then I asked Ossian to carry on with his story about the Herald. He had no wish to talk—his gaze was fixed on the repulsive gaping cavity which was to have swallowed up his home forever on the very next day. But hospitality was one of the islanders' inviolable laws, especially among the poor folk. For a while the old man stared at his knees, at the gnarled hands which rested there. Then he began.

'Well, all in all, there's not much to what happened next. After they closed the school, like I told you, Tommazo went wandering around the island, earning his bread as best he could. He'd teach a child to read and write here, he'd knock together a chest of drawers there, and he'd cobble a pair of shoes for a rich man somewhere else. And that's when he saw with his own eyes how the people were living. Just at that time, the Own-landers were politicking in a big way—out with the English, and lock the door behind 'em, they said. We could get along with our fish and our goats, we didn't need any foreign power, not a single soul who didn't belong, and we would live as our fathers had lived, celebrating our goat wakes on the quiet. The English chased them, caught them, and put them in the lock-up any time they could. In newspapers and on notices too it was forbidden to put 'own' and 'land' together—they had to be separated by at least seven words, or the censor would strike them out. That was how they thought to rein the Own-landers in.

'And so they tussled to and fro, and the poverty grew. The Turks gradually supplanted our goat wool on the mainland with the wool from their Angora goats. Nobody would have ours at any price. And when the refrigerator ships started bringing cheap meat to Europe from Australia and the Argentine, they stopped buying our fish, salt it or smoke it as we might.

'Of course, Tommazo wanted the English to get out of Minore and go to all perdition too, but the Own-landers vexed him not one whit less. I heard him style them stone-brows and pantless patriots. To hear him tell it, they would dine on stone if they had to, so long as it was our stone, Minoran stone. Tommazo said that the first thing that should concern us was living like human beings. He was for progress and he didn't care what kind, whether it was born on Minore or was borrowed from elsewhere. And for that, as he put it, we needed international cooperation and democracy. We weren't too sure what that might mean back then.

'I don't know if Tommazo would have managed to write down any of his thoughts—as a penman he was nothing to brag about—if it hadn't been for the Boer War. The English were in a pretty pickle at the beginning of the hostilities. They even brought reinforcements in from Australia. At that time, some hotheads on Minore decided that the hour had come. The British lion's claws were blunted, they said, and what the Boers in Africa had done so could we. We would push the Tommies into the sea and make the global Empire crack at every seam. Tommazo was well contented to become their leader. He was known on the island for all sorts of pranks, and especially for the trial about the donkey droppings. And so thirty-seven young lads in all went off with him to the caves near Santa Clara. For weapons they had only three hunting rifles, some knives and one big old Smith and Wesson revolver, which they had taken off a policeman in Santa Clara on their way to the caves. There were only four bullets in the revolver chamber, and such ancient bullets were no longer to be found anywhere else on Minore. But the lads thought that they would soon purloin all they needed off the English and that men would come from all over the island to join them in the caves.

'It didn't turn out exactly that way. The English left them alone right from the start, and very wise that was too. They didn't need any bloodshed, and they had enough on their plates overseas. The rebels didn't bother the Governor either. They just sat peaceably in their hideout. The English put up a guard post at the fork in the road near Santa Clara, so that the men in the caves couldn't go nipping off home to lollygag with their wives and stock up with victuals. And the rumour went round the villages that those families whose menfolk did not come home for Christmas would have their land taken off them the following year. It was said that there was too little plough-land on the island for women and children to be tinkering about on it, and it was said that the confiscated land would be given to those whose menfolk were home and taking care of the sowing. This was a sore blow to Tommazo's band. From November on, they did not conduct one single foray. The partisan band quickly began to melt away and he could do nothing to prevent it. I don't know, but maybe he could have got somewhere if, for instance, he had stolen into Antafagusta with his men by night before the guard post was put up, had seized the Governor and sent the King a message saying, "Your Majesty, give us self-rule or we will see to it that your Governor is gathered to his fathers." The King could probably have given permission for some sort of constituent assembly—he already had parliaments in all his colonies as it was—only tricks like that hadn't been thought of in those days. And who knows but what the King might not have given up his Governor so that later he could stretch the ruf-

141

fians' necks as the drums rolled. In those days, they still liked to punish offenses against the state with public executions.

'In any case, by Christmas there were only five men in the cave, counting Tommazo himself, with the hunting rifles and the Smith and Wesson revolver. They were no trouble at all to the English. I remember well the way they lived, because my elder brother was there. He had left home as a young 'un to become a cobbler in Bonegripe, which meant in plain words that he had no holding to take away. So he stayed with Tommazo in the cave and my mother sent me with food once a week. Sometimes Tommazo would give me a couple of minares and tell me to run down to the shop in Santa Clara and bring back herrings and rice or tea and sugar. I would go past that guard post and a mustachioed Englishman would usually wink at me and ask,

' "Well? Still sitting there?"

' "Still sitting there."

' "And let 'em keep sitting there."

'Tommazo started writing down his theory in the cave on the paper that was used to wrap the herring and on rice bags torn open and flattened. He began it out of boredom, I think. They used to make up four hands to play cards and the one left over was usually Tommazo. With all the many trades he knew, he never managed to learn how to play cards properly. He made mistakes and cheated, and was always the first out.

'That's where he thought up his International-Democracy, to spite the Own-landers and the English. Fortunately, the shopkeeper in Santa Clara—such a tubby, good-natured man—was no skinflint. He always wrapped the herring up in two big sheets of oil paper and weighed out the rice and sugar in bags made of thick white paper—far whiter than the paper they use today to make notebooks and textbooks. Tommazo wrote all over that paper in a tiny script, so as to fit more in. I remember him always having a black smudge of soot under his nose, and his back being bent from eternally sitting crouched over an oil lamp. Added to that, he had become fearfully hairy in the cave. It was a wild look he had. The portrait that they painted later and hung in official chambers—"The Herald in the Santa Clara Cave"—was just made up. There he's got flowing curls, like an Apostle, and a well-trimmed, knightly beard and he's wearing something like a Boer general's field uniform instead of the worn-out short pants and the goatskin waistcoat he really wore.

'What Tommazo's teaching is really all about, I cannot tell you. Perhaps you've gone into it? I haven't met anyone who's read it from cover to cover. Well, perhaps Ares Damian has, but he has a special reason. His father, old Petros Damian, was a dyed-in-the-wool huckster all his life and the courts were always after him for something. At the beginning of the Boer War he sold the English a big shipment of forage oats, and got a good price for it. Later they sent it out to the theatre of operations in Transvaal. I don't know what Greek or Corsican he bought those oats from, but he probably never set eyes on them himself. However it was, the oats were old and green-moldy inside, and a goodly number of horses died in the English cavalry and behind the lines. What with the gaps in the cavalry and the interruption of the supply train, the English lost a big battle at Magersfontein. There was a great fuss, and they set out in earnest to find the guilty party. It finally came to their minds to declare old Damian an agent of the German Kaiser and the Russian Tsar and shoot him. He got word of this, snatched up his moneybag and bolted in the night. There was nowhere for him to go on the island, so he made for Tommazo's cave. Tommazo greeted his new companion with open arms—Petros had, for all that, done harm to the English—and Damian was thus saved from certain death. Later, when they finally came out of the cave, the war had ended in victory and old sins were forgiven. There, then. And Damian's purse came in handy for getting victuals, because the shopkeeper did not let much go out on the slate.

'Once, when I was young, I set myself to reading what Tommazo had written as well, but it was too much for me. I only understood the parts where he had copied down songs and ditties of the open road, to show how the people felt about the authorities. My opinion is that Tommazo had the same ailment as many others who get by with little book-learning. He was so afraid of looking like a simpleton that he tried hard to screw all sorts of high-flown words and foreign lingo into his speeches and writings. I don't know if all was as it should be, but, looking at it on the surface, it made a right learned impression. Speak boldly, albeit out of place! But that's the reason why scholarly men rack their brains over his book to this very day. Otherwise, what would they have to study?

'In our history, that time is called "The Stand at Santa Clara". I dare say you've read of it. I read about it too, and I tell you I laughed fit to burst, especially when I got to the bit with Tommazo's homilies. Their life was not all that hard, nor did they deny themselves all that much—they weren't monks, not by a long chalk. One of Tommazo's sweethearts lived in Santa Clara, and she would visit him with her girlfriends on Saturdays and fetch down a good few bottles of mint liqueur. There's not a hint about that in the book, and nothing about the rice and sugar from the shopkeeper in Santa Clara either. If you believe the book, Tommazo and his men fed abstemiously on slugs and roots, and washed it all down with spring water. But I know that every time they crawled out of the cave into the fresh air on Saturday nights, they made such a row that the English guard would fire into the air to make them quiet down and not wake folk up.

'What I mean to say by this is not that Tommazo was a dissembler or a rogue. He simply wasn't at all the way they describe him now. For some reason they need for it to be that way...'

When I left Ossian, I was rather confused, which was not all that unusual. The life they lived was so different from the official account of those times. Ossian himself, like an old Indian brave, remained motionlessly ensconced in his miniscule, bare yard, whose stone wall had already been broached by a Consortium excavator's iron teeth. Fair enough, I thought: I'll take all these versions and make my own, a completely new one. I shan't refute the official story—that's asking for trouble—but I will liven it up with some details and clarifications from Ossian's narrative. And what a picture he made, too—a brave little Minoran Gavroche, fearlessly stealing by, in full view of the heartless colonial soldiery, carrying a simple willow basket (check if willows grow on Minore, and if not, what do they make their baskets of?) to those stalwarts in the cave, bringing them food and helping to thereby fan the flame of the struggle for liberation on the island. I was convinced that no one had written about it from that angle. It looked like I was onto a good thing.

I got stuck in a traffic jam on the way back. Dozens of cars were backed up and the road was partially blocked. There had just been a serious accident. On the side of the road there was a large silvery Firebird, completely totalled, which had, apparently, collided at top speed with a red BMW. One of the dark roadside boulders had fetched the speeding BMW up short. The fearsome impact had torn the car in two and the lifeless bodies of the passengers were scattered among the debris. The crowd of sightseers that had congregated was much subdued by what it had come to see.

Some people were pottering around the silvery car and a blue flame was flashing from a welding torch. That surprised me. It's not normal to play with fire anywhere near a car accident, because there'll be petrol leaks more often than not. I went closer, right up to where the policemen, firemen and Heaven's Orderlies were standing. After a few more spurts from the welding torch's blinding flame, I heard the clang of sheet iron being thrown to the ground and several of the men began to drag someone from the smashed car. I was pushed away, and that was all the better, because it was more than likely a grisly sight. In any event, one of the firemen, a very young lad, reeled to one side and ran behind his vehicle, one hand clapped over his mouth. Oh rubbish, I thought: I don't even need to shove my way in here. Thank goodness I'm not on the crime beat.

One of the policemen straightened up, holding the victim's identification in his hand.

'Stemo Kulamar, from Antafagusta,' he read aloud. 'Does anyone here happen to know a Stemo Kulamar from Antafagusta?' he asked the throng of people.

No one said anything.

Stemo Kulamar... Why does that name seem so very familiar to me? It's as if I have known this man all my life, although my memory yields no image, no face connected to his name. But, despite all that, the name is always here, always close at hand. It has a familiar ring to it. This is a perfect pain—I just cannot remember what I have on Stemo Kulamar, where I got it or when. I feel that if I concentrate just a little more there'll be a slight jolt and the secret of that name will be in my hands. But that's exactly what I cannot do, and the secret slips away from me, rolls off elusively, like a drop of mercury down a crack in the floorboards, and I have no means of getting it back.

Stemo Kulamar, who *are* you anyway?

10

The first person I recognized when I came round was Murana. She was sitting by my bed and crying soundlessly, unaware that I was conscious again.

'Don't cry,' I told her. 'Don't cry. Everything's going to be OK.'

'Your legs!' she said, beginning to sob.

I looked down my body. The blanket dropped sharply at the crotch and lay flat against the mattress.

I slowly turned my gaze to the ceiling. My eyes found nothing there to latch onto. The ward stared back at me, white and hopeless.

Now that familiar, intolerable pain was coursing along both legs. I had been paid back—crazily, unfairly—just for missing the point of a fatal omen.

From that moment I was seized by such despair that for several days I did not eat a bite and did not say a word. I avoided Murana's eyes. I felt that my life was at an end and that she had nothing left to hope for either. There was no consolation in anything. Several times I heard through my drowsiness the duty nurse snippily telling someone on the phone in the corridor, 'Kulamar? He's better already... No, no—he'll not be on his feet anytime soon!'

I wanted to rave and storm and shout, 'Why are you saying he'll not be on his feet soon, when you really mean that he'll never be on his feet!' I bit into the pillow and groaned. The nurse would think that the pain was back and would give me a morphine shot. That would instantly make me feel good and again let me pull back from all the horrifying things in my mind and plunge into a cool silence, into blessed relief.

Only much later, when I had clambered out of my pit of despair and could again take notice of what was going on around me, did I find out about the drama that was playing itself out at home just then.

When they telephoned Murana from the hospital and told her that I had been admitted after a car accident and was in a critical condition with my legs smashed, she had flopped onto the sofa with a moan and Tell, who happened to be around at the time, had a fit. He burst into sobs and wailed that this would be the end of him, because it was all his fault. After my visit to his father, he had made a secret wish that I would smash myself up in my car.

Murana and Roxana tried to assure him that there wasn't and could never be any link between what we want and what really happens, but to no avail. Tell was convinced that he had actually wished the accident on me. He told them that he couldn't prove it because you can't, not yet, but he just knew that he had. After the operation, when my life was still hanging by a thread, he couldn't keep still. Pale and wan, he fidgeted about the house, and later admitted that he had decided to do away with himself if I didn't pull through.

My condition improved, and little by little Tell steadied up. Then the leftist runners started coming after me again. They still thought that I belonged to them, and suddenly they had found that they needed me. At first several unidentified men phoned Murana, but she was evidently too uncommunicative, and her mournful reports that I was in hospital and would be there for quite a while didn't satisfy them. They were surely the ones who were phoning the hospital and pestering the nurses. A little while later, toward evening one day, a thin young stranger with a sparse, greasy mat of hair and a Christ-like beard caught Tell in an alleyway not far from our house and badgered him about where I had gone. Tell got a little rattled and said that I had been in a serious car crash and was in hospital, badly injured. Then he tried to get by.

His agitation made the courier suspicious. The boy blocked his way and said menacingly,

'And just suppose it's not that at all? Suppose he's just messed his pants and thinks he can wriggle away from us? Then let me tell you—the mangy dog that betrays the permanent revolution of the proletariat will get it in the neck!'

Tell, who was always easily nettled, flew off the handle at that point. 'You can take your revolution and stick it up your nose!' he barked, and tried to slip past.

But the leftist was quick on the draw. In the blink of an eye he had pulled a knuckleduster out of his pocket and smacked Tell so hard that the blood spurted.

'That's all yours, you bourgeois bedbug!' the lad yelled triumphantly, and took off.

Tell didn't have the build for fistfighting. His nose was broken and he needed a doctor. After that, the phone calls to the house stopped, but those to the hospital continued. Someone was trying to find out if I really had been brought in for treatment or if I was just lying low there.

I found out about all this later, when I returned home and set to digging Tell out from under the guilt he had loaded on himself. That took time and patience. But, surprisingly enough, it brought me some peace of mind and resigned me to my fate. I had to jolly him along like a child: it had all been an unfortunate coincidence, there was nothing anyone could have done about it, it could never have been foreseen. And anyway, it was completely ridiculous to imagine that any mortal man could make an accident happen. You might as well start believing in witchdoctors and house spirits.

It was a help to see Tell suffering on my behalf; it seemed to make up for all his past misbehavior. His nose had mended long ago, but he still wore a sticking plaster across the bridge, like a badge of honour.

147

With my insurance money I bought a colour television and a VCR, which were just appearing in the shops here at the time. The more money they gave people, the more luxuries they had to import. There were no colour broadcasts on Minore back then, but I had video cassettes. In the evening, Tell and I would settle down side by side—Tell on the sofa and I in my wheelchair—and watch a two-year-old baseball game from Philadelphia or a Bob Hope special filmed during the Vietnam war, in almost-living colour. We gradually learned those tapes off by heart, to the point where we could unerringly predict what would happen next, which of the players would catch the ball and everything. It was an odd thing. Maybe one of those lads running about the field so long ago had died in a car accident or fallen down a lift-shaft since then. But on my screen they ran over and over again across that yellowish-green field, a hundred times without a break if that was what I wanted. So, then, it was only their shadows I was seeing, but they existed—in almost-living colour—and I seemed to be developing a belief that those people behind the glass were real. I reckon that reality isn't important at all: it's what a person believes. After all, everyone perceives reality in his own way.

I noticed that after losing my legs, I particularly liked to watch people dashing about on the screen, running and jumping. Then I was with them, heart and soul. It was like running and jumping myself. The rest of my family didn't understand this at first. They thought that it hurt me to watch people with two good legs, and they insisted on getting me films of concerts that showed people from the waist up, standing stock-still and singing operatic arias. I got myself out of that one, thank heavens. High-pitched female voices do funny things to me. They strike through to the very marrow of my bones and listening to them makes my teeth ache.

The whole world really doesn't have to be cut off at the knees just because I'm a double amputee.

As soon as that thought occurred to me, I started feeling good. My high-mindedness filled me with pride—I mean, a petty person would have taken it quite the other way about. I was sometimes actually touched by my own open-heartedness.

The Antafagusta hospital and the embassy district face each other across the boulevard. Since it's usually very quiet across the way, especially early in the day before the receptions start, I was astonished to hear noise and gunfire close to the hospital one morning. If I had known then how determined the leftists were to get to me, I would most likely have realized that they were responsible for the shoot-out. I knew them well enough: forever and a day I'll remember that miserable black attaché case with the explosives that sat there for I don't know how long, all ready to blow up somebody's last resting place. But back then, in the hospital, I didn't have the foggiest idea what they were up to. All of a sudden, the gunplay started outside, and one of the windows in my ward had shattered into smithereens before I finally grasped that it was all for real. The duty nurse ran in and pulled down the blinds. When I asked her what was going on, she blurted out, 'They're probably chasing thieves!'

I had to be satisfied with that because she flatly refused to go and make any inquiries. How could she leave her patients when she was on duty? Supposing something happened to one of them—heart failure or a gastric torsion—and she was off somewhere? Really, did I want to make a murderer out of her?

And so I didn't find out at the time that a group of terrorists had taken over the embassy nearest us, had locked themselves in with their hostages and had presented the government with a set of demands. Not your everyday story, of course. I mean, ours is a quiet town, not like Chicago or even Amsterdam. We're not used to that sort of thing. But I would have cracked right out laughing if anyone had told me then that there had been a place and a job for me in that terrorist group. It was true, though.

The gunfire soon stopped, and after that I heard nothing but an occasional vehicle racing down the boulevard with a squeal of tires, and an old crate—one of the Saracens that the police were still running—rumbling past. I kept waiting for the duty nurse to come, but she, nuisance that she was, stayed out of sight. Then I went all weak again and dozed off.

I was back in my childhood once more, on the spring morning at the very end of the war when Samuel Arbis and I went out to throw some grenades. I don't remember exactly where we got them from, but it was probably from the air base. In the weeks before Leo Neckarborn flew off to England in a bomb bay, we had often nipped onto the base during his watch and rummaged about in the half-empty warehouses. If we'd been a bit older, we might have looked for clothes and food before anything else. For a long time after the war, half the population of Minore wore shirts and dresses made out of parachute silk. Never in all our lives had we been so well dressed. But Samu and I crammed our pockets with chocolate from the airmen's rations and sprinkled cartridges and shoved grenades down the front of our shirts. No one, including us, could have explained what we wanted them for, though the chocolate was easy enough to understand. We'd never seen the stuff, neither before nor during the war. Then, with Leo's help, we crawled back through the sagging barbed wire, our clothes bulging with hidden booty, while the seasoned Leo, sounding like a real old sweat, warned us, 'Watch you don't go and trip up. You and all your gear will go flying sky-high, and I'll be on the carpet for it!'

The metallic chill of the grenades and cartridges against bare skin made us all tingly inside. We had never had the good fortune to see anyone go flying sky-high.

We carted our loot off to the pit behind the Arbis' goat-shed, and carefully covered it with a tub lid and then with turf. But what were we going to do with it all next? The bigger our cache got, the more we wanted to do something with it. We couldn't keep on storing up ammunition indefinitely.

Our chance came without warning. One day the base commander put out the word for volunteers to report at the warehouses and help truck equipment down to the port. In addition to paying a fair wage, they would let people take the surplus food supplies and ammunition that the Americans didn't want. Since the Minorans had never been much used to getting anything for free, all the villages emptied on the instant. Even decrepit old duffers with one foot in the grave went to sign on for their pay—don't ask me what they were hoping to find there. Except for a few old folks who couldn't even be roused by greed, the only person left in our village was Aunty Glanda, my father's elder sister. She was an old maid, deaf as a doorpost, and nobody could even contrive to explain to her where everyone was going. Or perhaps they were afraid that with her hearing she might just manage to get run over. I had been left in Aunty Glanda's care before, when my father and mother went to the Antafagusta market. All I got out of it was the chance to drop in at Aunty's when I was hungry. She didn't chase me off, and I took care of the rest myself.

This was it!

I ran down to Bonegripe and shouted for Uri and Yessa. They came galloping out in a flash, all keyed up at the prospect of the adventure to come.

We had chosen an excellent place, according to our lights—out on the bare plateau, a long way from the village. No one could sneak up on us there; we'd always have time to cut and run. Samuel was carrying the grenades stuffed down the front of his shirt. There were two for each of us, with one extra for him because he was the leader. We stood behind the ruins of an old stone wall which stretched right across the goat pasture. In some places it was two stones thick, and in others three.

'These are the orders!' Samu barked, as though he had graduated from a military academy only the day before. 'We'll throw them in turn. I'll count one, two, *three*! Whoever has the next turn will throw the grenade as far as he can and then we all go flat on our bellies behind the wall. Anybody who stands there gaping will have only himself to blame if he gets hit with a grenade fragment!'

The grenades were round, with a ring on top. Samuel explained to us how to pull the ring out before throwing the grenade.

He threw the first one.

I flattened myself against the stiff grass and squeezed my eyes tight shut. There was a deafening roar. I stuck my head out from behind the wall and saw a cloud of smoke and dust clearing not very far away. Bits of stone and grass divots came drumming down on my back. There was a lovely sinking feeling in the pit of my stomach.

Everything went along swimmingly until it was Uri's turn.

150

Uri timidly lifted the grenade high over his head and let go of it with a great swing of his hand. But there wasn't much strength in his thin little arm, and the iron pear plopped to the ground not too far away.

'Down!' Samuel yelped in a fearsome voice, though we already had our noses jammed into the dirt.

There was no explosion. The silence went on for several incredibly long seconds. We began to raise our heads little by little, to peer out from behind the wall. The grenade was lying about twenty paces away, bedded on the stiff plateau grass which the goats had grazed level. It looked very small and not dangerous at all. There wasn't the slightest hint of the terrifying explosive force that slumbered inside it.

'Did you pull the ring?' Samuel asked Uri.

'I pulled on it and it seemed to be coming out, but then it got stuck, so I threw it because I was scared it was going to go off,' Uri babbled apologetically.

We were flummoxed. Uri thought we were silently blaming him. He stood up, hitched his short pants, and timidly put one leg over the remains of the wall.

'I'll go and get it,' he mumbled.

'Get back here, you twerp!' Samu hollered at him. 'You want to go flying sky-high or what? If you so much as blow on it now, it'll explode!'

Uri drew his leg back and stared at the ground. The thin, unhappy little thing—we didn't have the heart to tell him off.

'Let's chuck stones at it. Perhaps we can make it go off,' Yessa suggested, obviously trying to make amends for his bungling little brother.

We started tossing stones in turn. One of us would stand up, throw a stone, and hit the deck straight away. But we were scared to bits of the grenade going off, and we just couldn't seem to hit the thing. Each of us was in such a hurry to get back down behind the wall that we didn't give ourselves time to get a proper look at where to fling our stones. Only Yessa hit it, and then only once. The grenade rolled away a little but didn't blow up.

Then Samu decided, 'I'll shoot the blamed thing!'

He told us to lie flat and pulled our Colt—his and mine—out of his pants pocket. It was the thirteenth, not an even date, so the pistol was his that day.

'Now don't lift your bonces!' he warned.

Samu rested his pistol hand on the wall and aimed long and carefully. We gave him sidelong glances of fear and admiration: we'd never seen such a brave kid in all our lives. The shot clogged our ears, but there was no explosion. Samu swore under his breath and took aim again. To do this, he had to raise up a little, so as to get a better look at his target. We followed him with our eyes, not raising our heads an inch.

There was another shot, then another, and another. It was completely incredible that with all this shooting the grenade still hadn't gone off. The Colt was making such a deafening racket.

'Perhaps it's a bad one and it won't explode at all,' I suggested.

'I'll show it what's what!' Samu grunted as he took aim again.

Suddenly an explosion nearby shook the ground under me. I thought the stone wall was going to collapse on top of me. Something started crackling, fast and loud, on the stones. The grenade had gone up.

We waited another second, just in case, then got to our feet. Samu looked distinctly peculiar. There was a broad furrow down the middle of his thick, curly hair and the white skin was showing through. Slowly the furrow reddened with blood that was oozing down from the top of his head. A grenade fragment had gone straight through Samu's stiff mane like a razor and had scraped the skin at the very top of his head, leaving a little scratch. It never even occurred to us that the fragment could have gone through just half an inch lower.

'Now there's a hairdo to beat the band!' Yessa said, stuttering slightly.

Samu touched his head, looked in alarm at his bloodstained fingers and said, 'Hey, somebody bring a mirror!'

The hand holding the Colt was dangling nervelessly at his side. He didn't even think to put it back in his pocket.

There wasn't time to get a really good look at him or to go and find a mirror. Aunty Glanda suddenly popped up, mad as a whole swarm of wasps. We were all bunched around Samu and had completely dropped our guard.

'Oh, you good-for-nothing kids! Here's where you're doing your banging and crashing!' my aunty bawled, in the typically lusty tones of the hard of hearing. That yell probably carried right down to the air base, where they might not have heard the explosions and the shots. We gave a synchronized shudder.

Aunty Glanda's eagle eye promptly fastened on the pistol in Samu's hand. She obviously gathered that the noises which had penetrated her silent world had come from this manifestly unlawful object so, without a word, she snatched the weapon up, gave a broad swing and flung it away with all her might. Aunty Glanda was a strong woman. The Colt landed far down the slope and evidently slipped into a crevice. We crawled around until we were blue in the face afterward, but we never found it.

Then she gave us all a good crack on the head, not even going easy on Samu, who by that time had a rivulet of blood dribbling down the bridge of his nose. Little Uri, who was holding up his pants with both hands and didn't even have the sense to turn his head at the right moment, got the worst of it. His big head rocked so hard that his thin neck almost snapped.

'Why didn't you get your bonce out of her way?' I couldn't keep

152

from asking when my aunt, her punitive expedition at an end, was leaving with the satisfaction of a job well done.

'But I couldn't move my hands...' Uri whimpered. 'I had my second grenade down my shirt. Well, I thought that when she boxed my ears, the grenade would fall out and we'd all go flying sky-high!'

'Damned deaf old biddy!' Samu said, waving his fist at my aunt's back so hard that a drop of scarlet blood shook off the end of his nose.

It's funny, but the last time I met Samu in Antafagusta, he had a large grey streak of hair running right down the middle of his head. That was evidently the fragment's trail, brought to light by time.

And so our pistol was gone. The drunken armory officer had been sent home by then. Two days later we went to look for Leo Neckarborn, hoping that he could help us. But the American soldier we asked about him said, 'Nek? He's not here. He's disappeared!' And he gave a low, mournful whistle through his teeth. So we never did find out where Leo had vanished to. We could only suppose that he had perhaps come to a bad end somewhere, since he never set foot in Bonegripe again. Many years passed before we found out, each in his own way, that at the time we were asking about him he was already heading for England, crouched in the bomb bay of a Flying Fortress and trembling in the ferocious cold.

Again—or at last?—I was woken by the sound of shooting. A little while later the duty nurse came in with an injection. My lost legs were aching again.

'The police are going after some bandits. The place is heaving with them these days,' was all I could get out of her.

It wasn't until the next day, when Murana came, that I found out what had really happened. But by then it was already in the papers.

'Doctor, what's happening to me? Sometimes I'm inside myself and at other times I feel like I'm inside someone else—Kulamar or whatever his name is. I'm getting his memories and these completely crackheaded thoughts that I could very well do without. It's downright mad!'

The doctor looks at me for a long time, as if he's weighing up how much I'll be able to grasp of what he's going to say. Apparently my oddly phrased but not entirely illogical question eases his mind.

'The thing is, Yanno, we're far from well-informed on a lot of things too. Doctors are in the dark, as you might say, about the human brain,' he says slowly. 'Kulamar's here in the ward with you and you should know who he is better than anyone, especially now that you sometimes even know what he's thinking. I have nothing on him except his medical history. You were both sent into shock by the same explosion and now that you're in a sort of semi-conscious state it's possible that a bioelectric bridge, as you might call it, has arisen between your consciousness and his. It's an extremely obscure phenomenon. We're assuming that the severe concussion brought the bioelectrical fields of your brains onto the same frequency, so to speak, and that this has allowed the two of you to set up a direct link. I don't know, perhaps this is all too complicated for you?'

'It's all right. I'm more or less with you so far. Are you trying to tell me that this always happens to people who are concussed by the same explosion? On battlefields too? Or is there something pathological about our case? Are we mad, the two of us?'

'I don't know, my dear Yanno. It could be that a phenomenon like this has been observed so infrequently because victims of the same explosion with approximately the same degree of concussion are very rarely left alone in the same ward with nothing to disturb them. The distance between the two people and the absence of external disturbances and perhaps other factors too could be relevant to the construction of this sort of bridge. It's also possible that this particular ward, right here on Minore, is for some reason an especially suitable place for the connection to form. There might be something unusual about the earth's magnetic field, for example, or other force fields, or the intensity of cosmic radiation, or who knows what. Perhaps it's all due to sunspots. For the time being, all we can do is speculate.'

A dragging weariness came crashing down on me.

'Don't say it'll go on like this and half of me will be Kulamar for the rest of my days.'

'I don't think so. I'm assuming that as you get better your mental equilibrium will be restored and the phenomenon should disappear. Especially at a distance. We experimented by taking Kulamar out of the ward for several days, and the encephalograms have not been running parallel during that entire period.'

'Then get him out of here for good. Don't you have a vacant ward? Give me some peace—I need that to get better. Why do I have to keep on remembering all kinds of tosh? I'm tired to death of leading a double life!'

'Hang on, my dear Yanno, just hang on a little longer. The data we're collecting right now are extremely interesting. We're hoping to find a key to the study of human brain activity. Do you understand? You do want to help us, don't you? Besides, the police are hopeful that you might get a chance to pick up something pertinent to their investigation in Kulamar's memory-images. Unfortunately, he's in no state to tell them anything. I mean, it was your car they planted the bomb in and there's no doubt at all that they were up to no good. Now supposing he noticed? Then it's just a question of catching the culprit.'

I wanted to argue, to make a point, to insist, but my strength was all gone. The only thing that kept me calm was the awareness that I was still myself. Evidently the doctor was calling me 'my dear Yanno' all the time with the deliberate intention of dispelling my anxieties on that score. Gradually everything would settle down.

And I plunged back into things that had just recently happened—things I could remember with no difficulty at all. They were right there, right alongside me.

I went to the Figaro salon that morning in a perfectly lousy mood. The evening before I had gone to visit old Ossian in his new home and what I had seen there had upset me a lot. The old man was sitting in front of the seven-story building where they'd allocated him a flat. He wasn't sitting on a log anymore but on a red plastic Coca Cola crate. Ossian was staring dead ahead, his gaze vacant. There was an exact copy of his high-rise block across the road, with laundry out to dry on some of the balconies and dilapidated beds dumped on others. The building observed the old man through its one hundred and twenty-six absolutely identical windows.

Ossian seemed completely out of place among these standardized multi-unit buildings, like a random fragment of some former life. Strangers passed by, giving him astonished looks and trying to puzzle out why this outlandish old man was sitting there in the rubbish-strewn wasteland between the buildings. Evidently, it didn't even occur to anyone that there was no reason not to sit there on a crate.

'There's not enough air,' the old man complained. 'All the air inside has already been in and out of someone, and then out here the wind can't get around. My head's all muzzy from the bad air. No way to clear it.'

He was suddenly so much older somehow. I had to try something to distract him. Perhaps the past would bring him out of himself?

'Listen, you never did tell me what happened after Tommazo left the cave. How did he manage to get his theory about, and how did he become the Herald?'

Ossian's lips moved silently for a while. He clearly didn't want to get into a lot of lengthy explanations. But once again the obligations of hospitality got the upper hand.

'Well, what's there to tell? Like I said, when he finally came out the Boer War was over and everything stayed quiet for a long time. A bit later the Russians had a scrap with the Japanese, but that was right at the world's edge and naught to do with us. Tommazo began wandering about the island as he had in times past. He was an old man by then but educational societies had started springing up all over the place here, and they invited him to give talks. So he was hardly working at all, just prattling on at their society meetings for the most part. It brought in a penny or two.

'Sometimes the thing would even end up in a fight. You see, like I told you before, Tommazo was never stuck for words. Everybody caught it from him. He gave no quarter to the English or to the Own-landers, and they just didn't get the jokes, especially the crude ones. The Own-landers would pelt Tommazo with rotten vegetables and the English, the English police, weren't beyond warming his hide with their truncheons and tossing him in the clink. So, then, if there was ever a Saturday evening assembly announced with Tommazo as the speaker, anybody could go in good heart and be sure to have some fun. In those days, after all, there was no cinema. A travelling circus with a fair booth would come from Serana once a year, at Whitsun, and spend two weeks going round the island, but they still missed some places. Now and then the assembly would turn into a brawl. We young folks treated it like a sport and enjoyed going to meetings where Tommazo was to speak. And everywhere he went he would herald abroad some idea or other, and that's how he came to be called the Herald.

'But I'll tell you one thing—without Petros Damian's help, Tommazo would never have managed to publish what he had written and then not a single soul would have known anything about his theories. I mean, nothing sticks from just talking: words are carried on the wind. To the very end of his days, old Damian was grateful for the shelter Tommazo had given him. After his time in the cave, Petros started getting along famously in the world, as though by living in fear for his life he had paid the price of a winning ticket. Then he could show gratitude to the man who had saved him without putting himself out.

'Of course, you don't know the story of Petros Damian. He dabbled in trade and was forever racking his brains on how to make more at it. Wealth didn't come easy here, among all the poor folk on this island. And then he invented his famous Minoran mint tea. I have been told—and you can confirm this with Ares Damian as well—that old Petros had a lifelong habit of flavoring what he ate with all sorts of fragrant mountain herbs, to stop his food from tasting insipid. That was just the kind of mouth he had. He used to go out and pick them himself and bought up great bundles of them from the plateau dwellers at the Antafagusta market. They would be asking but a few coppers for a great armful. Those herbs, after all, grew everywhere up there. Usually the goats would eat them, and here was Petros paying for them, albeit a pittance.

'Petros dried and mixed the various herbs, and kept testing and testing until he found a mixture that he could brew like tea. Well, of course, it was a far cry from your famous Indian Darjeeling but it could vie well with the cheap Chinese brands. The tea had an uncommonly spicy aroma and it also eased chest discomforts because of the thyme there was in it. But what am I trying to explain to you for? You can try it yourself, if you haven't yet.'

I had seen the gilded green packets of tea labelled Damian Minore Tea, Ltd. in white, and I decided to check it out as soon as I could. I had thought that Damian owned an import company which just shipped tea in from Ceylon or India and packaged it locally.

'Old Petros had an excellent sense of smell. There was good cause for him to have a nose so large that he needed a specially made umbrella with a bulge at the front. But that was later, when he was rich and didn't know what to do with his money. As a young man, he just wore a cap with a big peak. He could get wind of a profit to be turned a thousand miles away, no matter how deep it was buried. In 1907 a crisis started up in England, and the price of tea rose beyond the poor folk's means. And so Petros made an agreement with some retailers of colonial merchandise in London whereby they took it upon themselves to become representatives for Minoran mint tea. The next year there was a strike in the port of Bombay and a lot of ships were late with their tea shipments to England. And again Damian, the old fox, was right there, on the spot. Through his middlemen he started offering shopkeepers sample deliveries for next to nothing. Then he sold a house he owned down by the sea in Antafagusta that he had inherited from his father. He sold it dirt cheap to a certain Doctor Thompson who had served with the colonial forces in India. Being asthmatic, the good doctor had to look for somewhere else to live after he retired, and he settled here on Minore. Then, in retirement, he began to indulge his wanton fondness for pencraft. He wrote all sorts of articles and sent them off to the London newspapers, and they even got published sometimes. And so, perhaps simply out of gratitude to Damian, and then again perhaps not, Doctor Thompson wrote that in comparison to Indian tea, which he had been studying for a long time, tea from Minore offered far greater benefits, especially to asthma or bronchitis sufferers. As you know, half the people in England have bronchitis—the dampness there and the fumes from their coal fires singe the bronchial tubes. So those newspaper articles very quickly made Damian's tea famous in England, and Petros started hiring more and more herb gatherers. Those blockheads on the plateau would bend over backwards to make a few coppers a day from him and were even glad to be paid anything at all for goat-grass. *They* thought that Damian was an idiot, while he went on dispatching ship after ship to England.

'Before the war, when he had a goodly sum of money in the bank, he even started placing announcements in English newspapers. The announcements said: "According to the most recent research, Minoran mint tea, all else aside, dissolves kidney stones, cures the gout, and is particularly beneficial in achieving weight loss." I think that if it hadn't been for the war, with the German submarines and all, Damian would have stripped the entire island to the last blade of grass, leaving nothing but stone. Moneygrubbing was his frailty.

'Then, just before the war, Damian made arrangements to have all Tommazo's writings from the herring wrappers and the rice bags printed up into a book. He had already bought himself a little printing press in the cellar of an old stone-built house. It had been rumbling away down there for forty years, day after day, and bothering the tenants. It was a lithographic press that he was using to print multicoloured wrappers for his tea, and he told them while they were at it

157

to typeset Tommazo's manuscripts too. I don't know how many copies they ran off. There was never any talk about that. I just remember that after the war they were still on sale in every shop that carried Damian's tea. Usually the booklets were stuffed somewhere between the household soap and the cans of turpentine. Their covers got all buckled and they were always flyblown. Damian never made anything out of it, which was unusual for him. But that must have been how he paid off his debt of gratitude.

'I think it would have made Tommazo melancholy indeed if he had seen his books lying around in village shops where not a single soul wanted to buy them. In those days there were at most but twenty-five or thirty people on Minore who could read the newspaper. But, as you know, at the end of the World War the island was visited by the Spanish *grippe*—they call it the 'flu now, but back then you never heard so much as a whisper about viruses. That was the illness that killed Tommazo. He was always traipsing about, and he would get chilled to the bone and soaked through. He was never one to stay put for long.

'He left nothing, and had no surviving relatives, so Petros ordered him a little crypt in Santa Clara, close by the caves where they had once been in hiding together. Some berate Petros to this very day, saying he was an old so-and-so who only cared about getting filthy rich. Well, be it thus or be it so—all my living life I've never been one to shove my nose into anybody else's pocket—but the one certainty is that Petros was no stranger to gratitude. Tommazo's crypt would have shamed neither duke nor count. Finely dressed steps and sculpture from here to there. We'd never seen the like all our born days. I don't know why they suddenly found a need to move his old bones from there to Antafagusta after so many years. That's probably not the last thing they'll think of, but my eyes, I'm glad to say, will never see it...'

Ossian's story would have been nothing more than a pretty good supplement to the colorful tales that the old man had already told me, if he himself had not been in such a deplorable state. His gaze, which had always probed searchingly into the distance, held no animation or interest in life any more. His eyes were fixed firmly on the ground. His strong, thickset body leaned toward the earth, overburdened by the years that had suddenly come tumbling down upon him. Some trees are too old to transplant, I thought.

The previous day's talk with Ossian still fresh in my mind, I sat silently in my chair at the Figaro salon and listened to the owner rabbiting on about some trivial scuttlebutt as he bustled around me. Finally he got round to the trial of Niarchos the shipowner, which had ground to a halt in a thicket of sundry legal subterfuges and endless appeals, since the defendant had no intention whatsoever of spending good money on raising his trash from the sea-bed, where the long-suffering steel hull of his old *Octavia* had been rusting quietly for a year now, poisoning the sea with cyanic compounds.

'The sea's big, but not big enough to allow that sort of thing, especially not on Minore's doorstep!' Eldon said crossly. 'If the sea dies, we can't live. Niarchos, of course, doesn't care two pins about that.'

A telephone rang in the back room and an assistant immediately poked his head out to call his boss to the phone. Scattering apologies right and left, Eldon went to take the call.

I didn't hear the conversation, but the barber came back in a flutter. He leaned right down to my ear and murmured, so quietly that anyone standing three feet away would probably not have heard a thing,

'I'll be finished in two minutes, then you hop to it. Things are happening. This is really privileged information, note you! You're the first foreign correspondent to hear about it. And in return we expect your cooperation in putting a stop to all this song and dance about the memorial. All right, then, listen. Fifteen minutes ago a gang of unidentified terrorists took over Leverkühn's embassy and are holed up in there. They've taken the ambassador and any number of embassy employees hostage, and in all likelihood they'll be putting out their demands soon. Quite a turn-up for the book. The police have the embassy building under siege.'

I left my car a block away from the scene, near where the police vans were parked, their blue lights flashing. A couple of scattered pistol shots came from the embassy building, but otherwise all was quiet. I went in closer, until a policeman stopped me. My reporter's pass was no help at all.

'No, Mr. Yanno,' the sentry said, after glancing at my identification. 'This is as far as you go—they're shooting over there.'

The officers were squatting behind the stone plinth of the embassy's hefty iron railing, peering from behind the columns at the building, which was giving no signs of life.

Suddenly the door of a nearby tobacconist's shop was flung open and the shopkeeper, pale with excitement, looked out, his head twitching.

'They're asking for a high-ranking policeman! They're on the phone ... you know, from the embassy!' he yelled.

Someone in uniform went pounding past me. I just managed to recognize the captain who had been at the Festival Hall that time, before he disappeared into the tobacconist's.

When he came out, he called a sergeant, gave a quick order, and stood there waiting. Seizing my chance, I went up to him, and, without wasting words, shoved two packets of American cigarettes into his shoulder pouch.

'Just a couple of things, captain. Who? How? What for?'

The terseness went down well.

'We still don't know whether they're rightists or leftists. Your guess is as good as mine—identical methodology, right? They arrived in stolen vehicles, captured the Ambassador in the garden, for all the world like picking a flower for a buttonhole, and hoofed it into the building. They declared everyone in there a hostage. We'll be finding out pretty soon what they want, because they've asked for an unarmed officer to come to the front door so they can hand over their demands.'

'What are they calling themselves?'

'Some sort of liberation vanguard. But you know as well as I do that they all have names like that these days.'

The police negotiator went through the gate, but the people inside the besieged building were obviously not expecting him. A shot was fired through a window on the ground floor. With the agility of a mountain sheep, the constable bounded behind a column.

'Bloody hell!' the captain swore. 'They're jumpy. For two pins they could have put a hole in his hide!'

He rushed over to his men. There was movement—practically a bare-knuckle brawl—behind the embassy windows. The police, meanwhile, were poking a white flag out from behind a column. They waved it for a minute or two, and then the constable appeared in the gateway again.

This time everything went off calmly. The policeman had hardly got to the door when it opened and a hand could be seen giving him a piece of paper. Then the heavy oak door slammed shut.

I managed to get a look at the paper before the captain sent the terrorists' communiqué to the chief of police. The demands had been typed, and the document itself had been creased along the fold-lines in a way which left no doubt that it had been around for a while.

There were five points:

1. to release Guido the Ragman from prison and hand him over to them;

2. to free from prison a total of nine terrorists—all named—who had been arrested at various times in various countries and were at present imprisoned in Basel, Duisburg and Graz;

3. to pass a law that forbade any further mineral mining on Minore in perpetuity;

4. to pay out five million dollars, in five-dollar bills with no consecutive serial numbers;

5. to book cabins for ten people on the *Maltese Cross,* allow the revolutionaries holding the embassy unimpeded passage to the vessel, and have Guido the Ragman waiting for them there.

If all the demands were met, they would take the hostages on board the *Maltese Cross* and free them immediately after the ship had left the port. If not, one hostage would be executed every three hours over the deadline, which was set at midnight on the following day.

'' was signed by the Vanguard for the Liberation of Minore,

VLM, a name that no one had heard before. The police captain scratched his head and commented that it was evidently worth scanning the newspaper files to find out about the nine terrorists whose release was condition number two. Perhaps that would make things a bit clearer. When asked about Guido the Ragman, he just flapped his hand dismissively. That finagler's life story was such a patchwork, he said, that it would be no big surprise if he had ties with the Galapagos Turtle Self-Defence Society. Nobody could tell for sure what gang he belonged to at any given moment, because he was forever changing sides.

Now silence reigned around the embassy. The terrorists had obviously assumed that the authorities would want time to consider the demands. When it got dark, they turned on all the lights on the upper floor and the lamps in the garden, so that the approaches to the building were well lit. They were apparently keeping watch behind the dark windows on the ground floor.

At any rate, they were on the ball. At around ten o'clock at night, when it was completely dark, one of the police officers, who must have been getting jittery with all the inactivity, made an unsanctioned attempt to get to the embassy back entrance. More than likely he wanted to check if they'd forgotten to lock it. A creeping juniper hedge, which the Ambassador himself had planted, covered his approach, but he had hardly touched the door handle when a shot roared out from the little pantry window above him. The policeman howled, went crashing through the hedge, and left the grounds at a fair clip. The bullet had come down, hit him in the nape of the neck, gone along the spine under the skin and had torn his trousers on the way out. The victim was bawling at the top of his lungs and the blood was spurting all over the place, but it was not, fortunately, a life-threatening wound.

After this, the chief of police, who had arrived on the spot in person, threatened to stamp hard on any other free-lancers. It was just a matter of waiting for the government's decision. An emergency Cabinet meeting was to be convened at midnight.

Shortly before twelve I left the silent embassy with all the lights on the first floor still glimmering restlessly. By that time it had become a veritable place of pilgrimage. The entire town had gathered, and people were jostling behind the police cordon, craning their necks. Something as fascinating as this was a great rarity in Antafagusta.

As long as the saga of the captured embassy continued, I went twice a day to the Figaro salon, where Dan Eldon, as he fussed around me and the other clients, worked hard to keep me posted on what was going on. He had obviously decided to corral me into scuttling the memorial scheme and you'd have to be some kind of ingrate not to appreciate the first-class copy he was providing.

Besides, I had struck lucky with this filing for once. My agency had been the first to get an overview of the terrorist activity in Antafagusta, and, since it was a time when there wasn't a single plane hijacking in progress anywhere and not a single multimillionaire's daughter was being held for ransom, we managed to find various buyers for the story and make a healthy profit on it. That even resigned me to all the blue-pencilling they did on my material. For some reason, editors always think I'm being too wordy when all I'm trying to do is get a bit more background into my stories. I'm of the opinion that, even though we're all in such a chronic rush these days, the reader sometimes still wants more than a choppy piece of telegraphese. He needs a bit of setting and mood at least—something for the emotions to work on. If that's not so, why are the glitziest soap operas so staggeringly successful in this rational world of ours? I always get the same answer: this, they tell me, is an agency for the propagation of information, not a society for elegant phrasemongering.

On the morning after the first emergency Cabinet meeting, Dan Eldon told me,

'The Cabinet's at loggerheads. Ron had a plan to take the embassy by storm—he says it's shameful to haggle with bandits—but the Minister of the Interior and the Foreign Minister started yelling that he would do that over their dead bodies. Terrorists are a cruel lot, of course—they'll squeeze a trigger as soon as spit. And if the slightest thing happens they'll put a hole into one of their hostages, and the gentlemen ministers were not about to sully their reputations with something like that. They didn't want to be made accountable by the whole world for any casualties there might be among those foreign nationals. And if Ron were to insist, they'd resign, and then there'd be a government crisis and the Own-landers would take over. Who'd be willing to let that happen? So Ron gritted his teeth and gave in.

'Then they started discussing how to meet the bandits' demands and what concessions they should bargain for. Guido the Ragman is the easiest of all. He's being held for questioning here and we can do anything we like with him. It's a lot more complicated with the nine foreign terrorists. There'll have to be simultaneous talks with several gevernments and nobody knows yet whether or not they'll be willing to make a deal. We'd be hard put to pressure them—what could we offer them in exchange, and, all in all, who are we to demand anything of them? The law to halt the mineral mining's no problem. Any law, after all, can just as easily be repealed as passed, and the Consortium wouldn't settle for anything less. The Consortium, furthermore, is our only hope for raising the five million. The government doesn't have that sort of cash, so it'll have to be borrowed.

'Well, so far so good—but that's not the worst of it. The most difficult part was getting cabins on the boat. There's not a single one to be had for love or money. It's the height of the season and there's a great ruck of tourists. All the places are booked solid and who are you going to bump without raising a scandal? The government can't do a thing about it. Finally, the Minister of the Interior came to an understanding with the Chief of Police who agreed to send out patrols on the day before the terrorists are packed off, to round up ten blind drunk Seranan tourists in the sleazier joints and underneath the arches, and send them to the cooler to sleep it off. They'll leave a day later. We could even apologize to them after they've had their little sleep but there would still be some free places on the boat that day. Now the Foreign Minister's hanging on the telephone, trying to winkle those nine terrorists out of the prisons in Basel, Duisburg and Graz. He's promising that Minore will pay any amount of compensation. He's never had such a difficult job to do in all his life.'

I went straight from the Figaro to the prison. I didn't know this Guido the Ragman, and I wanted to take a look at him. Perhaps he was the key to the riddle, since I had drawn a blank in my survey of the newspaper files. The nine named terrorists didn't belong to any one single group. On the contrary, they were a random sample of the bloody-minded brotherhood, from nigger-lynchers to the guys with the Little Red Books. Guido was the only hope.

The warden gave me an inhospitable reception. Foreign journalists were not supposed to meet with suspects. But I had had the foresight to arm myself with a bottle of Gordon's gin, a decent sort of drink, which in the blink of an eye took up residence in his desk drawer. After that he declared himself willing to make an exception for representatives of a friendly country's press. It just so happened that he was on his way to visit Guido with the news that he'd better get ready because in the very near future he was going to be handed over in fulfilment of one of the terrorists' demands. I could tag along.

I asked him to give me a brief rundown on this Guido person.

'Oh, he's an old client of ours!' the warden exclaimed with a certain kind of pride. 'We've had him under lock and key on at least fifteen occasions, not counting the times he's been in police custody. He doesn't stick to any particular line of work. He'll take anything that falls off the back of a lorry. In a word, an old-fashioned finagler and a jack of all trades, the sort you scarcely ever see any more. He gets caught more often than not. Some people are like that—they can't seem to get the hang of any job. He earned his nickname in one of his most famous fiascos. Once, many years ago, he hid in a department store and got locked in, and then, when everything was quiet, he set to work. He didn't have a torch with him—an unprofessional slip, that—and didn't dare put the light on either, so he got into the wrong department and jammed a whole cupboardful of children's flannel underwear and babies' nappies into his swagbag, thinking he was getting furs. I mean, they're soft to the touch as well, aren't they? He got out through a trap that led into the cellar, and he should have flown the coop at that point. No one would be likely to start a hue and cry over that sort of gear—they'd write them off as a stock-taking error, and that would be an end to it. But Guido wasn't of a mind to let all his hard work go for nothing. He decided to make at least something from it. So he went with his hulking great swagbag to the Antafagusta market and he might have turned a nice profit, because, thanks to his good offices, the department store had suddenly run short of those lines, and the shop assistants who had their wits about them had already slipped Guido's leftovers under the counter for their friends. Well, then, the ladies were queueing up to buy children's smalls from Guido but he went too far. He advertised his wares by draping himself about with romper suits and pinafore dresses, making it glaringly obvious to the policeman on the market beat that one man was mightily well stocked with small blue and pink garments. Had he started up a production line or what? On the other hand, you can see Guido's point too. It's his lifestyle—always at least two mistresses at once and if he didn't wet his whistle five times a day with a double mint liqueur, then, as he puts it, he'd crack up. That's why he's constantly stony broke.'

We walked along echoing corridors to the pre-trial detention cell. The barred doors were silently opened for us by stocky old men, not too steady on their feet, in weird black single-breasted jackets with high collars. Then they slammed the doors shut after we had passed through, with a sound that made me shiver every time. I asked the warden about them on the way back, and he explained that he employed people from the plateau exclusively and only the dimmest applicants at that. They were no trouble at all, never said a word to the prisoners and certainly never passed notes, were satisfied with a miserly wage and meekly wore out the old English warders' uniforms. The island, incidentally, had huge stacks of those uniforms since the end of the nineteenth century, when a shipment intended for Her Imperial Majesty's prisons in Canada, which were chockful because of the Klondike gold rush, had been dispatched to Minore due to a quartermaster's error.

Guido gave us a blasé welcome.

'All hail, thou god of the penitentiary!' he exclaimed, and in a rather supercilious tone at that. 'I'm glad to see that you don't neglect your charges. I have a little complaint to make. The mint tea that you serve us here every morning and every evening is vile swill, you know. It works like a laxative on me. And this happens every time I stay at your boarding-house. Isn't there some way, if only for old times' sake, to get me beer instead of tea? For long service, eh?'

Guido was a tall, well-built man. His high, intelligent forehead was framed with light-brown curly hair. You could tell he was a ladies' man, but you'd never have thought he was a failure. He seemed too self-assured for that.

'Steady on, pal,' the warden replied. 'Your cronies will soon be giving you more beer than you'll ever be able to drink. Do you know an organization that calls itself the VLM?'

Guido wrinkled his brow in thought, was silent for a moment, and then slowly shook his head.

'I'm scatterbrained, as you know perfectly well,' he said. 'Is it something run by vegetarians?'

The warden made an indeterminate noise. 'Hardly. Then this is just one big mystery. Certain terrorists have taken hostages in a certain place and are demanding that we hand you over, your own sweet self, in exchange. They call themselves the Vanguard for the Liberation of Minore. Does that still not ring a bell?'

Guido shook his curly head again, even more slowly than before and sort of reluctantly this time. There seemed to be a slow stirring of thought behind his forehead. Suddenly something dawned on him.

'They wouldn't happen to be leftists?' he inquired, not letting all his disquiet show.

'How should I know?' The warden shrugged. 'They probably favour one hand over the other. Sometimes, after all, it depends on the way you look at it.'

Guido's anxiety was visibly growing. His face turned gray and his eyes began darting about.

'But you aren't intending to give me up to them without my consent?'

'We brought you here without your consent. We can give you up the same way. When have prison inmates been consulted on anything? Anyway, the government has agreed to exchange you for the hostages.'

A different person now stood before us. Guido was looking at the warden and myself in turn with the alarm-filled eyes of a frightened man, his hands outstretched in supplication. All his cockiness had been whisked away.

'For heaven's sake, don't do it! I know what it is now—they're ultraleftists. Of course it's them. Who else would it be? And they'll skin me alive, if they don't rub me out altogether, but they will maul me for sure. They don't even go easy on their own!'

The warden screwed up his eyes.

'How do you know them? Come clean now, just like in the confessional, and then we'll see what might be done for you. But only if you make a completely clean breast of it. There'll be no one but yourself to blame if you fib.'

The warden and I sat on stools. Guido was squirming about on the edge of his bunk, as if trying to get comfortable, and swivelling his head from side to side. It looked as though his skin had suddenly become too tight for him and he wanted to crawl out of it. At last he pulled himself together and began.

'You know well enough that when I'm outside I end up flat on my behind quite often...'

'I can hardly imagine you any other way,' the warden chipped in calmly.

'Well, yes... And you also most likely know that when I'm not busy on a job I'm more often than not to be found on the market. Anybody who wants Guido goes to the market—the whole town knows that. So when I was hanging about the market one day, I made friends with this lad—a very pleasant fellow—who gave me the royal treatment in a bar and loaned me a few minares into the bargain. I often met up with him there after that. I didn't ask him his business—that sort of thing's not done here, you know that—and he kept mum about the loan. Either he was being gentlemanly about it or he had forgotten that it was spare change for a man of means. He introduced me to his friends, who turned out to be pleasant lads too. Then life just went rolling along. They would sometimes come round to my place and leave parcels for safekeeping. I had a look a couple of times, just out of curiosity. Once there were tubes and parts smeared with grease and another time there were cardboard boxes with some sort of hard yellow stuff, probably one of your chemical doodads. They told me they were ultraleftists, and all our politicians, they said, are rotten to the core and want hanging upside-down. And they're struggling for universal equality where everybody who's got nothing gets everything and everybody who's got everything is stripped bare. But what's that to me? None of my relatives are politicians, so I have no sympathies there, and to my mind that principle—dividing everything up—isn't so shabby. It'll do nicely. They were complimentary about my employment, too—all roads lead to the same goal, they said. It's just another way of undermining the power of the bourgeoisie, of giving people a fair share of the wealth. But what I liked best of all was that they brought whisky and gin to share round and always left the open bottles for me. I didn't even guess back then that it had all been pinched from the customs shed. They told me that later, when they started fussing about getting their loan back and threatening to shop me to the authorities.'

'And you didn't tumble to any of that before, you fathead?'

'I didn't think too much about it. I can't rattle off the criminal code from memory. But one time they came for me and took me to a cave up by the dry bed of Lake Nakhan. You know what a bizarre, hair-raising sort of place that is, of course. They have a sort of command post or staff headquarters there. There were some sullen bearded types sitting behind a table. The leader, though, was all transparent, pale in the face and white-haired, dressed in a grey three-piece suit. He was placid enough to look at, but make no mistake—those guys with the beards and the black jackets were leery of him.

'I started getting this rotten feeling, like being on a boat at sea, and that's something I hate with a passion. Then they said, "You've received from us a total of four hundred and ten minares in cash and twenty-seven crates of liquor. Can you repay us in full?" "Good sirs," said I, "perhaps that's all correct, but, you see, I just happen to be rather short of funds at the moment. Give me time and there's a good chance I'll get my affairs sorted out." "All right, then," said they, before I could finish explaining. "We aren't insisting. We've always stood right behind the working man. If you help us out with something, we'll be quits. But if you don't want to, or, even worse, if you blab, there'll be hell to pay. We'll strip your hide and make it into a big bass drum for a fireman's brass band. We had one who blabbed last year, so we hung him head down in a crevice and there he hangs to this day, all withered up..." That didn't leave me much choice but to say, "I'm ready to do whatever has to be done." They explained that they needed money to finance a very important operation. My job was to get that money by use of revolutionary force. They gave me a pistol. I was scared of it; I'd always kept well clear of firearms. They asked me if I could manage a motorbike. Well of course I can—I don't know how many I swiped when I was a nipper, and I have been known to wreck one or two and that's not something you forget. Well, then they gave me that white Suzuki. They put a new number plate on while I was there.

'You must have guessed that when they'd quite finished I went off to rob that darned bank on Adomar Street, where the women chucked me out and the motorbike did the dirty on me. Do you think I would have tried anything so risky off my own bat? All my life I've taken a quieter, more intellectual tack, as you well know.'

'And they didn't want anything else from you?'

'That's just what I asked—like, is that all? Not a smart thing to do, apparently, because then their puny leader grabbed a pistol from the table and starts banging with the butt. And he says, "When you haul in a sack full of money, you're sure to have shoved a few hundred minare notes down your shirt front. Well, fair enough—we won't quibble about that. Take it and good luck to you. But for that you'll have to nail a certain swine, a newsman by the name of Yanno, who's a toady to the bourgeoisie and rides around in a light blue car. You'll stick a key to heaven's door into his wheel and then you're free and clear."

I couldn't contain myself.

'A key to heaven's door? What the heck's that?'

Guido gave me an obsequious look. He didn't know me, but he evidently assumed that I was someone from the top and I could influence what happened to him next.

'It's a little piece of iron that's filed down to a sharp point. When you shove it into a tire there's nothing to see from the outside. It cuts away bit by bit as the tire goes round. It's usually stuck into the front wheel on the driver's side. The tire finally bursts at high speed, and that flings the car over onto the opposite side of the road, causing a head-on prang with an oncoming vehicle. That's where it gets its name from.'

'And why was Yanno, of all people, supposed to get one of these keys?' I persisted, suppressing a slight nervous shudder.

'I don't know. I mean, they never explain what people have done to cross them.'

'Are you afraid of them now?' the warden asked.

Guido nodded his head earnestly.

'They always go scatty when any of their things misfires, and they set out looking for someone to blame. Just like children. They have to have a scapegoat, somebody to take it out on. And I messed up. I didn't go through with my assignment and they sat around waiting for money that wasn't coming. And they'll never forgive that. So don't be beastly about it, warden—keep me here, nice and safe. I've made a clean breast to you. The whole business will gradually be forgotten and meanwhile I'll be doing whatever porridge the court sends me down for. I can't believe what a clot I was to get mixed up with them!'

The terrorists' demands just weren't being met. Guido the Ragman would have none of it. Of the nine terrorists on the list, only two—the most innocuous of all, who were being held in Graz—had been promised thus far, and then only on condition that the Minoran government would make the transportation arrangements and get them out quickly. The Consortium hadn't managed to raise the money—not the right kind of money, anyway. Perversely enough, several major banks had just received large deliveries of new five-dollar bills with consecutive serial numbers, in unbroken packets. Dozens of cashiers had to work overtime shuffling the packets up, adding old five-dollar bills, and counting the whole lot over again. When it became clear that the time limit was coming up far too fast, Ron Eldon's government asked the terrorists for an extension.

When this news reached the embassy, it caused quite a ruckus. Squabbling figures could be seen at the windows, gesticulating wildly. In the course of this domestic spat, panes of glass were broken in the door that gave out onto the terrace and one of the terrorists was pushed through it. Shaking his fists and swearing at the top of his lungs, he immediately scrambled back inside, obviously intending to give his assailant what-for. Two hours passed before the quarrel was patched up and the occupiers of the embassy announced their willingness to wait. At the same time they sent out another demand—food for twenty people and joints.

This last condition floored the official representatives. There was no source of supply for street drugs, since the stuff was illegal. But when the ranking police officer tried to explain this to the terrorists, a hoarse voice, full of an addict's pain and blind fury, yelled at him down the phone, 'Then heads will roll!'

As quandaries go, this was a bad one. It turned out that the government didn't have a single gram of marijuana. All the hauls confiscated from smugglers had been written off by the book and handed over to a stove-operator at Government House, who was supposed to burn the weed in the central heating furnace. There was no way of knowing whether he had actually done that or had funnelled the drugs back onto the black market. In any event, though, he didn't have so much as a shred left.

Finally, someone in the Ministry of the Interior had a life-saving idea. A group of policemen put on false beards and went down to the port in civvies to buy dope brought in by tourists, at whatever inflated price they were asking. The disguised custodians of the law got a very dusty reception there. The portside peddlers figured that they were competitors or even plainclothesmen on a secret mission to play havoc with the trade, so fists started to fly. One policeman got a big safety-pin stuck in his hip, and the poor wretch limped home from the port empty-handed.

The take was embarrassingly small—just two packs of Winstons stuffed with marijuana. They were passed into the embassy, whence five minutes later there came a demand for seconds, on the double.

The police officials brooded. It looked as though the hostages had fallen into the clutches of a bunch of junkies, and if that was the case, there was no telling how all this was going to end.

That evening, when I zipped into the Figaro again just before it closed, Eldon gave me the latest. The Health Minister had a team of doctors and pharmacists going flat-out to find some narcotic substances that would have the same effect as marijuana. A workshop was being set up at police headquarters, under the proverbial seven seals, where the drugs would be hand-packed into cigarettes.

'They're tired to death now, and what with that and withdrawal symptoms, they're on a short fuse. The slightest thing could set them off. They mustn't be provoked,' the hairdresser spelled out fretfully.

Thus ended the second day...

'So you're Stemo Kulamar?'

The doctor had come in unannounced, which surprised me. No one had been in my ward for a long time except Murana, my attending physician, the duty nurse and the nurse's aide. My case was perfectly straightforward: the operation had been routine, and it was just a question of waiting until the incisions healed. There was nothing to discuss or look into. All I needed was a bed and my food.

This new doctor's coat was sticking out in front, obviously covering something that looked suspiciously like a camera.

'I should be,' I grizzled, angry with this intrusion. I didn't want any visitors. 'Or do you switch patients about on the sly around here?'

'But I'm not from this hospital, so don't get angry about it. Then you are Kulamar, right? I'm from the newspaper. What can you tell me about the seizure of the embassy by the Vanguard for the Liberation of Minore?'

'Nothing more than you newspaper people have already printed. Do you reckon I've got a little pair of wings hidden under my bed and go flying over there at odd moments to see what's going on?'

'Of course, of course,' the reporter nodded pacifyingly. 'You see, though, now that it's all over the authorities have got their hands on a typewritten plan of the operation that must have been put together a good while ago. It says, and I quote, assault detachment B, led by Stemo Kulamar, establishes control over the offices in the ground floor right wing, the Consular Section waiting room and the lavatory. All individuals found in those areas are assembled in the Consul's office and held there. What do you say to that?'

'Listen, that's all hogwash. I don't know any Vanguard,' I snarled sulkily. I was fed up with this man.

'But they know you. Though admittedly your name had been crossed out and another name pencilled in, which means they changed the plan on the hop. The word is that they're ultraleftists, or champions of permanent revolution as they style themselves. Someone on the police force recognized their leader, though he had no papers on him.'

I suddenly felt that I'd had enough. Quickly, without wasting another minute, I had to tell him everything—the drug addiction, the cave near the dry bed of Lake Nakhan, the attaché-case with the explosives, the runners and their threats—so that at last the nightmare would let me go.

'Sit down!' I ordered the newsman, sharply enough to make him jump. 'Sit down and get out your notepad. You did come with a decent-sized notepad? There's a lot I want to tell you...'

'Is that Artur Yanno?' the telephone receiver asked gustily.

'Speaking.'

'We've got you spotted, you dung-worm! You'll pay with your own mangy hide for sounding off to the world about our revolutionaries!'

'What's it to be—a key to heaven's door in my wheel?' I asked, feeling well on top of things.

'That's our business. You've had your warning.'

The next thing I heard was the dial tone.

Yes siree—a charming way to be woken up at quarter past five in the morning! And then they go 'Oh, how interesting to be a foreign correspondent—always something going on, fascinating people on all

170

sides, receptions and conferences. A super life and excellent pay!'

I got dressed and went to the embassy. My police captain was just coming off the night watch, his eyes deeply sunken with lack of sleep.

'All quiet?' I asked.

'For the moment, yes. Just as the sun was coming up a little squirt in short pants and braces slipped out of the building. It looked like a kid. I had no idea they were holding children hostage in there. He trotted off double quick into the garden, but they noticed him and sent a couple out after him. The kid squatted down near a tap with a garden hose attached. I don't know what he was after—except maybe they're not giving them anything to drink in there. Only the two of them found him, punched him around and dragged him back into the building. We couldn't intervene—they might have shot him for all we knew. We've been strictly forbidden to intervene without a personal go-ahead from the Chief of Police.'

While we were talking, a window on the upper floor of the embassy crashed open and a long strip of cloth was flung out. It was a pale pink door curtain, and it unfurled out to show a multicolored scrawl that read: THE JOINTS OR 1 EXECUTION AT 13:00.

'Nothing but hassles over those joints. I've had it with 'em, 'the captain remarked. 'As if I don't have plenty of other things to worry about. I'll have to phone the chief again. Now, where am I going to come up with marijuana for them?'

Eldon greeted me at the Figaro salon, a look of mystery fixed on a face that was aglow with the freshness of early morning.

'There was a difficult meeting last night,' he said, looking conspiratorial. 'As you know, Damian and the Own-landers are demanding the government's immediate resignation, since it still hasn't managed to get the situation under control. It's nothing less than a godsend for them. But what can you do? The authorities are refusing to release the other seven terrorists. Only three and a half million in five-dollar bills has been scraped up so far, and the Vanguard isn't willing to knock their price down by more than two hundred thousand. And Guido the Ragman has issued an ultimatum: if they try to take him to the *Maltese Cross* by force, he'll slash his wrists. He's an honest Minoran, and wants to take the punishment he deserves right here on Minore.'

'A sticky situation. What's the next move?'

I was watching Eldon closely. To all appearances, he was feeling entirely optimistic, which didn't jibe at all with what he had just been telling me. He apparently had something vital up his sleeve.

The hairdresser busied himself with his razor for a while, testing my patience. All right, say nothing, I thought: then what will you do with your news? You'll spill it all sooner or later.

'Note you, it'll all be decided by this evening,' Eldon bent down close, having tried and failed to wait me out. 'Ron's come up with a gambit worthy of a genius. Only he could have thought up something like this. Ron's a really clever chap, a statesman, one in a million. Damian and the Own-landers are out of luck this time. All along they've just been wringing their hands—oh my, drug addicts, you can't predict what they're going to think of next, they could get mad all of a sudden and flatten everyone there! Ron intends to capitalize on precisely that fact. I just hope everything goes according to plan.'

I was intrigued.

'Explain in words of one syllable what it's all about.'

'Oh, it's a diabolical scheme!' Eldon, still holding out, was bursting with familial pride. 'At our house they used to say that Ron was as sharp as three foxes, and they were dead right. Anybody else in his place would have given up. I mean, it's impossible to meet the demand—at least, not before the time runs out—so you'd best just throw up your hands, step aside voluntarily for Damian and let him try and sort this mess out. With any luck he'll get nicely burned. But Ron marshalled his thoughts and found a way out—an incredibly ingenious way out...'

Realizing that Dan was trying to jack up the value of his news, I pretended that it didn't do much for me at all.

'But, strictly speaking, it really doesn't matter any more what happens. The kidnapping of the Ambassador has been a nine-day wonder, but no one particularly cares how it all ends. The world hasn't run short of news,' I remarked with airy unconcern.

'Don't give me that!' the affronted Dan exclaimed. 'Come along, now—if the hostages are released and the terrorists are picked up without harming a hair on anyone's head and not one of the conditions is met, wouldn't that be a brilliant operation?'

'And are you sure that it will turn out exactly that way?'

'Mr. Yanno, have I ever steered you wrong? You should know from your own experience that what you hear from me is always on the level. Unless, of course, something unexpected turns up.'

I held the skeptical expression on my face. His vanity wouldn't allow him not to talk.

'Very well, then,' Dan said after a brief struggle with himself. 'But I warn you in all seriousness and implore you to please keep this under your hat. We don't know where the criminals' accomplices might have planted themselves. If they get wind of anything...'

I nodded. 'I'm just trying to cast some light on what's happening. I'm not pushing out of line and I don't intend to spoil anyone's fun.'

'Then listen. Ron told the people at police headquarters to put something stronger than marijuana in the cigarettes—opium or the like, I don't know what exactly. Only when they smoke the muck it should cloud their wits completely and put them to sleep. Those people in the embassy are used to getting joints from the police by now, and everything's been fine so far. I'm betting that they'll smoke everything that's sent in, without a shadow of a doubt in their minds. And, to give them something to discuss, Ron ordered them to be told that the government wants them to drop their price by another quarter-million. They were given the story that the Treasury hasn't managed to raise the sum they want in dollars and has had to resort to borrowing money from abroad as it is. They took this completely seriously, tore Ron off a strip over the phone for being a tight-wad, called him a premier without two pennies to rub together, but all the same promised to give an answer later, after the next delivery of joints to the embassy. It'll just be a matter of sitting it out. They'll fall at our feet like ripe apples, you'll see!'

'And suppose some of them aren't junkies?'

Eldon shrugged his shoulders wearily. 'Then it's all a load of rubbish, and the best I can say is heaven only knows how it'll end,' he declared, a profound disquiet replacing his former animation.

I had something to eat and went to take up my post at the embassy bright and early, so as not to miss the most interesting part...

'Well, Kulamar, we're ready!'

The doctor smiles encouragingly, and so does the nurse. 'And why shouldn't they smile?' I think with an unexpected gush of despair. Murana's huge sad eyes are looking at me intently. Will I be up to it? For reasons that escape me, I imagine that there's sympathy lurking in those two smiles. That irritates me. My head starts buzzing and I have to make an effort of will to suppress some absurdly bitchy remarks that keep coming to the tip of my tongue. My personality's gone to the dogs since I lost my other leg. Apparently I can blame it all on an inferiority complex, or perhaps some important nerve networks were damaged during the operation and that's starting to show now.

I sit on the edge of the bed. Oh, how sick and tired I am of this bed; I've been wallowing about in it for so damn long! I'm wearing my best suit, which seems too big for me now. The trousers are neatly fastened up with safety-pins. These people have thought of everything. Just an arm's length away stands a brand-new wheelchair, its nickel and plastic glittering. This is the only way I'll be able to get around from now to ... the end. I jerk my head impatiently. My throat has gone dry.

The doctor and nurse come at me from either side and help me into the chair. Help me? They just take me under the arms and hoist me like a sack of flour. I don't weigh much without my legs. Only this is one sack of flour that can feel and think, worse luck.

I start wheeling myself about. I try going forwards, then backwards. The chair obeys me effortlessly. I turn around, roll myself to the window, look out of it, and come back to the center of the ward.

'It's not such a bad gizmo to start off with. You'll be able to take yourself anywhere you want to when you've got a bit more used to it,' the doctor says, breaking the tense silence. 'And then we'll see where we go from there. I read in a professional journal not long ago

173

that at a medical technology and prosthetics exhibition, which was held just recently in Houston, a leading firm brought out some bionic leg prostheses that caused quite a stir. They work just like real legs. We'll have them here too in a while...'

My throat has gone so tight that I can't make a sound. In fact, I should be thanking the doctor. He's done everything he could and I'm the one who started it by giving him an almost hopeless situation to contend with. But I can't say a word. The doctor and the nurse go away, leaving Murana and me alone together in the ward.

Murana comes uncertainly toward me. Now you're taller than me, my little Murana! I look up at her, and in her eyes, which were sad to begin with, I see grief so boundless that it pierces me like a knife. I'm like a helpless child to her now, with the one small difference that a child grows out of its helplessness and I get more helpless as time goes on. As long as I live, I'll be looking up at Murana, and other people will always be lifting me and supporting me. What kind of life is that?

In unbearable pain, I propel myself forward, put my arms around her and press my face to her breast, so I will see nothing and think nothing. We are surrounded by a dense silence and the glittering whiteness of the hospital ward. I squeeze Murana's shoulders so hard that she begins to cry.

We are the unhappiest people in the whole world.

Soon after I arrived at the embassy gates after leaving the Figaro salon, a van with a white flag drove up and turned into the embassy grounds. They were delivering food for the terrorists and their hostages (a list of ten, headed by Ambassador Leverkühn, according to verified reports). Among the supplies were Eldon's secret weapons, his Trojan joints.

Two clerks in white overalls stacked the boxes and crates onto the stairway at the embassy's main entrance and immediately drove away. Judging from their haste, they didn't feel too comfortable in range of the terrorists' pistols. I picked up a pair of binoculars and trained them on the front door. Alongside me, a police photographer was aiming his telephoto lens in the same direction from behind the bare trunk of a plane-tree. The files needed updating, and they'd have to turn out now.

The door opened and two figures dressed in black emerged. I just couldn't seem to make out their faces, and I began hurriedly fiddling with the focus. The photographer behind the tree was just about to start snapping away but instead he sighed and lowered the great long cylinder he was holding.

The terrorists were wearing black turtle-neck sweaters with the collars rolled up to their eyes. There were simply no faces to see. They made a business-like survey of the delivery and began hauling it into the building. Everything stayed calm, with not a hint that a tense siege was under way. OK, then, we'll wait.

As evening came on, more and more journalists gathered on the boulevard in front of the embassy. Dan Eldon evidently had plenty more blue-eyed boys, or perhaps there were other channels for the dissemination of especially important information. At about seven o'clock a television trailer came bowling up and fifteen or so people spilled out of it. The cameramen promptly began lining up good angles, while the assistants and technicians dragged the cameras about and the lighting crew started setting up their equipment by the iron fence, so that when the moment came they could flood both the garden and the embassy building with light. A familiar photographer—the one with the huge glittering aluminium box slung from his shoulder—made a game attempt at sprinting through the embassy gates, but was headed off by the police. Quick as a wink then he shinned up a nearby tree, and shortly thereafter a lens that put one in mind of a grenade-launcher barrel came poking through the leaf-cover. If I'd been a terrorist, I would have assumed that it was a gun sight, just to be on the safe side. It could be a danger, which so far had gone unnoticed.

Everyone waited for it to begin.

The police had been conspicuously reinforced. While one armoured car had previously been deemed enough to barricade the embassy gates, today another had appeared. It hid furtively behind the trees, its gun pointed toward the embassy. There were clumps of policemen all over the place, armed with submachine guns and wearing the plastic-visored helmets that are usually only brought out when there's trouble on the streets. The atmosphere got more uptight as the minutes ticked away, even though nothing had happened yet.

I went looking for my police captain. What I wanted to find out most of all was how they would know when it was time. Who would give the signal? Did they have a mole in the embassy? This time the captain was peculiarly close-mouthed: he simply didn't want to talk to me. The usual allotment of cigarettes had no effect whatsoever. He mumbled that he himself didn't have a clue and kept repeating that we'd see when the time came and that no word had come down about anything out of the ordinary happening that day. Only after a flat brown bottle of Ballantine's excellent whisky had made the trip from my briefcase to his shoulder pouch did he loosen up. He took me to a car that was parked some distance away, switched on the radio, rolled up the windows and even took a quick look under the car for eavesdroppers, and then whispered so quietly that I could hardly make out what he was saying,

'You know, of course, that there are microphones all over the place in the embassies. That's just how it's done, like everywhere else in the world. The security service listening post is running three shifts to keep tabs on what's going on in the embassy. When the time is right and they're all good and ready in there, we'll be told about it over the radio. Simple, isn't it?'

Yes it was—unusually simple. They eavesdrop on Ambassador Leverkühn in the normal course of events and on his kidnappers when things get strange. I mentally christened myself a perfect ass for not having the sense to find out who worked at the listening post and get pally with them. That's where my prime scoops would have come from. Now it was definitely too late and all I could do was sweat out the developments with the others. Somebody once said that anyone who wants to be a real journalist has to keep on learning all his life in order to make the grade more or less by retirement age, and he knew what he was talking about. It's sad, but true.

The police were getting ready for the finale. Patrol wagons with barred windows arrived and pulled up to wait some distance away. Some high-ranking officer appeared at the side of almost every policeman. This bothered me. Surely such an influx of big brass would put the men's nerves on edge? Before you knew it, they'd do something dumb and the whole cunning plan would be ruined.

The minutes dragged on endlessly, as they always do when you're waiting for something. In their impatience, the photo journalists started up a fusillade of shutter-clicking at the blank evening sky and the trees outlined against it.

At last and finally the long-awaited signal was received, a fact I realized the moment I heard a police walkie-talkie snapping open. Everyone was on tenterhooks.

It was quite dark. True to form, the terrorists had punctually switched on the upper-floor lights and the lamps in the garden, and in the garden spotlights I saw a group of people filing soundlessly toward a fire escape on a corner of the building. Everything moved fast, without a hitch or a foul-up, like in a film. The two leaders braced under the ladder while the rest vaulted over their bent backs with the swiftness of well-trained athletes, and disappeared into the darkness. Evidently they were intending to penetrate the building from up top, through an attic window or a skylight, taking advantage of the element of surprise.

Everything was still quiet inside the building. No one had noticed the assault group. The two police officers who had given the rest a leg up melted into the darkness, evidently to take their assigned back-up positions.

I waited for the shooting to start. The terrorists can't be that dense, I thought: harebrains they're not! Just one unfuddled guard would be enough and it *was* a bit much to expect them all to be out. The shot that started it off would decide everything.

The cameramen trained their lenses on the silent building. The light crew, waiting for the go, had their fingers poised over their 'on' switches.

But instead of gunfire from the building there was a muffled and growing hubbub which was more like a barney belowstairs than a skirmish between policemen and armed criminals. Everyone was on the ragged edge. The Minister of the Interior was watching the go-ings-on from a black vehicle parked under the trees on the boulevard. Dark as it was, I identified him by his spectacles, with their heavy, angular frames. The Chief of Police got up onto the armored car and, like a military leader, scrutinized the battleground from that vantage point. The reporter in the tree suddenly let his fingers relax and drop-ped one of his numerous cameras onto the road with a clatter. It was like a bomb going off. We all stood rooted to the spot, our eyes tracking over to the embassy gates.

The first to snap out of it was the policeman posted under the tree. He went over and picked up the broken camera, holding it by its strap with two fingers, then looked up.

'Done for, right?' he asked sympathetically.

Smothered curses came from the tree in reply. The police officer went off with a measured tread and carefully lowered the camera into a litter bin.

At that moment the lights went on in several ground-floor win-dows, the front door crashed open and a vague figure appeared in the doorway.

'We've got them!' came the triumphant cry.

All the lighting equipment and police spots flashed on at once. The still cameras began clicking like mad and the video cameras start-ed chattering. It was very much like a pack of hungry dogs pouncing on a pile of bones. I quickly moved in closer. People pushing from be-hind jammed me up against the railings. No one was being allowed into the grounds.

One by one, with their hands locked on top of their heads, the ter-rorists came through the open doors of the embassy. The dozens of lights aimed straight into their faces dazzled them and they walked blindly, feeling their way with their feet. They had to pass through rows of policemen with submachine guns at the ready, to reach the gates where three patrol wagons were waiting for them, their doors flung wide-open. Before getting in, they were individually instructed to throw down their weapons. Their submachine guns had been taken away inside the building, so now pistols started thudding onto the as-phalt as if dumbstruck reporters were dropping one camera after another.

They were strange-looking people. I had always thought that kid-napping and terrorism were the business of well-trained professionals, self-styled acolytes of James Bond, but the individuals who stood weaving in the embassy grounds, shuffling from one foot to the other, were males of indeterminate age, dressed in little more than rags. Any one of them could have passed for a cheapjack sharpie but cer-tainly not for a mobster. Some of them were doped up to the eye-balls, which must have been due to those sneaky joints from police headquarters. But even allowing for that, it took an almost impossible effort of imagination to see these people as the bandits who had had the authorities trembling in fear for three long days.

The terrorists came weaving through the gate one by one, while the police captain standing next to me let out umpteen exlamations of astonishment.

'Who would have thought it?' he said at last, staggered by what he had seen. 'I know all those faces. Everybody in this Vanguard is one of Antafagusta's registered marijuana users. And we've arrested them all separately, in the port or on Britannic Boulevard, I don't know how many times.'

A sudden shot roared out followed by several more, fired all at once. Someone in the police ranks dropped with a groan. The call went up for a doctor.

As one of the last terrorists in the queue was tossing his pistol down, his trembling finger had quite accidentally pulled the trigger. The gun went off with a loud bang which the police sharpshooters were quick to answer, and even before anyone had had time to work out where the stray bullet had gone, the luckless prisoner had taken four hits in the body and the legs.

The Minister of the Interior's black car pulled away and hurtled off, as if on a signal.

The last person they brought out was a bearded young man dressed in black from head to foot. He was the only one in handcuffs, which meant that he must have put up some resistance. Now he was sobbing, his face buried in his hands. Nervous shock, I thought: and no wonder—he's been staring death in the eyes. But as the young man was being led to the patrol wagon, I heard him muttering deliriously,

'Troglodytic strategists, dingbats... The very idea of conducting a serious operation with a bunch of vagrants... Screw the lot of 'em! With ten real people, I'd have cleaned up...'

Big, ill-tempered tears were coursing down his cheeks into his beard.

It was a lot like the Film Festival on Britannic Boulevard, with flashbulbs popping, cameramen pushing people aside to get a clear shot, and reporters with tape recorders doing live-action interviews under the blistering hot lights. Meanwhile, they were starting to bring the hostages out of the embassy one by one. Crumpled clothing, gray faces. Leading off was Ambassador Leverkühn himself, in the short Tyrolean pants he had been wearing when he was captured. The eidelweiss flowers embroidered on the bib between his braces shone out in the glare of the spotlights, as brilliantly white as his round kneecaps. Leverkühn manifestly felt ill-at-ease in this unseemly attire. He was putting on a brave front and trying to smile, but it was patently obvious that he would have liked nothing more than to slip back inside and lock himself in. Perhaps his inappropriate outfit would cause him even more unpleasantness.

The flock of newsmen descended on the miserable, exhausted hostages like a swarm of bees.

I stood at one side, biding my time. None of this interested me in the slightest now. Let the journalistic lightweights beaver about: everybody wants to snare some original turn of phrase or paradox for his dinky little filler. For me it had all ended the minute the door had swung open and it had become clear that someone, yet again, had fallen victim to his own human weakness.

I suddenly caught sight of someone I knew. It was Delia. She strolled unhurriedly to and fro along the pavement, as though she were waiting for someone, and watched the free-for-all in the embassy grounds with a slightly superior smile on her face. Seeing me, she nodded in an unexpectedly amiable manner and, realizing that I was in no hurry to go over to her, headed toward me.

'How're things?' I mumbled awkwardly.

'Not too bad, you know,' she replied, with frisky self-assurance. 'I'm getting married!'

True as I live, it was a whoop of victory.

'Re-e-eally? Congratulations...'

'And do you know who he is? He's in the media business too, and does a lot of travelling. He's an entertainment editor for Radio Luxembourg, on temporary assignment to Minore. We're leaving next month, after the wedding.'

'You've had a stroke of luck, then,' I remarked with unfeigned relief.

'What did you expect? There are still some real men in this world!'

There was a tinge of reproach in that. I couldn't think at first how to respond and, anyway, what defence would work against that kind of accusation? But then Delia said in a completely different tone of voice,

'And still, it could have been you...'

She said it in an odd way that made me terribly uncomfortable. I was all eaten up with shame, as if an intimate secret had been shouted from the housetops, but where that feeling came from I didn't know.

'I'm evidently not made for marital bliss,' I said lightly, and immediately sensed how revoltingly contrived that sounded.

Delia's lips curled into a scornful grin.

'Tell me, though, how's your knocked-up girlfriend from the port getting on? Do you actually have her home address?' she asked caustically.

She didn't wait for an answer. Everything was clear enough as it was.

Delia began to laugh derisively, flapped a hand at me in an unmistakably supercilious manner and went off, swaying on her stiletto heels. I felt completely atrocious for some reason, although Delia's words had made it quite plain that she considered the matter closed and that, consequently, there was no longer any danger of her making things unpleasant for me. I should have been glad to be rid of her, but something was preventing me from feeling smug.

And in the depths in the garden that surrounded the embassy, far from where the reporters were scrambling about and shouting at each other, little Ambassador Leverkühn was standing in his short trousers and, oblivious to what was going on around him, was watering his neglected flowers. The stream of water pouring from the hose glittered iridescently in the light of the television lamps.

'Yanno, Yanno—listen carefully to what I'm going to ask you. Do you feel any change in your condition?'

He wants something from me again. Why is he making it so hard for me to rest, to rid myself of this leaden weariness? There's nothing for it but to try and answer him. He'll not leave me in peace, no matter what. I concentrated. Changes? I feel too woozy to detect any changes. I tried to go more deeply into the sensations I had recently been having. Wait a minute—is that it?...

'It seems that Kulamar's consciousness is gradually ... going away. If I'm not mistaken, it's cutting in far more rarely now and for shorter lengths of time. But I couldn't swear to that. Perhaps it just seems that way... And anyhow, I often don't know the difference between things that are really happening and things I'm just imagining...'

'It's probably true,' the doctor says encouragingly. 'The encephalograms are showing the same thing. Chin up, Yanno, you're starting to come out of the shock you got in the explosion.'

We're silent for a while. One thought is worrying me.

'And how is he?... Kulamar?'

The doctor gives me a serious look.

'Badly off, very badly off.'

I start to hurt, as though he's somehow talking about me too.

I was not in the greatest of moods when I went to the Figaro salon that morning, but a failure to show up could have been interpreted as an admission of guilt. The *Antafagusta Post*, the International-Democrats' newspaper, in yet another editorial about the national fund-raising drive for the Herald's memorial, had taken the government firmly to task for bureaucratic shilly-shallying and harped on about the role of selfless donations. My services were mentioned on that score—once I was referred to by name and once I appeared as 'a friendly foreign journalist'. I was hopping mad about the casual way they kept dropping my name. Admittedly it's not easy to get a journalist to promise that he'll never quote you on the record without your permission, but all the same... I realized that this could only thicken the clouds that were already hanging over me.

And so it was. While pampering my chin with a hot towel, Dan Eldon shook his head sympathetically and said,

'You're such a nice client—always level-headed, no airs and graces. It's a real pity to lose you, and that's the honest truth. I mean, with some of them it's out of sight, out of mind. A week later you've forgotten they exist. So many have come and gone. It's different with you, and that makes me sad.'

'What are you getting so sad about all of a sudden? I have no intention of leaving yet. My contract still has time to run.'

'And how much depends on us these days, my dear Mr. Yanno? As social systems become better organized, more universalized, man becomes increasingly less significant. It's difficult to come to terms with that. You want to retain your individuality most awfully, but there's nothing you can do about it. There's always some higher power that interferes in our lives, changing things whenever it sees fit.'

'What are you driving at? Do you do some fortune-telling on the side, and know more about my future than I do? As I see it, I've done everything humanly possible to avoid making any rash moves that would give them an excuse to have me deported as an undesirable alien, though there seem to be more of those points in Minoran law than in any other system ever.'

'That's all as may be, my dear Yanno, but surely you aren't assuming that'll get you off the hook? You must know, for example, that foreign correspondents accredited to Minore are subject to an annual re-registration procedure. It just happens to be coming up, and, to my knowledge, the press section of the Interior Ministry has been advised to tread warily on the extension of your current status. Now do you understand?'

I had never dreamed of worrying about something like this.

'And all because of the nonsense about the memorial?'

'My dear Yanno, you've caused so much unpleasantness already. Have you read today's papers? Of course, you have. You came through the door looking as though you knew everything. You see, instead of using the handouts from the Ministry of the Interior press section to write committed articles which show Minore to be a front-runner among small nations, you meddle in things that don't concern you and create nothing but unnecessary annoyances for other people. And that despite the fact that you were warned! So, pray tell, why should our government love and cherish you?'

He was stomping around my chair, signalling his disapproval with sheer busywork.

'Hmmm... But there must be some way of making them change their minds?' I said, putting out a feeler.

Dan was still stomping about with a disgruntled look on his face and didn't answer me for a long time. I guessed, though, that he had something up his sleeve, or else why would he even have bothered to start the conversation? I get kicked out and that's the end of it!

'I don't know,' he rumbled. 'I really don't know... No one has authorized me to offer you any conditions... But I think I might presume to put in a word for you with Ron if you were to distance yourself publicly from the deliberately obstructive campaign that Damian is whipping up. Your first step is to insist that the newspapers stop using your name. While that goes on—as in today's issue, for instance—there's nothing to talk about...'

I thanked Dan for his advice and promised to see what I could do. As he watched me leave the salon, his round head tilted to one side, he looked despondent enough to give the impression of having become attached to me in his own way and being genuinely unhappy about my impending departure. It was probably pure hokum because Dan was a tough cookie, after all. But nonetheless it pleased me to imagine that some kind of fellow feeling had grown up between us. I felt sorry for the barber and wanted to do something to cheer him up.

I gave Damian advance warning by phone, and went to see him.

He had me meet him at his clandestine flat on the outskirts of town. Two others—the heavy-set chauffeur-cum-bodyguard, and Damian's deputy, Dr. Ingoberto Reus—were there too. Damian was pretending to be not in the least bit ruffled by my unexpected visit, but Dr. Reus had his sharp nose up in the air, like a dog on point.

It was the first chance I had had to get a close look at Damian's most intimate associate. Dr. Reus was a little fellow with a ratlike face. He wore very small boots buffed to a glittering shine and splendidly well-tailored suit. As if to counterbalance his foppishness, Reus was a bundle of energy, forever sitting down or abruptly leaping up, taking a few quick steps, stopping and rocking back on his heels. The doctor fixed his conversation partner with sharp eyes, and an omniscient smile never left his face for a moment. He evidently felt defenseless without it. Reus' mannerisms conveyed abounding effrontery masked by good upbringing.

Damian poured his usual round of mint liqueur and said genially,

'Down the hatch, then, and you have my undivided attention, my dear Yanno. You can tell me everything that's troubling you. You're among friends here and not one single word will leave this room.'

Pull the other one, I thought: because I know that this whole flat is jam-packed with microphones. Only this time I have nothing to fear from them—on the contrary, I hope the conversation comes out loud and clear. I'd like nothing better than to have it well circulated. Let the hidden microphones do me a favour for once!

'You see, esteemed ex-premier,' I began on a subdued note, 'I find that you've taken me for a ride about this memorial. Did you ever tell me that you were intending to use it as a way of overthrowing Eldon's government? Did you perchance let me in on the connection between the phosphate quarry and Tommazo Oon's burial chamber? Did you warn me that this whole business reeks of a domestic squabble?'

Damian and his deputy exchanged meaningful glances.

'Where did you come up with all that?' Dr. Reus asked.

'Never you mind. I have my channels.'

Damian looked me over appraisingly.

'You know,' he said, 'I don't see anything unusual about taking on temporary allies in a political struggle. On the contrary, it would be unforgivably stupid not to do so when the occasion presents itself. It's always been like that. We haven't done you any harm with it now, have we?'

'Oh, knock it off! I've just found out that because of this convoluted affair—in which you well and truly exploited my gullibility—the government intends to show me the door for being a troublesome foreigner. This wasn't at all what I had in mind and I don't propose to just sit around and let it happen.'

'Don't worry—you only have to hang on for a little while until I've formed a new government. You have my word that we'll give you a better deal than any other foreign correspondent.'

'I'm afraid that by then I'll have forgotten what Antafagusta looks like,' I responded gloomily.

'Then what do you think we should do to assist you directly at the present moment?' Dr. Reus, who had been rubbing his hands throughout all this, inquired softly and ingratiatingly.

'First you can count me out right now. My name is no longer to be mentioned in connection with this business, as it was in today's paper. That irritates some people upon whom certain things depend. The rest of it I'll handle myself.'

Damian gave a paternally reproving shake of his curly head.

'You can't be serious! I mean to say, it all began so marvellously well. No, no—now that we've started something that's turning into a truly international movement of solidarity, we can't give up even one publicly known supporter who has been on our side since the very beginning. There's the question of honour, if nothing else! And don't forget, too, that Eldon's government still hasn't caved in. We need to lean on them hard so that they'll abandon the idea of transferring the ashes, and sanction the monument.'

I looked at him. He gave every impression of having actually persuaded himself, for the moment at least, of the grandeur of this crusade of his. But perhaps he was just a better actor than I had thought.

'Listen, Damian,' I said, unable to resist the temptation. 'How in blue blazes do you intend to cope with the situation? Suppose Eldon's government, whom you're trying to lumber with this memorial like a cat with a clothes peg on its tail, does fall as a result and the International-Democrats get in, which, incidentally, is by no means a sure thing? I mean, you'll inherit that wretched memorial and it'll trip you up too. A month or so later the Consortium and its billions will give you the boot as well.'

Damian and Reus again exchanged glances and started laughing quietly. They were enjoying themselves.

'That won't happen to us,' Damian declared, glowing with self-satisfaction. 'Never in this world! Eldon won't fall because of the memorial, after all, but because he's deficient in ingenuity and scope!'

'And you aren't?'

'You insult me, my young friend! Don't you think we proved that by the way we tracked you down the moment you set foot on Minore? And don't go pretending that it didn't surprise you in the least. I'll warrant you wondered how we knew about you when I called you in your hotel room that first evening. But, as you see, our assumptions were correct. You've assisted us substantially and for that we are, of course, somewhat beholden to you. I say again that we're prepared to settle our accounts as soon as we come to power. But you must agree, all the same, that it was a deft move.'

'Well and good, but it seems to me that you had a simpler time there than you will have in warding off pressure from the Consortium.'

'Who said anything about warding anyone off? The Consortium will get its concession and my government will remain as unshakeable as the Vatican conclave.'

'I don't get it. What'll happen to the memorial and the burial vault? Will you have them demolished when you come to power?'

'You're as unimaginative as Eldon!' Damian said reproachfully. 'I thought you were shrewder than that, but I was obviously mistaken there. Very well, then, you've proved your loyalty and I'll respond with trust. Just remember, though, it's your life on the line if this secret gets out! You must have heard about the way they saved the tomb of Abu Simbel in Egypt when they were building the Aswan Dam? We'll go about it the same way. We'll cut the burial vault, along

184

with its foundations and the memorial, out of the bedrock, split it into blocks and take it wherever we fancy. *My* Finance Minister will earmark twenty or thirty million from the phosphate remittances to pay for it. Then let Eldon kick himself all round after the event for not having thought of it himself!'

Perhaps he has thought of it now, I said to myself maliciously, imagining the tapes revolving in the cellar of a neighbouring house.

'So you intend to carry on as before? You don't propose to meet me halfway?'

Damian poured us all another mint liqueur and made a helpless gesture.

'I can't, my friend. You have to understand that there's no way we can thin our own ranks right now of all times. Otherwise before you know it, Eldon could be panicked into deciding everything at a stroke and the Herald's weary bones might turn up in Santa Clara in a jiffy. We wouldn't have time to put together a written protest, much less collect any signatures. Tough it out—what else is there to do? In politics someone's always having to pay the piper. Party interests can't make any allowance for individual concerns.'

'Gentlemen, you are putting me in a very undesirable situation,' I said, switching to my official tone.

'Life is like an endless tandem heat, with someone sticking his bum into somebody else's face all the time,' Damian said philosophically. 'The most important thing is to get the front seat. But don't take it badly—there isn't room there for everyone, no matter what!'

Damian was revelling in having the upper hand. I kept a hold on myself and left him convinced that I had resigned myself to the inevitable.

'Bear in mind that you and I will be working together again!' Damian, highly impressed with himself, cautioned me as I left.

Ingoberto Reus accompanied me to the entrance, his heels clattering as he pranced right and left, opening the doors for me. When we got into the lobby, he nodded back toward the room and said, rubbing his hands,

'The old man's ridiculous at times, but remember what he said about the tandem. Those are truly prophetic words!'

That's about the size of it for a person like you, eternally stuck in the back seat, I thought spitefully.

As I had expected, two days later, Dan Eldon's mood underwent a radical change. He chattered about this and that, and affably abused the fiendishly astute Niarchos, who had, belatedly and inexplicably, managed to get hold of the necessary papers which proved that the *Octavia* had been sold on the very eve of her last voyage, to some company which wasn't even listed in the international register. Later inquiries had shown this to be one of those flash-in-the-pan business ventures which are calculatingly set up to carry out one single commercial operation and then immediately shut down. The firm to

13–1298

which he had sold off his obsolescent *Octavia* had declared bankrupt-cy and been liquidated after the ship sank, so there appeared to be no one to take the rap over the raising of her cargo. Without a shadow of a doubt, the documents were nothing but a well-executed forgery, but Niarchos had money to burn and it would take just about forever to get an expert opinion on them. In the meantime the cyanic com-pounds went on dissolving into Minore's coastal waters.

When the other clients had left, Eldon leaned toward me and whis-pered,

'It seems that you're not so badly off. Ron has suddenly changed his mind. He has decided to cut short all the arguments and put up the memorial. You see, he's thought of a way which will allow him to do that and still stay on good terms with the Consortium. So you can hope for the best. Oh, you know, they always said at our house that Ron was as sharp as three foxes!'

'Did you manage to put in a word for me?' I inquired.

'Don't worry. Everything's going to work out for the very best,' the hairdresser said, looking secretive, and with a quick snip of his scissors he took off a tuft of hair that was sticking up from the back of my head.

A baffled Murana handed me the envelope.

There was no name on it and no address. A photograph cut from the newspaper and glued to the envelope showed me lying propped up in a hospital bed, a gray blanket pulled up to my chest, my arms at my sides and an evil look on my face. And the caption read: 'Stemo Kulamar, who has made some sensational disclosures on the activity of ultraleftist groups, seen here in the Antafagusta Municipal Hos-pital.'

The envelope contained a piece of paper folded in four and speckled with wildly uneven lettering. I had to look at it more closely be-fore I realized that the entire text had been pasted up using bits of sentences, words and letters, also cut from newspapers. Not a single stroke had been done by hand. There was big type and little type, capital letters and lower-case letters, and different colored type too, all brought together in a rollicking carnival of words. But the contents of the dispatch weren't likely to buck anyone up. It said:

'Stemo Kulamar!

'YOu manGY DOG YOur dAYS aRe numBERed! You'VE WRIT-ten yOUr OWn senTENce. DEAth tO THe trAITor! AOM.'

I didn't show Murana the letter. I just told her that some anony-mous correspondent was having his say about my interview, and didn't like my style. But as soon as she went out shopping, I phoned the police. The desk clerk's voice was drowsy, and it took him a long time to figure out what exactly I wanted from him. He had it fixed in his mind that I was complaining about some kids who were raising hell next door. Then he started nagging at me to come to the station

186

in person, and finally agreed, very grudgingly, to send an inspector round. To get that far, I was obliged to threaten him with a complaint to police headquarters. That did the trick, although I'm in no way convinced that a complaint would have got me anywhere.

The inspector arrived. Fidgeting with ill-concealed impatience, he skimmed the letter, obviously in a hurry to get this over with. Then he tossed the paper onto the table and announced,

'It's a kid's prank, more likely than not. You have kids in this block? Of course you do—every block has some. They're terribly fond of playing at secret societies, at gangs, you know. There was a time when I liked to do that sort of thing myself, and it's especially good when you manage to put the wind up someone. They got the idea from your interview. You talk about secret goings-on, about a command post in a cave near Lake Nakhan and all the rest of it. So they're playing at real-life gangsters. Kids are at the bottom of this, no doubt about it.'

'I don't think so. I have reason to fear that this is the doing of great big grown-ups and that they really mean everything they've written. Did you read my interview carefully?'

'Yes, I did.'

'Then you ought to know that this kind of game is played by very grown-up kids and that it constitutes a danger to society.'

'Yes, but that all depends,' the inspector remarked. 'There was plenty in your interview that went unconfirmed.'

'How was that?'

'Very simple. The police got information from another source besides you, someone in the pre-trial preliminary detention cells, you know. They planned a major operation, down to the last detail, and the day after your interview appeared, a beefed-up police squad, supported by an armoured car, mounted a sweep on Lake Nakhan. You see, you obviously stretched it a bit in your interview. I understand, of course—press attention and all that—but we turned up no command post there and not a single terrorist, much less a weapons cache. All we found was an empty cave, a couple of broken chairs and rubbish in the corners. I'm not disputing, of course, that someone had been there at some point. It's possible that there were some sort of secret meetings there once, but the cave has been abandoned for a long time. Mind you, I'm not calling you a liar. It's just that your information's out of date.'

'If you got confirmation from another source, why did you wait until the interview appeared? You think they don't read the papers?'

'Oh, Kulamar, give it a rest! I can well see that in your situation things look a great deal more dramatic than they actually are, but I advise you to burn that stupid note and forget about it. Don't let childish larks get you worked up. Excitement's not good for you in your state of health.'

'And if I still insist that you take the case on?'

'Then I would refuse. Absolutely, on principle. Even leaving aside the question of who would compile such a letter and why, this case has nothing to offer at all. Judge for yourself: what do we have to investigate here? There are no starting points—no stamps, no handwriting samples. It would be yet another unsolved case, and we're up to our necks in those as it is. No, really, spare us that—all it does is lower our percentage of solved crimes and that's precisely what they use to evaluate our work. We have to report on a routine basis to the Ministry of the Interior. So, you can see for yourself that I can't oblige you.'

'Then you definitely don't intend to take any action?'

The inspector shrugged impatiently.

'What action would you suggest? And against whom?'

And with that he left.

When Tell came home that evening, I showed him the letter. He looked black and touched the fresh scar on the bridge of his nose. Then he nodded and said that he would keep his eyes peeled from then on. I asked him to get the rifle with the rangefinder down from the wall, and started giving it its first good cleaning after a long period of neglect. I intended to keep it by my bed. There was a touch of fear in Tell's eyes as he handed me the rifle, but he did what he was told without giving me any cheek.

Sleep wouldn't come either that night or the night after. The whole time I was listening for someone forcing the lock on the door or coming over the balcony. I saw myself as a pathetic nonentity with nowhere to go for protection or support. Intolerable pain used to course down my lost legs at night. Now that I was getting an even bigger grant, we had all the money we needed, but that gave me no pleasure at all, and when I lay wide awake at night, watching the shadows playing their secret games, I was haunted by the oppressive, compulsive thought that in return for that money I had agreed to let them whittle me away like a pencil. Now there was only a little stub left and soon that would be gone...

'Well, Yanno, how are we today?' the doctor asks jauntily, giving me a searching look.

'I get the feeling that I've been Kulamar's medium again,' I reply, straining my memory as hard as I can to make it snag the visions I've just been having, which drift away like a smoky haze as soon as I come round.

'Yes, I know. The encephalograms have been running parallel, and that hasn't happened in quite a while. Try to remember if there was some kind of threat made to you, a hint about some possible use of force.'

I concentrated. A sense of impending danger washed over me. But I just couldn't work out where it was coming from. Perhaps, simply by talking about it, the doctor had put me in fear of a threat I knew nothing about. As my thoughts roamed helplessly in the darkness, I became increasingly aware that the danger was somewhere close, nearby, on the other side of a thin partition. But there wasn't a single opening, not so much as a chink, in the wall. I couldn't see the danger that was threatening me, but my agitated senses could feel it radiating. That's what the danger did—it radiated. I strained with every nerve, but I could not bring back Kulamar's fear: it had settled in a shapeless lump somewhere in an unmapped part of the brain. Ruefully, I told the doctor so.

'Yes,' he said in a resigned voice. 'This is another place where the human brain has to get along without our help. It's evidently pointless to expect any direct results. When you black out, you repeatedly experience individual snippets of Kulamar's life, but they never stay with you, and you're unable to generate anything consciously at any later stage.'

I could have told him that.

'Perhaps the experiment should be discontinued, doctor? I can feel this double life sapping my inner reserves. It's hard to take.'

'Yes, yes—we'll be discontinuing it soon. Just a little longer to go, my dear Yanno.'

I wasn't at the baseball match where the Serana team subjected the Antafagusta All-Stars to a crushing defeat. To me, first of all, baseball is simply boring. And, secondly, there's no way I can sit for hours in a mob of roaring, chomping, sweating people—now sitting, now on their feet—in a concrete dish of a stadium that's filled to the very brim. Call me a confirmed individualist, but that sort of mass entertainment gets me down. Yet all Minore is baseball-mad. There's not one pop singer or film star who's anywhere near as well known as the top baseball players. Their portraits are on sale in all the newspaper kiosks and were used to decorate women's swimwear until the bottomless style came in. Sailboats and streets in new housing developments are named after the current champions. True, the streets are renamed every year on an order from the town council if the championship changes hands, but perhaps that's all to the good, since it keeps things interesting and the town sort of stays abreast of the times that way. Mayor Amora always keeps a fresh nameplate on some street corner, ready to be ceremonially unveiled when official guests are in town. A while back, shortly after beginning my stint on Minore, I asked Carlos Martinez, a long-time resident, for his explanation of this wholesale lunacy.

'The game gives them a chance to let their emotions out,' Carlos replied, tugging at a sleek beard that could have graced a Castilian grandee. 'Apart from that, what do they have to get excited about? The future? But the future's beyond anyone's control. Everything here depends not upon fate but simply on how long there'll be phosphates on the island and how much the Consortium will pay for them. Politics? Politics, like sport, is the province of professionals. They shut out the dilettantes, and fleece any chance guest who happens by, like a soft touch at the roulette wheel in Monte Carlo. And, that being so, the man on the street couldn't care less what the ruling party at any given time calls itself. That's not going to make any difference whatsoever to his life. They think—and, I'd hazard, not without good reason—that the power play of politics is exactly like a play in the theatre. The ending was written down word for word by the playwright long ago and no matter how much inspiration, how much inventiveness the actors bring to it, nothing can ever be changed. Sport, on the other hand, is something that they can really get into. It could just as easily have been bullfighting, for instance, but the fact of the matter is that there's nowhere to raise bulls on Minore, as you know yourself. In sport, and only in sport, no advance decisions have been made and the victory goes to the strong. At least, that's what they think...'

'That's what they think?'

'Of course, my dear fellow. All the baseball teams on Minore have long been exclusively comprised of professionals, and they have to live on what they earn. So the prizes and bonuses are divided fairly, making sure that no one gets left out. A long time before the game they come to a gentlemanly agreement on which of the teams will win this time, which one will lose, and what percentage of the take each team will get for it. It can happen that if the stronger side is supposed to lose, they'll get twice as much as the winners, to make up for having thrown the game. After that, all the coaches and players have to do is stage-manage the thing well and put on a good show, to create a perfect illusion that there's a competition going on. Under no circumstances should the spectators be able to tell that a deal's been struck. That's a hard and fast rule. They're not about to bite the hand that feeds them.'

'So, then, the whole thing's pure skullduggery and emotional manipulation?'

'Like any theatre. The only difference is that sport involves a much larger number of people and gets them a lot more involved than the most interesting plays. Or is it time, perhaps, to ban everything but improvisational theatrics from the stage? All the parties on Minore, without exception, take it in their stride. Whether Eldon or Damian's in power, the baseball teams will still pull down their bonuses. How else could it be? After all, if those one hundred thousand people didn't roar their hearts out and use themselves up twice a week at the ballpark, who knows—they might suddenly get it into their heads to take up something else that threatens a great deal more peril to the social fabric. To demand, for instance, an account of how much the government has made, and from whom, for putting their island on the export market.'

In any event, nothing could have made a baseball fan of me. But, that notwithstanding, the Minoran government had nothing to fear from yours truly, which meant that I could be allowed to put my mind to other things during the times when the place turned into a ghost town, silent except for howling choruses of delight or despair that rose from a thousand windpipes and soared over the dish-shaped stadium.

Despite all this, I got a full report on the Serana-Antafagusta match.

When it became obvious that the Seranans had the edge, the more hotheaded and patriotic fans went haywire. The Antafagusta side soon discovered that there really is no place like home. The first bottles thrown at the players were intercepted by policemen posted on the other side of the chain-link fence around the playing area. The Antafagusta police force has a squad specially trained for that purpose, made up entirely of former basketball players who must be at least six feet tall. Their job is to stand facing the spectators during the game, target individuals who are winding up to throw something and go up to catch all the missiles that come flying over the fence. I heard tell that three years ago one agile sergeant even caught a grenade with which an impassioned fan was hoping to blow the opposing team's pitcher to pieces. True, it didn't leave much of the policeman at all—mostly buttons and buckles—but the game was able to continue after a brief pause. The sergeant was given a state funeral which, as the story goes, attracted a massive crowd, and all the newspapers, irrespective of party affiliation, ran an obituary which held up the deceased, whose photo appeared alongside, as a splendid example of the selfless sportsmanship that reigns on Minore.

No explosive devices had been brought into the stadium this time, but there were so many bottles that the police were overwhelmed. By the last inning, when the Antafagusta team was inarguably beaten, a veritable hurricane began to rage over the playing area. Broken umbrellas, legs from benches, boots, bits of fencing and Lord knows what else came showering down from the stands along with the bottles and chunks of brick. Eyewitnesses asserted that a certain number of artificial limbs and crutches, sacrificed by their owners as an expression of their indignation, were even observed in flight. All this whirled over the players' heads with the fearsome roar of a freak tornado, continually spattering them with bits of debris. The players kept slipping on broken glass. All the countless direct hits so stupefied the players that they could no longer determine when the ball was really coming at them, which caused continual arguments with the officials and held up the game. The stands roared and raged, but the real explosion came when the umpire, whose whistles were no longer having any effect on anyone, took a personal decision to send a hurt Minoran back to the bench. The player had been cracked on the head with a brick, which could have done him a serious injury if he hadn't been wearing his helmet, and had also taken a bottle in the midriff

191

just a second before the ball hit him. The infuriated player howled that it was the umpire who had been smacked on the noddle with the ball, and he could just bugger off. At this point the hitter got into it and decided the argument by the convenient means of taking his bat and whacking the umpire's legs hard enough to add him to the disabled list right there and then.

After that things got completely out of control. The spectators poured down in a solid black mass from the stands, knocking over the television cameras and breaking the glass in the press-box windows. Once they'd pushed their way to the fence, the most frenzied fans started going up it, poking their fingers through the little open squares in the netting. One of them, in a flood of tears, was trying to bite through the galvanized wire, and knots of people had gathered around the struts and started to pull them up. The shouts of the policemen as they drove people back from the fence drowned in the howls of the crowd. Even if those in front had wanted to move back they could never have done so, because of the thousands madly crushing in on them from behind.

The umpires stopped the game and told the teams to get off the field. That instruction, given by men who remained eyeball-to-eyeball with the rabid crowd, was less of an incentive to the players than their own survival instincts. Both teams disappeared at a spanking pace down the tunnel that led under the stands. The deep-throated roar of the crowd storming the fences rang in their ears, and their hearts were gripped with fear. The casualties, limping and dragging badly bruised legs, brought up the rear. No one wasted any time getting changed: they just scooped up armfuls of clothing and sports holdalls and piled into the buses that were drawn up to the changing-room door, before the maddened spectators could figure out where they had got to. In all the chaos, one of the Antafagustans took the wrong bus, which had pulled away by the time he realized his mistake and couldn't stop because the fans were in hot pursuit. The poor thing plastered himself against the back window, hammering on it with his fists, but the glass held. His face was wet with tears. His whereabouts were still unknown by evening on the following day.

The prize-giving and closing ceremonies of the international match were held in secret at the far end of the town, where the Ministry of Culture and Sport had hurriedly rented a school gymnasium. To prevent the local vigilantes, who were tearing about all over the place, from getting wind of this, the children were sent home after lunch, carrying a message that large colonies of Colorado beetles had been discovered in the school garden, which was to be fumigated, and this meant that everyone in the vicinity would have to be evacuated and a police cordon thrown around the school.

The Serana team, covered with a collage of sticking plaster, was secretly bussed in at dusk and lined up in the gymnasium. The Minister himself gave an inspired speech about the meaning of true sportsmanship in international relations and the role of sport in the reinforcement of friendship and mutual respect.

The Antafagusta team had refused to take part in the ceremony. The players had announced that the very sight of those self-satisfied Seranan kissers made their fists itch and they could not vouch for their behaviour. On express orders, their place was taken by the state-appointed Antafagusta head coach, whose official excuse was that the team was attending a psychotherapy session which was part of the training program and could not be rescheduled. He conveyed the team's very warmest regards to rivals every encounter with whom in the sports arena was a source of genuine pleasure to all concerned.

At that time, the entire Antafagusta team, including the reserves, was sitting in a tavern called the Golden Mint-Leaf, dolefully knocking back double shots of mint liqueur and discussing the vicissitudes of life. They began by coming to the unanimous conclusion that there's no justice in this world. Then they all sat there long-faced until one of them had the brilliant idea of putting a lead casing on the ball to be used in the next Serana-Antafagusta game, so that anyone who got hit with it would be laid out permanently and put up no arguments. They were all enraptured by this stroke of genius. The bitterness of defeat started to go away, and everyone ordered another double mint liqueur to celebrate.

The Serana team's prize was a sturdy bust of the Herald, presented in the kind of large, goatskin box that's made only on Minore. The bust was carved out of phosphate rock; brown highlights shimmered over it. It was one of the locally-produced works of art which the Antafagustan artistic community was entitled to offer for sale in unlimited quantities to the Ministry of Culture and Sport, that being their way of going for a slice of the phosphate revenue. Truth to tell, the works of art they put up for sale were never screened by anyone in the ministry. That wasn't part of the ministry officials' job description, and they wouldn't be paid for it. Besides, it would have been completely pointless, since the only purpose was to spread the phosphate income about. On the first Thursday of each quarter, the artists simply delivered their new works to the ministry's main auditorium and vestibule, where they were counted. Then the sum allocated for the given quarter was divided by the number of works received. After this, the crafters could go to the cash desk, while haulers took their works down to a warehouse from where, as the need arose, some would be picked out as prizes, as gifts for visitors, or as exhibition pieces. Most of them were subsequently donated to the exhibition venue, which freed up the ministry cellars for new purchases.

It certainly was a very handy system. The artists didn't have to take account of anyone's taste or of market prices. They could produce entirely as they saw fit—a lot or a little, well or badly. Nobody was constrained to violate his creative persona with vain attempts to screw his expertise to the sticking point or overemphasize the ideas underlying his creations. They had a completely free hand in what they did. There were, however, still some discontents, who complained that jumped-up sleazeballs were deliberately opting for concepts and themes that would make their works stand out and thus be selected more often as exhibits and souvenirs. Incidentally, I dare say, that's inevitable. Since time began, after all, people in the world of art have been casting a far more keenly jealous eye on their neighbour's workbench than upon their own canvases. In any event, the sculptors who specialized in busts of the Herald, of which there was always an ample supply, had become objects of envy and targets of criticism.

I got an unexpected look at the Serana team's grand prize—the bust—in the customs hall of the steamer passenger terminal. I went down there late on the following day to see off my old friend Carlos, who was starting out on the *Maltese Cross* for some home leave after a two-year posting.

'I would never have let myself in for such a long journey,' Carlos admitted in the press bar before going aboard, 'if I didn't want, albeit for a while, to shake off the revolting feeling that minute by minute the scrap of land under my feet, in this great expanse of salt water, is being clipped up and sold one piece at a time. Soon you'll be having to balance on one leg, and then one fine day you'll flop into the water and start bobbing about on the waves, hoping against hope that a ship will come by before the sharks do.'

The Serana baseball players, still a mass of sticking plaster, happened to be having their luggage examined at the customs barrier at the time. My eye was caught by something brown and curlicued between the legs of the mob at the barrier. At first sight I thought it was a dog, which made me wonder who would have brought one of those to Minore and why, since there's nothing to hunt on the island. It was only when the baseball players spread out that I saw it was a sculpture of Tommazo Oon with the officially sanctioned curly beard. Its brownish phosphate tints had put me in mind of an Irish setter.

There was a large decorative goatskin box on the table and a dispute in the making. The players were waving their arms and trying to get some point across to the customs official, who was listening to their arguments with professional distrust, shaking his head negatively all the while.

Some young chaps with unexpressive, unmemorable faces were dodging among the passengers in the hall, quietly muttering, 'For sale? For sale? Anybody got anything for sale?'

Suddenly the Seranan coach turned his attention to one of them, was much surprised by something and promptly grabbed the peddler by the lap of his red and yellow promotional jacket.

'Mr. Ecks!' the coach shouted, loud enough for everyone in the place to hear. 'How are my briefs with the picture-pattern doing these days?'

The hustler gave the coach a look filled with hatred. As if to avoid a blow he knew was coming, he drew his head into his shoulders, which made him look a lot like a cornered rat. All of a sudden he jerked abruptly to one side and there was a sound of plastic material tearing. Leaving the lap of his red and yellow jacket in the astonished coach's hands, the lad plunged into the crowd. He crouched down as he ran, so that only a slight movement in the crowd showed the direction he had taken. A few other trade enthusiasts bolted for the door at the same time, evidently afraid that this might be some kind of trap.

The coach was too busy to go after him, and it was hardly likely that he wanted to anyway, because in the meantime, the dispute between the customs official and the players had heated up. Driven by curiosity, I moved nearer and saw bottles of mint liqueur lying like logs in the box. The customs official obviously considered that there were too many. Minore had stringent restrictions on the export of mint liqueur, to protect the foreign trade monopoly. The players were shouting in the disgusting, highly-strung voices of spoiled children that it was everyone's luggage, that there was a whole team involved, including the reserves and the coach as well. Divided between the lot of them, the number was exactly right.

Then the coach decided to put a stop to the argument forthwith. He slapped the customs official on the shoulder and said in a moralizing tone,

'What's the point of getting so picky about details, old chum? After all, my players are going home winners!'

That was exactly the wrong thing to say. The customs official's face immediately went stony, turning into an implacable mask. It was clear that there was to be no further conversation with him. He puched the box aside so decisively that the bottles packed inside it clinked together.

'Confiscated,' he announced, with a metallic edge to his voice.

'The heck it is!' the coach, never one to stand on ceremony, said dismissively. 'Bring the box, you guys, and let's get on board. We're late.'

The nearest player tried to grab the box but the customs official had evidently foreseen that contingency. With astonishing speed, he grasped it and hung on bodily. The lanky athlete wasn't strong enough to shift it from the table.

'Up and at 'em!' he hallooed.

But the customs official had already waved in the policeman on duty, a shortish sergeant wearing a uniform with carefully polished buttons and a new dress cap decorated with braid. Fully mindful of his dignity, the sergeant approached the customs barrier, and, in a formal tone of voice, asked them not to obstruct the customs official in the pursuit of his duties.

A six-foot-tall Serana baseball player came bearing down on the sergeant, his chest stuck out.

'Snooks to you, kiddo!' he drawled tauntingly with a broad grin. 'Hush up and shoo!'

The policeman went pale.

'Stop this disruptive behavior!' he demanded.

The baseball player, who had a sticking-plaster cross on his eyebrow showed his gums like an old camel and spat between his teeth. From his height of six feet, he hit the toe of the sergeant's polished boot with staggering accuracy that bore witness to thorough training.

'You're under arrest!' the sergeant screeched in a high falsetto.

'Well, I never!' the baseball player said in surprise. Then he lunged forward, grasped the policeman under the arms and lifted him high above his head. The sergeant snatched his cap off so that it wouldn't go flying. An instant later, he was sailing across the customs hall, to the waiting area with its upholstered seats. Still in a sitting position, he landed on a chair with a fearsome crunch. It tipped over and he went toppling onto the floor, right at the feet of the flabbergasted onlookers.

Meanwhile, the customs official had drummed up some help. The policeman on duty in the concourse outside the glass door came running in, alternately blowing his whistle and reeling something off into a transmitter he was holding to his mouth.

The ensuing melee frightened the other passengers so much that they cleared the hall, their buttons popping off in the crush at the door. Being loath to deprive myself of such a spectacle, I hid behind the bar, where a scared bartender was hastily removing bottles and glasses from the counter and shelves. His fear was not ill-founded, since sports holdalls and suchlike pieces of hand luggage were already flying from all directions.

The Serana team would have had a quick victory in the customs hall too, had not a minibus containing a police patrol come speeding up, its siren wailing. The fresh contingent dashed straight into the hand-to-hand fracas. Soon three shortish policemen were dragging the baseball player with sticking plaster on his eyebrow—the one who had first tried to pull the box away from the customs official and then had tossed the sergeant right across the hall—toward the police vehicle. Justice was thus seen to prevail. The police were working on the very simple assumption that removing the ringleader would calm the others down with any luck, but if it didn't, then a few more could be picked off and crammed into the patrol van. While that one was being dragged toward the vehicle, the other guardians of law and order held back the Seranans, who were going all-out to free their team-mate. Since the police were a bit outnumbered, the van driver slid out from behind the wheel and recklessly rushed off to help.

The Seranans immediately made the most of their tactical advan-

196

tage. Two of them, removing themselves from the fray, slipped through a side door and climbed into the police van. When the captured ball-player was brought out of the customs hall, the van started to move and took to coasting back and forth, with the police and their detainee either tripping after the departing vehicle or hopping aside so as not to get run over. The two baseball players drove the police van around until the other Seranans had recovered the captive by force. The police, who looked really undersized alongside the strapping athletes, were reduced to attacking from the rear. At every opportunity, they tore the Seranans' motley artificial leather jackets from the back slit to the collar, so that before long all the athletes had what looked like enormous wings fluttering at their backs.

An inquisitive crowd of passengers and those who had come to see them off had gathered, forming a semicircle that stretched first one way and then the other, as the focal point of the brawl shifted. The crane operators on the wharf stopped loading and began rubbernecking out of their glass hutches. The porters dropped the passengers' luggage just anywhere and congregated close to the fighting, staying well out of it themselves but offering plenty of support and roaring as though they were at the ballpark.

At that point, the nippy little Ingoberto Reus appeared on the scene. I don't know if he just happened to be down by the port or if someone had called his office for a mediator and legal counsel, seeing as how the conflict had taken such a nasty turn. Over time I had become convinced that Dr. Reus always showed up wherever there was a commotion, thanks, more than likely, to his impeccable lawyerly instincts. The first thing he saw as he came bounding, out of breath, around the corner of the customs hall was a police sergeant who, having been pinned to the wall by three brawny baseball players, was left with no choice but to haul his pistol from its holster so as to fire a warning shot.

Dr. Reus froze in his tracks. Boundless fear showed on his inquisitive, sharp-nosed face. For all that he loved to witness affrays and disturbances of any kind, there were two things that scared the living daylights out of him—poisonous snakes and gunfire.

'Down! They're opening fire!' he squealed, so loudly and piercingly that everyone who heard him would later assert unanimously that there really had been shooting near the customs hall. Nothing else could have given everyone present such a turn.

The zest went out of the fighting. A minute later, the Seranan base-ball players, putting up no further resistance, allowed the police to herd them back to one end of the hall. Everyone was suddenly feeling the worse for wear, and embarrassed too. The floor was littered with torn off buttons and buckles, and scraps of cloth. The onlookers started to disperse, as if on a signal.

The captain of the *Maltese Cross* communicated his impatience with a blast on the ship's whistle. The deep-toned sound pealed over the customs hall and soared off into the evening town. It was already half an hour after the steamer's scheduled departure time. The booms of the portside cranes creaked into action.

An atmosphere of general reconciliation reigned. Everyone seemed to have agreed to mark it down as a drawn game. Dr. Reus fussed about for a little while, first with the police squad leader and then with the Seranan coach, after which the players were allowed free passage to the steamer. The bone of contention itself no longer existed. The decorative goatskin box had been knocked off the table during the fight and now lay on its side in the center of a nine-feet square puddle of sticky dark-brown liquid over which two wasps, of unknown provenance and already intoxicated, were circling.

Solitary and superfluous in the middle of the rubbish-strewn customs hall stood the brown bust of Tommazo Oon. Someone had evidently back-heeled him in the nose, which now lay on the floor next to the statue.

As the baseball players, without so much as a farewell glance at their prize, began to file toward the back door, which gave onto the wharf, yet another little bloke with an unmemorable face thrust his mousy snout from behind a door-post.

'For sale? Would anyone have anything for sale?'

I emerged from behind the bar, got the bartender, who was busy with the inventory of his broken glassware, to pour me a double whisky, and made for home. That was it for the day.

Rounding a corner, I unexpectedly ran into Dr. Reus. We both stopped dead, as though rooted to the spot. Then the doctor recognized me, bared his yellow teeth for all the world like some kind of rodent and snorted spitefully,

'Judas!'

'What did you say?'

'You sold us out! We trusted you, confided in you, and you went and told everybody in town! Eldon's found out about our plan, he's sure to take advantage of it now, and the whole splendid idea we had for the memorial is down the drain, and it's all your doing! And you have the gall to look people in the eye after that?'

What a laugh!

'Don't you think Eldon has a thousand channels of information that are more reliable than me?'

'That won't wash!' Ingoberto said with another peevish snort. Then he flashed a hate-filled glare at me and clumped off in his childish little high-heeled boots, vanishing into the depths of the car park.

13

After the threatening letter, I didn't so much as poke my nose out the door for two or three weeks. I kept imagining enemies on my tail. I was upset, said sarcastic things for no reason at all, rolled my wheelchair from one window to the next and kept a tense eye on everything that went on around our block. My blue boat was fading forlornly on the shore. Gale-force winds had already half-covered it with sand. Come next spring there'll probably be nothing left but a small sandy hillock and no one will even know what's hidden beneath it, I thought, and I decided that it was fair enough for it to be buried. Since I'd never row out to sea again in my life, the boat might as well not exist. It gave me a gloomy sort of pleasure to think that the world around was gradually falling apart and would go to pot with me.

I caught such a lot of shady-looking pedestrians in the rangefinder of my rifle from my stake-out behind the balcony railing during those few days. They didn't have the foggiest idea that they were standing under the barrel of a loaded gun, and that the only thing between them and the unexplainable moment of no return which strikes like lightning and goes by the name of death was my curved index finger. Sometimes, if they didn't leave straightaway and I had to hold my aim for a long time, that finger began to tremble dangerously.

I never once thought to put myself in the place of those people, those strangers. To me they represented only a danger that had no name and no face, an unreasoning threat which had to be parried, so I conscientiously held them in the crosshairs. What business did they have to be standing and gawking near my house? An honest man is sure to know the exact address, and he heads that way, eyes front, not scrutinizing other people's houses.

On the other hand, perhaps I'm just imagining that there's anything odd about it? Perhaps it's a perfectly normal, everyday human condition? Isn't life so arranged that you're always a target for someone or something and it's just your good luck if you remain ignorant of that fact up to the very moment when that curved finger trembles? But then it's too late; you're beyond bothering.

I exercised to strengthen my arms during those days and, by endlessly scooting about here, there and everywhere, I learned to control my wheelchair perfectly. It was now like an extension of my body. I had stopped running into things, and felt completely independent, as I had long, long ago, when I stood on my own two feet. My self-confidence firmed up little by little, and I was no longer the pathetic cripple I had been when I left the hospital.

Then it happened. The leftists—the ones whose threatening letter had not given me a moment's peace—made the false move that finished them off. They took on the Consortium. Anything else would, I dare say, have been forgiven them, but not that.

Furious with their failure at the embassy, the leaders decided to kidnap Hamilcar MacPherson, the chief executive officer of the Consortium's Minoran branch, as the best way of getting their demands met. They had evidently worked out that none of the local politicians carried enough clout for that. They had lost their catspaws—the junkies who had been my companions in misfortune—in the embassy adventure, and so this time, like it or not, they had to send out some of the activist fanatics from their underground organization. All else aside, they were no doubt also goaded by the fear of becoming complete laughing-stocks. As it was, the newspapers were sporting caricatures of bearded conspirators, and 'leftist' and 'failure' had come to mean the same thing. They had to put on a display of strength and give everyone a good scare.

The operation was launched on Monday morning, when MacPherson was being driven from his villa to work. The leftist assault units came charging out of alleyways in vehicles they had stolen the day before, and blocked off his car. They bounded onto the roadway and started such a shoot-'em-up, with pistols and submachine guns, that you'd have thought a hundred anti-aircraft guns from the almost-forgotten war had unexpectedly been returned to Antafagusta and all set to firing at once. MacPherson's poor chauffeur was instantly riddled with bullets, and his bodyguard died too, but not before he had ventilated the lung of one of his attackers. MacPherson was driven away to an unknown destination.

A veritable tempest ensued. Within three hours the Consortium board of directors had presented Eldon's government with a tart ultimatum: if MacPherson was not swiftly found and freed alive and well, and if the culprits were not caught and severely punished, the Consortium would start shutting down all its economic activities on Minore within twenty-four hours. All the employees would be airlifted out by helicopter and the island, which had proved incapable of guaranteeing the safety of Consortium personnel, would be left to starve quietly to death and gradually sink beneath waves that Niarchos had spiked with cyanide. So serious was the threat that the government immediately mobilized an investigative task force and assigned every detective, spy and street agent to it. Road-blocks went up everywhere and the *Maltese Cross* was taken out to sea, so that no one could stow away in any of her bunkers.

It was the gunman with the shot-up lung who cracked the case wide open this time. While he was bolting with the other kidnappers, he told them his wound was a mere scratch, since he knew very well that urban guerrillas have an iron rule which says that anyone who is seriously wounded has to be shot on the spot by his own side so that he won't be captured and give the others away. There had been times when he himself had heatedly upheld that rule, but, now that he was directly concerned, he was afraid. The reality of death is a lot more scary than theorizing on the mortality of others. The wounded man put an incredible amount of energy into fooling his confederates, but later, in their hideout, he became so ill that they had to dispatch his younger brother on the quiet to get a doctor. The doctor showed up, gave the injured gunman first aid and promptly told the police. All Minore had been in a tizzy over the kidnapping in the hours since it had happened.

It was child's play from that point on. They didn't torment the wounded man with interrogations or threats; they just told him that if he talked they would take him to the hospital for proper treatment and if not they would leave him there and he could put his trust in the good Lord, because they had no time to mess around with him. They had his accomplices to find. He hurriedly told them everything he knew—and more besides, as was later discovered—and on Tuesday night, without firing a single shot, the police overran a new leftist command post in the caves at Santa Clara and got MacPherson out. The entire hard core of the organization was seized in one fell swoop, taken to Antafagusta and thrown in jail.

The paper said that on the morning when MacPherson's kidnappers were brought to the prison, Guido the Ragman, who was being held for questioning in connection with a bank robbery, blew his top. He upended the bowl containing his morning cereal over his warder's head and scalded him with tea to boot. Prior to that he had twice returned his tea with an official complaint, and he kept demanding that they send down some hot tea. Later, when asked why he had behaved that way, he replied that he wanted to be moved into solitary, because he had no intention of sharing a cell block with those cannibals. After that he was transferred to the prison hospital, for a thorough psychiatric check-up.

The Wednesday when the papers ran the entire story was a big day for me. I hid my rifle under the bed, opened all the windows and felt that I was really breathing for the first time in ages.

That evening I persuaded Murana to come out for dinner with me. She was terribly surprised, but pretended she wasn't. I think she was afraid that I wouldn't be able to cope with it all and would mope about, expecting her to help me. But it was as though I had sprouted wings. I bowled from the bathroom to the wardrobe and back, shaved carefully, and put on my best shirt. Little by little, my perkiness spread to Murana, who had at first been watching me with a bemused smile on her face. It seemed to take years off her, and she started hunting out a dressy outfit that had been gathering dust in the cupboard for a million years. Even Roxana, who never got excited about anything, was caught up in the swing of things and did what she could to help us.

We went to the restaurant in the Archipelago Hotel, because I wanted the very best. It was early on a weekday evening, and the

14–1298

place was empty except for two men sitting at a far table—one bald with a thin, straggly fringe of hair around an egg-like pate, and the other an ash-blond, probably a Northerner. They ignored us and we took no notice of them.

I don't remember ever enjoying a meal so much; everything tasted incredibly good. I'd never had anything like it, especially not the lobster meat fried in sesame oil. Even Murana at times forgot how inescapably sad she was, and burst into hearty laughter.

Then we danced. The band had just come on, the musicians had spent a long time carefully tuning up, had tried out their instruments and the amplifier, and had finally swung into such a jazzy beat that I couldn't resist. I was a new man that day.

The circular parquet dance floor was entirely at our disposal. The music played for the two of us alone. Everything had vanished, leaving nothing but those sultry, tantalizing sounds. Murana was dancing around me, her body twisting and straightening, off in a world of her own. My arms would raise high above my head, imitating her movements. I whirled, soared, rolled up, and unwound again like a spring. The wheelchair I sat in had come alive: for the first time in my life I had a pair of black wheels fully under my control. They heeded my every movement, carrying me and supporting me, their lord and master. Murana was swaying and whirling close by. My gaze never left her for a moment as she moved passionately to the jazzy tempo. The people in the band were unable to tear their eyes off us and couldn't have stopped playing if they'd tried. It was our dance, and all we wanted was for it to continue, to continue and never end.

Murana was undulating on the parquet like a flame having broke loose. Her dance brimmed over with heartache and sensuality. I kept up with her, my heart pounding madly, and we whirled and whirled, oblivious to everything. The outside world had ceased to exist for us. The patterns and symbols that my chair wheels were drawing on the empty parquet would until very recently have seemed well nigh impossible.

We ourselves could never have ended that crazy dance. And it was only when an overstrained guitar string snapped with a plaintive twang and the instruments fell silent that we stopped, soaking wet and gasping for breath, and gazed around with unseeing eyes. The echoes of the music still trembled in the air and my conscious mind had yet to recall that I had no legs...

'May I? I'm sorry, I've forgotten your name, Mister...'

'Yanno,' I say, putting an end to the torments of Professor Umbermann, who was standing by my table, shifting from one foot to the other.

No one in the Archipelago Restaurant, free tables galore, but for some reason he has to sit with me. Well that's all right—the place really is too deserted, and obviously this reverberating, starched loneliness is more than a lot of people can stand.

The egg-pated Professor blinks his eyes gratefully, sits down, and spends a long time trying to get control over his hands, alternately putting them on the table and dropping them back onto his knees.

'I think we've met somewhere before...' he says tentatively.

'A number of times, Professor. Once at the IEA meeting and again on the polder, when you were looking for worms. How's it going with the mutants?'

Umbermann flaps a hand dejectedly.

'They exist, of course. They have to exist! There are no missing links in the natural world. They're here somewhere—that's a certainty—though not for me this time round, unfortunately. I only managed to find two specimens, and neither was any good. One had been squashed on the road and the other had been chopped into bits and put on a village kid's fishing hook! And when I started trying to find out where he'd dug that worm up, he got the willies, started bawling and ran off. I don't know—do you suppose he thought that he'd done something illegal? You wouldn't have chanced to hear about a law against digging up earthworms here? Perhaps I asked the wrong way, didn't use the right tone? I chased off after him, but that just made things worse. The kid roared so loudly you'd have thought he was being chased by the hounds of hell. Who could have scared him like that? I can't run worth a darn—there I was huffing and puffing and trailing behind, and he disappeared, as though the earth had swallowed him up. There are crevices all over the place up there on the plateau. An outsider could never search them all. He'd evidently hidden in one of them and rolled into a ball like an earthworm during a drought. Fat chance of finding him!'

'So you lost him?'

'Right. And what was I to do—pull those pitiful scraps off his hook? They were no good to me. I only need a single worm, but it must be in one piece and viable. I wandered around the area for a whole week, on the lookout all the time. I grubbed about in a hundred places and never found a single worm. And all the boys look the same. I caught seven of them but never laid hands on my angler. He must have been lying doggo the whole time. He'd evidently heard from the others that I was roaming about and asking everyone where I could find earthworms. And the unanimous answer was that they'd never seen an earthworm, and had always used mosquito larvae and goat dung for bait. Can you imagine how terrified those people are? I made a point of telling them that I'm a scientist and whatever they used for bait—slugs or anything—is fine by me, if only they'd show me where the worms were. I said I needed them desperately for a scientific project. I even offered them money, and it was no use at all!'

'A real conspiracy of silence.'

Umbermann wiped his perspiring forehead.

'In the end I managed to find an old man who was a bit quicker on

14*

the uptake. He'd accompanied an English expedition to the Minoran plateau before the First World War. I don't know what the English were looking for. It's just their way—always looking for something somewhere. The passion for discovery runs in their blood. Well anyway, that old man considers himself a scientist to this day, so he compared notes with me as though we were colleagues. He shook his head and said there was nothing he could tell me about earthworms. That wasn't his department. But as for the fact that no one wanted to help an outsider to find anything, that he understood perfectly. It's the instinct for self-preservation, pure and simple. He says that some people once turned up in Bonegripe and took to asking ever so politely if there was any good sand around there. The local half-wits proceeded to escort them to the outskirts of the village and showed them the sand. Nobody begrudged it them. But that was how it started, and now there's no sand, no shore, no Bonegripe even. It's all been dug up by mechanical shovels and exported overseas. We've learned a lesson too, he told me, so I hate to put it like this, my dear colleague, but you're wasting your time. The next day, on my way to the village to see him again, I heard one of the little tearaways shouting, "Hide, you guys—the egg-pated spy's back!" That's when I decided to drop the whole thing. I knew I'd never get anywhere with them.'

'But is there really nowhere on Minore where you can go for some scientific back-up?' I inquired, mostly out of sympathy for the Professor, who looked genuinely downhearted.

'They have an enormous, sumptuously appointed Minoran Institute of the Natural World,' Umbermann told me. 'You think I haven't been there? I went within a week of my arrival. Their brief covers everything to do with the natural sciences. They have a staff of seventy-four, all with degrees, as well as a whole army of lab technicians, lab assistants and field inspectors, a large budget and modern premises. And do you know what they do there? They maintain card files on every single aspect of the natural scene on Minore. They have identically-formatted cards on insects and birds, minerals and plants, invertebrates and topography. When I found out about that, I clapped myself on the forehead. Now you're set, I said to myself: you just request the cards you want and read in black and white everything about earthworm habitats, population densities, and, who knows, maybe even species distribution! After that it'll be plain sailing—take your jars, get out into the field and collect as many as your little heart desires. What child-like faith! I absolutely did not know the system. Anyone who isn't familiar with the system is worse off than a blind man, a deaf man, and a madman all rolled into one. In this day and age, the system is all. You can't imagine what's really happening up at the Institute. They go on and on filling in those cards, then put the cards into large boxes and stack the boxes on racks, all higgledy-piggledy! Sometimes they have big meetings to discuss how to do an even better job of filling in even more cards. They mount an expedition, collect their material, and, without a care in the world, start scrawling new cards. Not an ounce of systematization! It would have taken me at least a year digging around in those boxes to come up with any earthworm cards—and that would mean I'd been lucky. Maybe you could rummage about for two years and come up empty.'

'I'm probably something of an ignoramus when it comes to science,' I admitted. 'But what's the point of all this?'

'That's just what I asked them. Minore's dwindling away, they said, and our urgent task is to accumulate, by hook or by crook, the total corpus of information about the island. We'll have time to systemize it and break it down when waves are rolling where we're standing now. If we omit any little detail at this stage it'll be lost forever. That's what they said. Anything they do to organize the material is, according to them, an impermissible waste of time and energy.'

'But it'll be murder to sort all those mountains of data when they get round to it. Perhaps they're hoping that machines will have been invented for that purpose by then? What do you think?'

'I don't know what I would have thought if I hadn't happened to spend some time with the deputy director in the private bar at the Institute. We were discussing my work. He acknowledged to me that a clever man knows better than to eat all his bread at one sitting, or at least not before a Consortium excavator has gobbled up the last strip of land here. What's going to happen to us if we do that? he asked me. If we wind up our work now, compile the catalogues and make the card files available to the public, we could all be out of a job. Or they'll scramble to find something else for us to do. Who needs it? Besides, it's not the thing to hurry a serious scientific endeavor. As it is, the material we've collected will do nicely for us and for our children, who are still going to primary school. Nobody could ever accuse a scientist of being too nit-picking. And he slapped me on the knee, as if to say that I'm not one whit better, only I'm such a slyboots that I'd never admit it...'

'And so you found nothing?'

Umbermann shook his head wearily.

'One of the staff members with a master's degree seemed to remember coming upon the earthworm card when he was dusting several years ago. But where? In which room, on which shelf? It's a vicious circle! Perhaps he just wanted to make me feel better. But I'm out of time now. My grant's expiring and I have to go home and get back to work. Of course, I've laid the theoretical groundwork, and I do believe that someone's bound to find those mutants in the end and crossbreed them. Earthworms are too important to be neglected. That's mankind's great hope. They're capable of saving him from hunger—which is more than you can say for fertilizers. I'll never tire of repeating that unreasonable quantities of fertilizers will end up killing all the soil's biomass! But, you know, it's not particularly satisfying to feel like some kind of humus that later generations will grow on. I'd have liked to have reaped the benefits of my own idea. If only I'd had a modicum of luck here on Minore!'

The Professor stared at me miserably. He might have carried on unburdening his aching soul, but at that moment the band, which had come on to do its regular evening spot, started to play. At first the noise was loud enough to bother us, and by the time we'd got used to it an improbable dance had begun—a dance that I can still see in my mind's eye.

All of a sudden there appeared on the empty dance floor a shapely woman with long black hair and a legless man in a wheelchair. They turned to face each other and slowly, unwillingly as it were, they began to sway to the beat. At first it was as though they were trying to overcome a mysterious resistance, were trying to rouse themselves from a torpid sleep. Standing there in place, gradually quickening the smooth movements of their bodies and arms, they had the look of water-weeds, caught and twisted by a current that was seeking to carry them away, to tear them from the river-bed. The music grew louder, the beat picked up, and suddenly both dancers broke away. They had forgotten about the empty, comfortless room, and I doubt that they had ever noticed us at all. The woman was whirling and swaying, moving closer and drawing back, retreating from her partner's grasp, while he bounced like a spring in his wheelchair with his arms raised high, as if imploring heaven for mercy and forbearance. The legless man was unbelievably deft in his pursuit of the woman. His wheelchair had come alive, had been transformed from an invalid's cumbersome getabout into a responsive instrument, almost a fair replacement for real legs. If there wasn't a dash of the supernatural in this, then it was a bionic miracle. The man and the woman had given themselves over entirely to the dance. Their bodies and arms spoke; they cried aloud of a craving for life and the heartache of unlived days, of lost joys and hopes. In their state of oblivion, the couple were trying to bring back even an iota of what had been frittered away and the sight of them started up a heavy-hearted yearning to have the unfeasible and the unthinkable—all of it—come true for them.

Umbermann followed the dancers with a fixed gaze. There was a feverish glint in his eyes. A man wishing for the impossible always subconsciously lives in hope of a miracle.

It's a tragic thing when a legless man dances. The human spirit rebels against physical infirmity; the human being tosses out a challenge to the invincible; and for an instant he contrives to wrestle down fate. That's the way it seems to us, at least, because really nothing can ever repair that sort of damage—neither willpower nor even time, which has absolute power over many things.

The band suddenly fell silent with the pitiful sound of a broken string, and the dancers stopped short. There in the middle of the deserted restaurant they became small and ordinary again, although a second before they had filled that entire space with themselves, with the towering grandeur of their emotions. The difference was staggering.

'Did you see that?' Umbermann whispered. 'Fantastic!'

The legless man and his lady melted away over on the far side of the room. The shadows swallowed them up, and they disappeared from sight behind countless chairbacks and the glittering whiteness of tablecloths. A few moments later I was wondering if they had been there at all or if the whole thing had been a hallucination.

We were silent for a while. Suddenly Umbermann livened up.

'So you're leaving too?'

'What makes you think that?'

'I heard about it completely by chance. I was in the Foreign Ministry visa department yesterday. You know, of course, how they always get things snarled up there and nothing's ever done on time. The place richly deserves its unofficial title—the department of hamfisted services. I queued for two hours to get an exit visa stamp. But you know yourself how they work there. You'd never see anything like it anywhere else. I think it's all because of the phosphate revenue. No one has any fear of losing his job, so what's all this nonsense about work? They chatter on endlessly, make personal telephone calls, amble from room to room, and have parties. And in between times they very reluctantly attend to the public, who, as they unfailingly give us to understand, should be awfully grateful for the favour. And you can't do anything about it. That's just the way it is—you have to have a stamp so you've no choice in the matter. And it would be possible to put up with all this, you understand, if we were out in the sticks, living with the headhunters in Papua or something. But no ... they'd have us believe that this is a civilized country! Yes, well, anyway... So I'm standing in a queue, counting the petals in the plaster rosettes on the ceiling and I happen to hear your name being mentioned on the phone. The clerk even asked them to say the surname again and repeated "Yanno, journalist". "But he hasn't been in here yet," says the milady who issues those stamps. Then she says, "Understood. So long as he comes in soon, of course we can get it all done straightaway. Whatever you wish." I'm sure it was someone from the very top, because otherwise milady wouldn't have been cooing like that. Mere mortals just get the rough edge of her tongue. So congratulations—you've evidently got some influential patrons here.'

'But are you sure they were really talking about me?'

'Absolutely. I know I'm absent-minded and I couldn't even remember your name at first just now. But as soon as you said what it was, it smacked me right between the eyes—I knew I'd heard that name very recently. And there, you see, I've remembered at last...'

He chattered on for a while, but I'd had more than enough of it by that point. It wasn't long before I excused myself, saying I had some urgent business to take care of, and dashed straight to the

207

Figaro, leaving him to finish his supper alone.

Dan Eldon was just closing up. The assistants had already lowered the bars over the windows and striped jailhouse shadows lay across the pavement. He wasn't particularly surprised to see me. At the same time, I felt a certain wariness in him, and even a kind of hostility, which was not normal for him at all. His little hazel eyes watched me intently. It was like being observed by a bear holed up in his den.

There was no time for preambles.

'I've heard rumours that someone's keen to have the paperwork for my departure taken care of posthaste. Have you heard anything about that?'

'But naturally, naturally I heard something in passing, my dear Yanno,' Eldon replied, as slow and easy as you please.

'And what do you say to that? Why didn't you let me know about it? I'm completely confused now. Didn't I take your advice? You told me yourself...'

'I told you that everything would work out for the very best,' Eldon interrupted with a Jesuitical grin.

'So it's for the very best to give me the boot, correct? What have I done to deserve that?'

'You see, Yanno, it all depends on the point of view you take,' Eldon, wily as a cat, replied. 'What looks one way from your point of view could look quite differently from ours. After all, you can't go round insisting that Minoran interests should invariably coincide with yours, can you?'

'Save it, Eldon. National interests? Who've I thwarted?'

'Er, yes ... you simply haven't had much luck here, Yanno. You've collected too many adversaries and you've turned into a troublesome foreigner. Do you know what a pain in the neck a troublesome foreigner is? I think you'd do well to book a ticket on the *Maltese Cross* as soon as you can. You never know how nervy some people might be... And if you have any problems, I can help. I've got some pretty good connections in the steamship business. They get their shaves here too. You want a more detailed explanation? Oh Yanno, Yanno—you still have that endless, fatal newsman's curiosity, that urge to get down to the hidden mainsprings! Well, all right—I can run down the more essential points, since you insist. I just don't know how much good it's going to do you. For example, the Own-landers don't like you because you're an internationalist and you're rude about their beliefs in your articles—troglodytic nationalism, indeed! With Ron, it goes without saying. You've caused him a slew of headaches more than once, as you well know. And to cap it all off, Damian, your friend of old, is vexed with you now for some reason. You must have managed to tread on his pet corn too. So who's left to support you? Then there are the security service reports—unbecoming conduct with several female Minoran nationals, conversations for a purpose or purposes unknown with senile old men, the gathering of derogatory rumours about our past and present. And a lot more, up to and including the bribing of public officials. Well, what do you say—isn't that enough to make us want to get rid of you? Are you still surprised?'

'All that twaddle's a far cry from reality. It's harking way back into the past and it's not true, insofar as I can decipher any of it. If that's the way it is, I'll pull all the necessary strings to get the stupid decision rescinded. But I can't apply myself to anything unless I'm sure that there isn't something more serious lurking behind it.'

Eldon gave me a long, searching look . Then he draped a towel he'd forgotten he was holding over the back of a chair and said slowly, almost sadly,

'It's not worth trying to pull strings. They won't budge. Ron recently met with Damian, and Damian suggested a reconciliation. They've come to some kind of agreement.. True, I can't tell if it'll result in a real coalition or not, but in any event they are intending to cooperate. Ron says that you've done too much digging around in things that should be kept under wraps, that you've found out certain not entirely pleasant details, and that's not something you can gainsay. So there you have it, my dear Yanno.'

It was hard to breathe and for an instant a red wave washed before my eyes. So, they've made a pawn of me—a pawn that can be sacrificed without turning a hair as soon as that suits somebody's purpose. It's quite possible that I myself have at times performed manoeuvres that were less than irreproachable from the ethical standpoint. That's pretty sure to be the case. But all the same I've done nothing to deserve this sort of treachery. If I go home now, ahead of time and essentially because I've been expelled, I face an extremely unpleasant carpeting back at the agency. Matters of prestige are a ticklish thing. And in any case, I only need to blot my copybook once and that's the last overseas posting I'll get for years to come. I'm only one candidate among many. The years go by, the youngsters come on...

'So, Yanno's the sacrificial lamb on the altar of Eldon's reconciliation with Damian!' I said, with a bitter grin.

Dan spread his hands, an oriental half-smile on his face.

'Is it all that unjust? High-powered politics demand sacrifices.'

A diplomat would have stopped the conversation right there. But I'm not a diplomat, for good or ill. And so I decided it was time to see if I couldn't spook the people who were playing fast and loose with my life, although in fact I could hardly be much of a danger to them.

'But don't the esteemed fathers of the state, the big-daddy politicians, realize that, after being so roughly handled, I might let slip everything I know? How do you see it, Dan—do I have enough to raise a little storm around Minore? On an international scale, let's say? I mean, if I think a while, I'll bet I can come up with some diabolically funny stuff that would look good in an essay, perhaps, or a pamphlet.'

Dan's smile turned into a frozen grimace. He suddenly put me in mind of an old Mongol.

'There are things that gentlemen don't talk about,' he grated.

'There are things that gentlemen don't permit themselves to do!' I shot back triumphantly. 'Otherwise they're no gentlemen and deserve to be dealt with accordingly.'

Turning on my heel, I strode firmly out of the salon. Dan took a few hasty little steps after me.

'Watch yourself, Yanno!' The sound floated quietly from behind.

Badly churned up, I parked the car near the polder so as to get a breath of sea air and calm down. I had to think carefully through everything that had happened and map out what I was going to do next. This time I could make no mistakes.

In the direct light of the sun, which hung low in the sky, the gray plain of the polder swam in a silvery haze. It was hard to see the line where the land stopped and the water's unsteady glint began. Squinting, I forced myself to look right into the sun, which sent a pain shooting through the optic nerve. That pain was something I just had to have. What a mess I was in, with no way out! Minore had swallowed me up, had sucked out all the juice, and now, when I was no longer necessary, was intending to throw me away without a second thought. And I had wanted to do this bizarre little island some good. How naive of me!

Just a little to the right of the fiery sun, something moved. Overcoming the blinding light in my eyes, I made out two figures. A man and a woman were strolling along the outlying dike, and from where I was standing, from a distance, they looked so carefree and so much in love that my heart tightened with envy. People on the skids shouldn't look at people who are happy.

Tearing my gaze from them with an effort, I scanned the entire, introverted desolation of the polder until my eyes rested on the far bay near Cape Cataracta. There, on the shore, rose a seven-storey residential block. Some of the windows were open wide, the drawn curtains fluttering in the breeze. The building looked empty, lifeless. The tenants had hidden themselves away somewhere, leaving the building to itself. It seemed to have opened its own windows without human help, to let out the stifling air that had built up inside. One felt the kind of barren emptiness that's found at midday only in towns far to the south.

All of a sudden I was stabbed by a reflection, a ray of light so sharp that it could almost have been a laser beam. Something was glittering blindingly behind the wall of one of the balconies on the second floor, and there was nothing it could be but the glint of the setting sun in a binocular lens or a gun rangefinder.

And what if it really is a rangefinder? What idiot would take it into his head to aim for no good reason at people walking on the polder? Has the world gone that mad? Suppose they're aiming at me?

The warning note I had heard in Dan Eldon's voice suddenly rang in my ears. I started feeling uncomfortable: this was evidently no place to retrieve my poise. I almost ran to the car, my very skin alive with the sensation of those sights tracking me. Was it a camera or a gun that was going to make the shot? How stupid, I scolded myself: what's your hurry, you great jerk? And I carried on running.

As I hurtled away from the polder, making rather better time than usual, I happened to catch a fleeting sight of a car I knew—a low-slung, dark-red Porsche—parked in an alley. An incomprehensible sound, a sad, chipped little noise, fed into my growing panic...

'I'd like to speak to Mr. Stemo Kulamar.'

What a strange feeling. I'm the one saying those words but at the same time I can hear my voice from the outside, slightly distorted, coming through the telephone receiver, as if there were two of me. I don't know why this is happening.

A woman's voice, rather husky and attractively low-pitched, answered. She asked me to wait, then an entire eternity seemed to pass before Kulamar came to the phone. I had a flash of irritation as I wondered what was keeping him, but I pacified myself immediately. Go easy, now—perhaps he's still not feeling too well. The report said that Kulamar had been interviewed in hospital after a car accident or something like that... And the picture, as I remember, showed him in a hospital bed.

At last he picked up the phone.

'Kulamar speaking.'

'My name is Yanno, Artur Yanno. You've probably not heard of me. I represent a major foreign press agency here on Minore. Please don't be surprised by my contacting you like this. It's just that I need to get some background which you can probably provide, if your recent interview is anything to go by. I would like a spot of honest, unembellished help in understanding something that's happening on the underside of political activity, of party infighting here on Minore...'

'Take a long run off a short pier!' the voice barked down the phone in an outburst of rage. 'I don't want to hear another word about that rotten interview! It's given me enough trouble as it is.'

'Wait!' I appealed, afraid that he was going to cut me off. 'It's terribly important to me. And not just to me, rest assured of that. You have nothing to worry about—I give you my word that under no circumstances will I ever reveal the sources of my information. I'm the only one taking any risks here.'

'And what makes you so sure that I'll agree to tell you anything, even if I know?' the voice at the other end suddenly asked wearily.

'You think everything's really OK here on Minore?'

'And can you make it OK?' he responded, quite reasonably.

'No, of course not. And nor can you. At best, it'll take the wider public consensus—international pressure, let's say—to get anything done. That's why I've taken this thing on. You don't think I just happened to fall into it because I had nothing better to do?'

Deep inside I was a little ashamed to have trotted out the personal axe I had to grind, though it had been that or nothing.

'No. I don't want to,' Kulamar said, after a moment's thought. 'I'm sick to the back teeth with it. I want some peace.'

'Good God above!' I cried in absolute despair. 'What's going on here? Don't say that old Ossian was the only real man left on Minore and now he's gone the rest of you don't give a damn!'

'Ossian? Did you really know old Ossian?' Kulamar asked.

'Where do you think I got all those stories about the Herald that don't exist in print?'

'He told you that?'

'And who do you think fed me the details of the donkey dung trial, for example? What was my published source for that?'

Kulamar was silent. I had more or less decided that he was slowly and soundlessly putting down the phone, but, as I savored the bitter taste of failure, he suddenly said in an unexpectedly firm voice,

'Good enough. Ossian was the most evenhanded and courageous man in our village. He stayed there alone, wanted nothing to do with the phosphate money, and he only left when the excavators were eating up the very ground under his feet...'

'He told me a lot without my even asking. He was always saying that people should know everything and then no one person would be able to hoodwink everyone else into submission. But there's just one thing the parties really care about—making sure that people only know what the politicians want them to know and remain blissfully ignorant about the rest of it. That's the worst damage their damned politicking can do!'

'And he was right...' Kulamar said slowly, and I realized that he was deep in thought.

'Unfortunately, his information was limited to people who passed away long ago,' I added after a short pause.

'Where and when shall we meet?' Kulamar asked decisively.

'Let's not put it off. Tomorrow at twelve, on Herald Square. I drive a bright blue Datsun, with a number-plate that ends in 08. Is that all right with you?'

'I'll remember.'

'See you then.'

The phone had given a couple of those characteristic clicks during our conversation. I noticed it, but it didn't put me out at all. They can listen as long and as hard as they like; I've burned all my bridges. Let them bluster away in impotent fury, because I'm ruthless now and plan to give no quarter. In the few days remaining to me I'll seek out everyone who has any inconvenient secrets to tell. I'll bundle all that explosive material together and I'll lash out so hard that there'll be some permanent political injuries. They'll have to find new front-liners. Thus far I've never made a practice of going around unseating politicians, or even premiers. These are the biggest stakes I've ever played for. As God's my judge, it's my turn now!

An instinctive fear crept into Murana's eyes.

'Don't go, Stemo! Where's it to be? I'll go with you if you want to go so badly.'

I embraced her with my right arm and clapped her encouragingly on the back.

'You're worrying about nothing. That's silly. All I've done is arranged a meeting with a very interesting person. No, no—don't be scared. I've finished with the junkies and the terrorists. This is a serious man, a foreign journalist. Besides, I think he can help Tell. I mean, you know that the lad wants to be a newsman, and he needs someone to get him in with the editors.'

Murana gave in, as always, but the hand that stroked my shoulder still trembled with unspoken fear. I can feel that touch to this day.

When I left the arcade and emerged into Herald Square, which was drenched with sunlight, I was momentarily blinded. I had to stop and give my eyes a chance to get used to it. A little while later I moved on, scouting about for that bright blue Datsun with the number-plate that ended in 08.

Then my eyes happened on the chap in the striped suit. I'm still convinced that there was something fishy about him, because otherwise he wouldn't have been tinkering with the door lock on that grey Datsun. He was trying a key. Then he hopped off and started casing another car door. He was rushing about the square, glancing all around. I still had my eye on him when he stopped in the very middle of the square. I rolled quietly toward him, the parked cars hiding both me and my wheelchair from his view. Sometimes it's useful to be short; tall people are rather more noticeable. The chap in the striped suit opened a car door, and that's when I saw that it was a bright blue Datsun with 0 and 8 on the numberplate.

Could that be Artur Yanno? If it was, then to my mind he was an extremely shifty-looking newspaperman. I'd need to be careful with him, no matter what he said about Ossian. And if it wasn't him but some lowlife trying to steal the car, I still had time to scare him off.

I rolled closer. The striped back had disappeared behind the car. A door slammed and suddenly there was a bright flash, like a bolt of lightning... And then once more nothing but a buzzing darkness... nothing but backtracking over and over again to events of long ago...

I left the car in the square and went across to a small shady cafe under a colonnade. It was only just after eleven, and there was no sense in burning myself to a crisp in the sun. I could take my time over a couple of cups of coffee and think out how to manage my conversation with Kulamar. I had to discover as much as I could in this one encounter, because I'd hardly get the chance to meet him again. I had been too roiled up to think all this through at home, and anyway, I didn't want to sit by the telephone in case someone from the Foreign Ministry started trying to track me down.

The clock was striking twelve when I stepped out into the square again. The doors in the Town Hall tower opened and two goats came out, moving slowly along iron rails. They made a dignified turn to face each other, then they lowered their horns and banged heads. Twelve times they would bend their knees and crash their gilded horns together, move back and do it again. I paused for a moment and watched them for the umpteenth time. You had to credit the witty artist who had restored the goat-figurines following the fire several years after the war, when a careless town council clerk had forgotten to unplug his coffee-maker and burned down the entire Town Hall tower. One of the goats had a hooked nose and curly hair, while the other's protruding upper lip and the bald patch on the back of its head were easy to spot. People could not fail to recognize the two butting rivals as Damian and Eldon. Whole families came at midday to watch the clock strike, and the children were told, 'Now we'll see Damian the goat banging heads with Eldon the goat.' I think the authorities would have done something to modify the figures a long time before, had they not been afraid to admit by so doing that the hint had been taken.

It's true that Mayor Amora once had the people on the square notified that the old clock was to be dismantled. The mechanism was purportedly too ancient and worn out, and there was no longer anyone capable of repairing it. The crowd took the message in, then started breaking down the Town Hall doors. Amora hid in the attic, while some very cross Antafagustans went to the home of the centenarian who had served as watchmaker at the British High Commission and had trained in London on no less a timepiece than Big Ben, and dragged him out. The craftsman, like a wizened old relic, was hauled bodily by four robust butchers to the tower and there personally pulled out the stick that had been thrust through the huge cogwheels by some dutiful junior officials on the town council. The people on the square waited patiently, and then the sliding doors opened again and the goats locked horns, whereupon the general rejoicing began. The ill-starred stick was subjected to a public burning in the middle of the square, and after that no one ever dared to raise a hand against the clock.

The square was blindingly bright after the dusky cafe. The air above the iron car roofs vibrated and coiled, so that the buildings on the opposite side of the square seemed to be pulling away from the ground in plain sight and floating off. In the Town Hall tower, Damian and Eldon locked their gilded horns for the eleventh time.

I got going. In front of me there appeared a round-shouldered back

214

in a striped jacket, hopping between the cars and paying no attention to the sounds coming from the clock. The person in the jacket acted as though he'd lost something but didn't really know what it was. His behaviour made me feel rather odd.

I unhurriedly set out to follow the striped back to the center of the square, where I had left my Datsun. Kulamar—the one who was to help me take my next step towards revenge—would show up at the car any minute now. They'd never be sorry enough for the way they'd treated me! I stopped for a moment and again glanced back at Damian and Eldon with their golden horns. They had just finished banging heads for all to see and were slowly returning, cheek-by-jowl, into the black innards of the tower. The iron gates closed solemnly behind them.

The striped back suddenly stopped and bent over, but I didn't suspect anything even then. It was only when the back straightened up again and a bright blue car door glittered that I began to feel alarmed. I hurried forward, still not completely convinced that it was anything to do with my car. With the corner of my eye I caught sight of a man in a wheelchair, who was much closer to the car than I. At that moment the door slammed loudly.

And then the explosion hit...

'Get ready, Yanno. They've come for you,' the doctor says, with a certain firmness creeping into his voice.

'They've come? Who?' I'm caught by surprise and I can't help but show it.

'Heaven's Orderlies. They'll take you down to the port. The government has made a booking for you today on the *Maltese Cross*. You're able to get around now, if you use your stick. You don't have to stay in this hospital to complete your convalescence.'

'Hold it! What about the explosion?'

'Oh, Yanno—what does that matter now? You're alive and that's the most important thing. All the substantial evidence was destroyed by the explosion, and the investigation's been called off. There's nothing left of the poor devil who was planning to pinch your car and ran foul of the bomb that had been planted there but a scrap of striped material from the back of his jacket and the heel of a shoe. You'll be paid the insurance on the car, and the government has even given permission for you to be reimbursed in foreign currency. What more do you want?'

What more could I want?

'Tell me, though—how are things with Kulamar?'

The doctor looks away.

'We've transferred him...'

He leaves, so that I can get dressed in peace. They've had the foresight to leave my clothes folded on a chair.

Suddenly an unexpected thought comes into my head. Wasn't it this very evening, exactly a year ago, when I disembarked from the *Maltese Cross* to set foot for the very first time on Minoran soil? Somehow it has never occurred to me to think about that before. I've been busy with a thousand other problems. But if that's the case then this has most certainly been an absolutely extraordinary year of my life. What year, though? My thoughts scatter in every direction. From the crannies of my memory floats the fact that in the Orient every year is named after an animal. Yes, that's how they do it... So then, what's the name of the year I've spent on Minore?

My lips themselves suddenly find the words I need, and I say them under my breath,

'The Year of the Donkey...'

Hearing my escorts' muffled coughing outside the door, I start getting dressed.

The circle is complete.

So long, Minore.

Tallinn, 1978